Sport Media
A Trinity Mirror Business

Published in Great Britain in 2007 by:
Trinity Mirror Sport Media,
PO Box 48, Old Hall Street,
Liverpool, L69 3EB.

Executive Editor: KEN ROGERS
Editor: STEVE HANRAHAN
Art Editor: RICK COOKE
Production Editor: PAUL DOVE
Sub Editors: JAMES CLEARY, ROY GILFOYLE
Designers: GLEN HIND, BARRY PARKER,
COLIN SUMPTER, JAMIE DUNMORE, LEE ASHUN,
ALISON GILLILAND, JAMES KENYON
Writers: CHRIS McLOUGHLIN, GAVIN KIRK,
DAVID RANDLES, JOHN HYNES
Sales and Marketing Manager: ELIZABETH MORGAN
Hall of Fame statisticians: ERIC DOIG, DAVID BALL, GED REA
Alan A'Court contribution: IAN HARGRAVES
Main photographs: Trinity Mirror North West & North Wales/ Liverpool Daily Post and Echo

ISBN 9781905266203

Printed and finished by Broad Link Enterprise Ltd

'It would be very **flattering** even to be in the running for the **Hall of Fame** when you look at the heroes who have already made it and the **quality** of some of the **greats** who have missed out. To see all the **legends** in one place would be **very special**.'

– Steven Gerrard

Enjoy a trip to Reds' heaven along road of Anfield gods

By KEN ROGERS

There have been heroes and legends since time immemorial. The Ancient Greeks had Achilles and Ajax, the latter a fearless warrior rather than a world famous football club in Amsterdam.

The Romans had Hercules. Celtic folklore told tales of Arthur, Lancelot, Galahad and Merlin the Magician.

The fans of Liverpool FC go misty-eyed at the very mention of **Dalglish**, **Rush**, **Hunt** and **Liddell**. They are part of an exclusive group that stand tall amongst that band of football 'gods' who have graced the fields of Anfield Road and who now stand, side by side, in the 'Official Liverpool FC Hall of Fame.'

This book is the definitive salute to the 22 men in Red who have been inducted into this unique 'club' - an honour that guarantees each of them a place in the annals of Liverpool history. Their stories and the process by which they were elected are told in this book.

Liverpool FC first invoked the 'Hall of Fame' selection process in 2002. Outside of the Anfield family, many people would have been surprised to discover that an elite sporting body like the Reds did not already have a Hall of Fame.

But when you have got so many greats, how do you begin to separate a star from a legend and a legend from an immortal?

We all have our own idols and woe betide anyone who seeks to question your hero's credentials.

With this in mind, LFC had to set absolute parameters for its illustrious judging panel who were asked to name just two players from every decade between 1892 and 2000 for the Hall of Fame with a forward plan to reconvene to name two more giants for 2000-2010.

So why not two from one fairly straightforward era, but three or four from another more complicated timespan - like the supremely successful Seventies and Eighties when the Reds won everything in sight?

The view from within Anfield was that this could undermine some other decades. As important was the logic that a strict limit of two for every ten-year spell would instinctively add to the exclusivity of the project.

After all, to get into the Liverpool FC's Official Hall of Fame should be the most difficult thing in the world.

"No compromise" was therefore the mindset of every member of the panel - made up of Chief Executive **Rick Parry**; record-appearance holder **Ian Callaghan** (a key

counter-productive because of the quality and status of some of great candidates who were not elected. **Kevin Keegan** did not get into the Hall of Fame. **Emlyn Hughes** didn't get in. Nor did **Graeme Souness , Tommy Smith** and many other Kop idols. The list goes on.

In reality, the question immediately answers itself. It is this very fact that demonstrates the prestige of the Official Liverpool FC Hall of Fame. It is not just about those who made the final 22. It's actually a measure of the sky-high standards of the club and a tribute to every playing hero.

There are other things to consider. The Hall of Fame project, far from overlooking people, actually served to highlight the achievements of every single member of the Liverpool playing family via the 'Scrolls of Fame' - the starting point to debate every decade. People who had not been talked about for a hundred years were suddenly back in the Anfield spotlight.

Equally, the feats and exploits of the teams from every era were suddenly being re-examined with each decade thoroughly researched and featured in the official club publications and local press.

This whole process would spell out the obvious. To have worn the famous red on just one occasion is a real badge of honour. To have worn it 857 times, like 'Hall of Famer' **Ian Callaghan**, is taking it to a whole new level - one that separates heroes from legends. Quite simply, the 'Hall of Fame' epitomises the stature of one of the greatest football clubs in the world.

figure within the LFC Former Players Association); former star **Brian Hall** (who runs the club's Public Relations Department with powerful links through to the fan base); **Phil Thompson** (European Cup winning captain with one foot on the terraces); **Alan Hansen** (European Cup winner and a man with a full grasp of Liverpool's national stature via his role with the BBC).

You will read more about the panel and its remit later in this book. You will understand how it operated, what statistical information it analysed and how it listened carefully to the fans.

It would be a reasonable question to ask if the elitist nature of the 'Hall of Fame' might somehow be

It reminds us of the standards demanded by the Reds on a daily basis. It is the definitive celebration of the club's remarkable history. It will ultimately provide a focal point as fans prepare for the emotional leaving of historic Anfield for a fantastic new home in Stanley Park.

Who will step forward in the future to grasp the mantle of the greats?

This story has still to be written. For now, enjoy the journey that follows into Anfield folklore and be proud that Liverpool FC's Official Hall of Fame is simply in a class of its own.

CONTENTS

STEVEN GERRARD and JAMIE CARRAGHER on the heroes who have entered the Hall of Fame

The Official Liverpool FC Hall of Fame is packed with legends from the past, reflecting the period 1892-2000.

However, the Hall of Fame is not just about the heroes who have gone before. It is the club's intention to elect two new players into this supremely exclusive "club" every decade moving forward.

This, in itself, sparks a great debate about the current and more recent giants who will be in the mix when the panel ultimately sits again to weigh up the claims of a host of magnificent candidates. These would include the likes of Michael Owen, Sami Hyypia and that band of Anfield brothers who have played their part in the Rafael Benitez revolution that is already part of Anfield folklore, not least those who were central to the legend of Istanbul. >

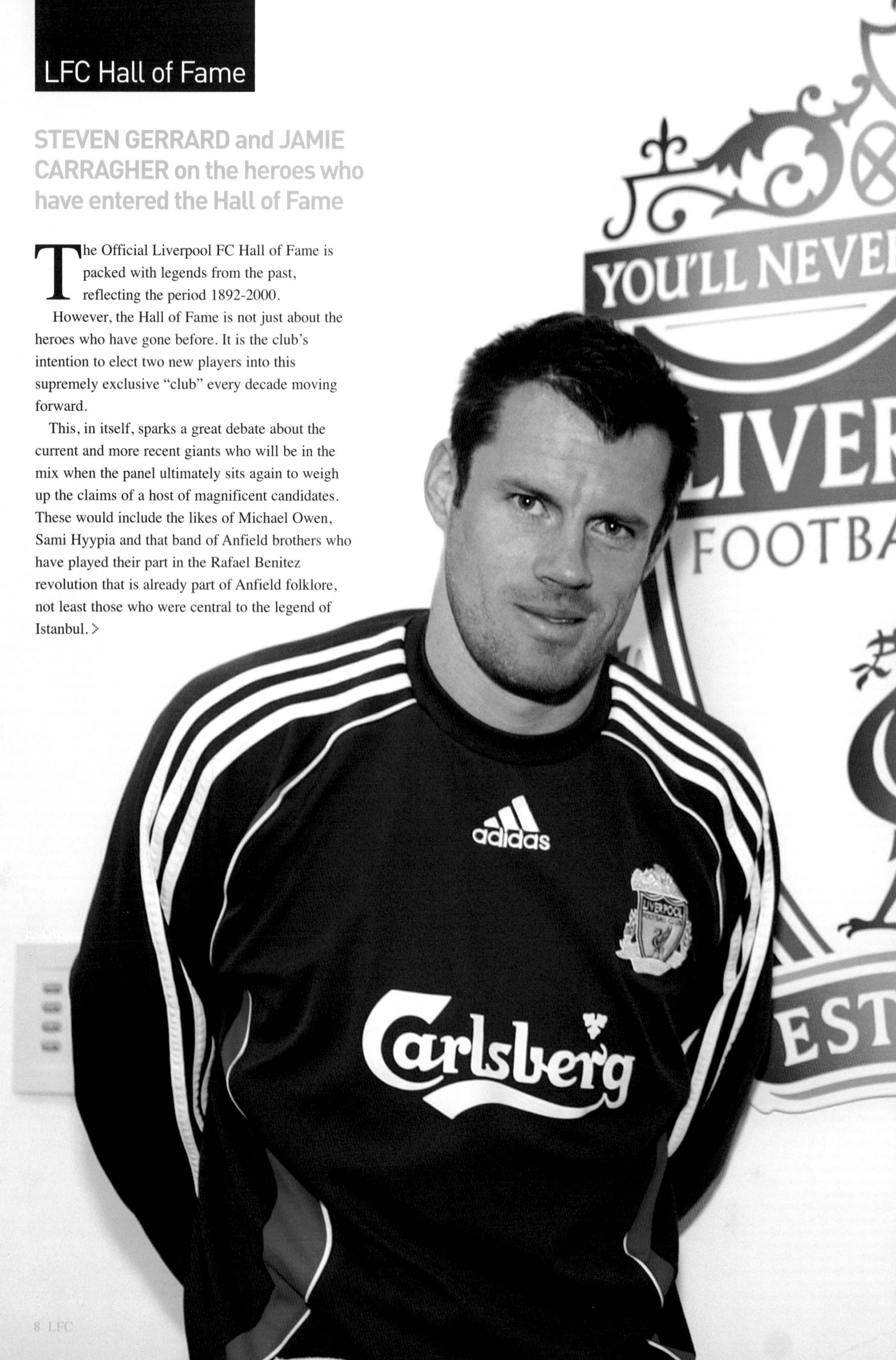

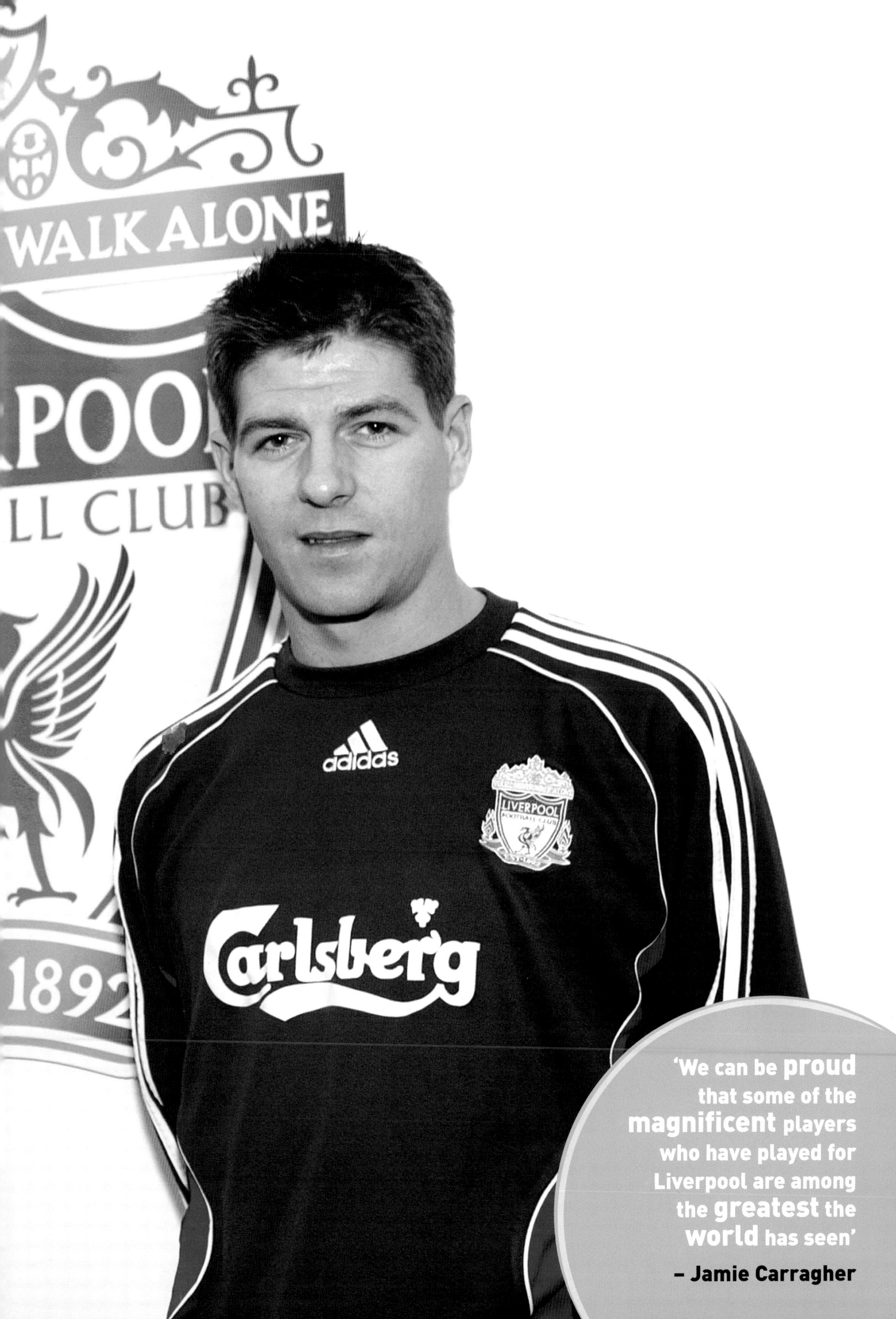

'We can be **proud** that some of the **magnificent** players who have played for Liverpool are among the **greatest** the **world** has seen'

– Jamie Carragher

> Of course, there are two other names who will dominate the panel's thoughts, conjuring images of Scouse power at its very best.

Steven Gerrard's world class qualities and his success in leading the Reds to Champions League glory in Istanbul are already part of Anfield folklore. Standing alongside him, Jamie Carragher has not just been a massive influence on Liverpool, but has demonstrated the kind of staying power that has inspired a deserved testimonial year.

In the following pages, Stevie and Carra reflect on the club's history, the legends who have inspired their own football development and the importance of the Official Hall of Fame.

Liverpool FC's incredible history is clearly very important and a string of European Cup triumphs have developed the club's world brand. How important are the achievements of the past in inspiring the dreams of the future?

Stevie: Our history is very important. The reason why the club is so big is because we have been so successful down the years.

It's important to the likes of Jamie, myself and the other players that we try to continue that success story so that, in years to come, there will be new things to talk about and revel in.

Carra: Obviously Liverpool FC has a great history, going right back to the very early days when the club first started. Bill Shankly arrived in the Sixties and things really took off. It means we now have worldwide support and there are not many clubs who can say that. We can look back at some of the magnificent players who have played for Liverpool and be proud that they are also among the greatest players the game has ever seen.

Who are the heroes you instinctively think about yourselves from your younger days?

Stevie: When I first started going to Anfield and watching games, I was probably round about nine to ten years of age. John Barnes and Peter Beardsley were the two star names at Anfield at that time. Obviously, there were many great players in that era because we used to win the league all the time, but it was Barnes and Beardsley who stood out for me.

Carra: Of course, I was an Evertonian as a kid so the one who used to annoy me most was Ian Rush. He was always scoring against Everton. He then joined Juventus and we thought he was gone for good, but he returned and was at Anfield for a very long time. He was one of the greatest goalscorers the game has ever seen. There were tremendous players in that era, many who didn't get into the Hall of Fame, but Rush and Barnes in particular were special.

Stevie: Yes, Barnes deserves to be in, possibly because Beardsley went to Everton. If he had stayed at Anfield for a few more years he would have had a great chance of being elected to the Hall of Fame. But there were many candidates because >

Scourge of Everton: Ian Rush!

> Liverpool have been lucky to have had so many great players. I wouldn't have liked to have been on the panel, trying to choose just two from each decade from so many true greats.

John Barnes is a double Footballer of the Year and so perhaps that highlights the kind of standard needed to influence the panel.

Stevie: His type is so hard to come by now. You look at the England situation. We are crying out for another John Barnes. Top class stars who can play on the left are hard to come by. Barnes was the best for such a long time, creating goals and scoring goals. He was just so good to watch and so exciting. He was a player you would pay any amount of money to see.

Jamie, you have been at Anfield for ten years now, long enough to be granted a deserved testimonial. Are there Liverpool players who are very special to you, looking back on your time at the club?

Carra: I first came here when Kenny Dalglish was manager. We used to come and watch the training when we were kids. There have been so many great players along the way and there have also been people who not only played for the club, but who joined the backroom staff to give tremendous service to Liverpool. You think about the likes of Ronnie Moran and Roy Evans who gave Liverpool FC almost a lifetime's service.

When you look back to the club's pioneering years, specifically 1892-1900, there was a player called Matt McQueen who not only played in goal, but also turned out in almost every other position in the team. He was an incredible all-rounder who also became the club's manager, a record that ultimately earned him a place in the Hall of Fame.

Stevie: All those positions! He's a bit like me then, wasn't he! But seriously, that always happens if you are a versatile player. If you can play in different positions, it's a big help to the manager. Jamie and myself have experienced that over the years. It also helps you to get you in the starting eleven as well, which is all-important!

Carra: Obviously, having the ability to play in different positions was as important years ago as it is now. Possibly it's even more important these days. There are big squads and with the possibility of injuries the manager has to change the team and so it's important to have players who can operate in different positions.

To get in the Official Liverpool FC Hall of Fame demands very special qualities, highlighted by someone like Ian Callaghan who still holds the club's appearance record, having played in 857 games. That's a phenomenal achievement. >

Club men: Ronnie Moran and Roy Evans (top, in the Bootroom with Phil Thompson, Steve Heighway, Hughie McAuley and John Bennison) stayed at Liverpool for many decades while Jamie Carragher and Steven Gerrard have enjoyed many successes on the pitch together

'There have been so many **great players** and people who not only played for the **club**, but who joined the backroom staff to give **tremendous service**'

Stevie: Yes, we were talking about this with the manager recently, saying 'How did Cally manage to do that?' It's such an unbelievable achievement to play that number of games. I mean, Carra has been in the first team now for nearly 10 years and never misses a game through injury. He's an ever-present in the starting eleven. But even if he played for another 10 years, he probably would not match or beat Ian Callaghan's record.

These were players who bridged history and often played in several different positions to show their versatility.

Stevie: It's more than that. Cally was one who came at a very young age and showed real loyalty to the club, staying up to the age of 35. He deserves credit for that.

There were only three players who were elected into the Hall of Fame without debate.

Loyal servant: Ian Callaghan earned praise from Steven Gerrard while Jamie Carragher can't believe how many games Cally played!

Stevie: Let me have a guess. Billy Liddell?
Yes!
Roger Hunt?
No! He was elected into the Hall of Fame, but the panel debated other candidates from Shankly's great first team before ratifying his name.
Kenny Dalglish?
Yes!
Was Ian Callaghan one?
No, you got the first two. Like Roger, he was also elected after debate about other candidates. In fact, the third one was legendary goalkeeper Elisha Scott who played for Liverpool for over 20 years between seasons 1912/13 and 1933/34.

When you held the European Cup above your head in Istanbul, did you feel that you had somehow finally cemented your own place in Liverpool history?

Stevie: I don't think that comes into your mind at the time, but

HUYTON
CUP
MORIENTES
19
TheFA.co
Carlsberg
Carlsberg
8

> playing for Liverpool – and because of the history and how successful they have been over the years – there is always a pressure that you have got to go out and win trophies. It's a relief and a weight off your shoulders when you manage to do that. It means you have provided a big trophy and some great memories for the supporters and the club.

Carra: As Stevie said, you don't think about it at the time, but you realise that people will look back on that moment and say that your career was a success, not least because the Champions League is so difficult to win. Personally, as soon as you win it you want to go out and do it again, as well as winning the championship, because that is what this club has been built on. Our predecessors won four European Cups before us and many championships and so we want to add to our honours list before we finish.

Hopefully it's going to be a long time off, but how would you both like to be remembered by the fans?

Stevie: It has to be for winning trophies and being a successful player. When you've finished and fans are talking about you, it's important that they can look back and say: 'He was a good player and he won this and that.'

What about your actual playing and leadership qualities? How would you ultimately want these to be remembered in the future?

Stevie: I think Jamie and myself always go out and give it everything for the fans, even if we are not playing well. I think our supporters recognise that.

Carra: I just want fans to look back and say 'He gave it everything'. I want to win more trophies so that the next generation will look back at us and say that we helped to take the club to the next level.

As Liverpool FC prepare to leave Anfield for a fantastic new stadium in Stanley Park, the Hall of Fame debate will open up again with two new players inducted for 2000-2010. The club will then stage a spectacular event on the pitch at Anfield to formally induct everyone who has been selected for the Official Hall of Fame. Possibly this will be the last official thing that ever happens at historic Anfield. What would it mean to both of you if, at the end of that process, you were up there alongside the likes of Dalglish, Rush, Barnes, Cally and the rest?

Stevie: It would be very flattering even to be in the running when you look at the heroes who have already made it into the Hall of Fame and the quality of some of the greats who have missed out. To see all the legends in one place would be a very special day. Of course, it would also be very sad to

be saying goodbye to our famous old ground, but it would also be a tremendous opportunity to revel in all the great Liverpool memories while saluting the players who have contributed to the club's success. It would be great if me and Jamie were in contention for those two prized places.

Carra: We are just so proud to be playing now. I was lucky enough to play with stars like Ian Rush when I was in the reserves. Obviously I played a few games with John Barnes as well. They were legends of the club and heroes to us and I'm delighted they were named in our official Hall of Fame. It would be great for us to be involved in something like that.

LFC Hall of Fame

INTRODUCING THE PANEL

LIVER POOL
FOOTBALL CLUB
Mizuno
umbro

Starting the debate

When your job is to pick out 22 legends from the many heroes who have represented Liverpool Football Club, you need a good panel of judges . . .

Liverpool Football Club's Hall of Fame process saw an intriguing group of individuals come together as a respected panel to assess and discuss hundreds of potential candidates.

The club was determined to cover all the angles with this crucial group of individuals. Firstly, it was vital to have someone at the very top who could ultimately take key recommendations back to the board of directors (Chief Executive, Rick Parry). Then the club wanted someone who had commanded respect and influence in the dressing room (former captain and Assistant Manager Phil Thompson). In came another skipper and famous Red with a national media profile (Alan Hansen). It was also crucial to have someone with a powerful link with the fans and the local community (Brian Hall). And LFC wanted an individual steeped in Liverpool FC tradition who commanded the total respect of every single supporter (Ian Callaghan). Cally, of course, played over 850 times for the mighty Reds.

You can rest assured that they all took this challenge extremely seriously and listened intently to supporters' views. Naturally, a panel member who was a former player could not vote for himself.

There is no doubt that the panel revelled in the challenge. Alan Hansen said: "When you go through the players and look at the legends who did not got into the Hall of Fame, it shows the remarkable strength of this club.

"It is unfortunate that we could only name two players for each decade, but this is what makes the Hall of Fame so prestigious.

"The standard of players who have worn the red down the years has been of the highest quality. You tend to remember those who you watched yourself, but when you go further back you realise just how many legends we have had at Liverpool.

"That part was interesting for me as I sat on the panel. There was so much to talk about. That was the thing that stood out. We sat there and said to each other: 'How can we possibly leave him out?'

"It was tough at times, but it simply emphasises our strength as a club."

Hansen believes that the Hall of Fame will ultimately become a real focal point for fans visiting Anfield. No formal decision has been taken yet as to how it will finally be displayed, but it could help to mark key sites like the old Kop in the future when the stadium is rebuilt in Stanley Park.

Alan said: "I think this will spark a whole new debate with the fans who, once again, will be heavily involved."

Of course, Hansen's own input into Liverpool's glorious past will be forever remembered by supporters. He said: "To play for Liverpool was wonderful. To later become captain was one of the true highlights. I played in three great sides.

"The first, the late Seventies team, was probably the best. We conceded just 16 league goals in 1978-79 and scored 85 to win the league."

Just to mention that team brings back wonderful memories for Liverpudlians. Ray Clemence, Phil Neal, Ray Kennedy and Kenny Dalglish were ever-presents that year. Hansen played in 34 league games, having missed the start of the season. He would take the No 6 shirt off Emlyn Hughes and make it his own.

Graeme Souness was immense in 41 games and Thommo only missed three. You think about Alan Kennedy, Jimmy Case, Steve Heighway, Terry McDermott, David Johnson, David Fairclough and Sammy Lee. It was a formidable squad packed with vision, >

'The **Hall of Fame** debate gave us so much to **talk about.** That was the thing that **stood out.** We sat there and said to each other: 'How can we possibly **leave him out?'**

When selecting the Hall of Fame panel, the Reds were determined to conjure up a body of individuals steeped in the great Liverpool Football Club traditions. They looked at a wide range of important factors before coming up with Ian Callaghan, Phil Thompson, Alan Hansen, Brian Hall and Rick Parry. The panel covered off all the angles.

IAN CALLAGHAN played in over 850 games for Liverpool and is a leading figure in the Former Players' Association. Cally has the total respect of every Liverpudlian, was beyond reproach as a player and remains of the most respected figures in the world of football.

PHIL THOMPSON is an inspirational former Liverpool and England captain and was a driving force within Gerard Houllier's backroom team. Thommo eats, sleeps and drinks LFC and has a real feel for the club and its history.

ALAN HANSEN was one of Liverpool's greatest-ever players, a tremendous captain and a man with a national media profile. He helped to take the Hall of Fame debate into a wider area. Alan's football opinions are always thought-provoking.

BRIAN HALL is another respected former player who still plays an important role within the club as a key contact with the community. Brian has a real feel for grassroots opinion.

RICK PARRY is not just the club's Chief Executive but also a lifetime Liverpudlian. He took the panel's views - and the recommendations of the fans - into the boardroom for ultimate final ratification, highlighting that this whole project had the full support of the club at the highest level.

NOTE: If a former player /panel member was nominated in his own right as a possible Hall of Famer, he naturally could play no part whatsoever in that element of the debate.

skill, strength and pace - a potent mix that swept all before it.

Alan said: "Funnily enough, we won the European Cup in '78 and '81. The teams later won doubles and trebles. The '84 lads claimed the treble under Joe Fagan and then in '86 we grabbed the double under Kenny.

"Every player in each of those teams was extra special, but I still look back to the invincible team of 1978-79.

"As soon as you put on a Liverpool jersey, it fills you with pride. It was because of what Bill Shankly had created and what Bob Paisley had followed up with. You saw the famous 'This Is Anfield' sign as you came down the tunnel and it was extra special.

"You went out walking tall. The people behind the team played their part. Shanks had been inspirational for previous teams. Bob had such a great eye for the game. Joe Fagan commanded so much respect. He was also a great coach and a great manager in his own right.

"And we should not forget Ronnie Moran, who was with the club for something like 46 years. He was Liverpool through and through. All of them were different in their own way, but they all contributed to the history and the success of the club.

"When work needed to be done you can rest assured that it was done. But they also encouraged us to laugh. That helped build the great team spirit. This is what I miss most. It's not the training. It's the going to training and everything that surrounded it.

"The people in charge deserve our total respect for building that togetherness, closeness and camaraderie. If you take these things on the pitch, you've always got a chance."

'In **our minds** we have been picturing stars back out there on our **famous pitch.** Hall of Fame has brought the **legends** back to the fans and I think this has been a **wonderful** thing'

Fellow panel member Brian Hall said: "As fans, we sometimes pick out the highlights as they relate to a club, rather than assessing the global picture. What Hall of Fame has done has put the whole of the picture together.

"You suddenly grasp the immensity of our club and its history, the success and quality of the players. The whole thing comes into perspective.

"There has always been a great empathy between the football team and the supporters, going all the way back to the beginning. Hall of Fame has focused our minds and served to re-emphasise the collective bond between players and fans. Many of our heroes of the past are no longer with us, but this process has brought them back into our famous stadium.

"In our minds we have been picturing them back out there on our famous pitch. Hall of Fame has therefore brought the legends back to the fans and I think this has been a wonderful thing.

"We do have a long and successful history. The modern generation of fans inevitably concentrate on those stars who featured in the immediate past. But these fairly modern heroes are just part of the total history package.

"And it's not just players we have been talking about. It has enabled us to reflect on people like our founder John Houlding, whose big house still stands close to the Centenary Stand, backing on to Stanley Park. The whole process brings it back to supporters. It further cements the spirit between everyone connected with a football club.

"I was fortunate enough to wear the Red. I wasn't the greatest player the club has ever had and I won't be in the Hall of Fame, but I played my part in a very successful era and I have a tremendous pride in that."

Brian added: "Hall of Fame has actually highlighted the input of everyone who has pulled on a Liverpool shirt, be it for just one game or 800 games.

"When I look back, I was an 18-year-old who had no real interest in becoming a professional footballer. Suddenly I found myself on that famous Anfield stage and I was lucky enough to play at Wembley and many of the great venues in Britain and in Europe. It was a fantastic experience, something I was very proud to be a part of.

"I work behind the scenes at the club these days and so I am at Anfield just about every day. It means that I am constantly reminded about great days and wonderful memories. I was a central part of something special along with a group >

A game of opinions: Alan Hansen (above) relished the Hall of Fame challenge. Below: The panel enjoy a joke

'I spent some time getting my **own thoughts** together about the Seventies because I wanted my **nominations** to be absolutely **right . . .** there were many **unsung heroes'**

of other players and we all treasure what we achieved.

"When the club asked me to sit on the panel, I was thrilled. I know they wanted a wide-ranging forum. I'm the former player who these days has strong links with the fans. It's my job to reach out and touch people through our community activities. Alan Hansen was a great player from the past who brought a national profile to the table with his media work.

"To look around the panel and see Ian Callaghan alongside you was tremendous with his 800-plus Liverpool games behind him and all that knowledge. Then there was Phil Thompson, providing a link to the past and also a recent link into the modern dressing room."

Phil Thompson's whole life has revolved around Liverpool Football Club as young fan, Kopite, first-team player, European Cup-winning skipper, reserve coach, assistant manager, caretaker manager and then, having come full circle, devoted fan once more.

He brought a lifetime's experience to the Hall of Fame panel and was able to speak powerfully and knowledgeably as the red-hot debate unfolded. However, never was he more animated than when he was talking about the sensational 1970s.

"What did the Seventies mean to me?" said Thommo, inviting himself to revel in a golden era. "Absolutely everything! I was involved from the outset as a young player and finished the decade as club captain. It was a fantastic time for me and for the fans. We won our first European trophy, the UEFA Cup, in 1973, beating Borussia Moenchengladbach. It was an incredible occasion.

"I'd played in the semi-final against Tottenham, but watched the two-legged final against the Germans from the touchline as a substitute from where I was able to study Bill Shankly. The first leg was actually abandoned because of a waterlogged pitch at Anfield. Shanks, having suddenly recognised a German weakness in the air, left out Brian Hall and brought in John Toshack to exploit the situation when the game was replayed 24 hours later. It was a masterstroke. We won comfortably 3-0, but they were a very good side with world-class stars like Bonhof and Netzer. In the return they gave us a torrid time and we were two-down and clinging onto a 3-2 aggregate lead early in the second half.

"Shanks was walking up and down the touchline, pointing his finger in the air and pointing to the fans. It was as if he couldn't watch what was going on. The character of the players to hold on and win that first European trophy was magnificent and I remember the supporters spilling onto the pitch on the final whistle and swamping the lads.

"It was astonishing. We would win

Long running debate: Marathon man Ian Callaghan (above) and ex-skipper Phil Thompson

five titles through this decade (including 1979/80), the FA Cup and, of course, our first European Cup in 1977 when we once again beat Moenchengladbach.

"On a personal note, good can always come out of bad. I missed that Rome final after having a cartilage operation. John Toshack also sat it out because of injury. But the following year I was privileged and pleased to play against Bruges at Wembley as we retained the trophy, which was a great achievement.

"It was an incredible time for Liverpool. While I missed the '77 Rome final, I have to say that it was possibly the most emotional night in the history of the club, until Istanbul of course.

"I will never forget seeing that giant embankment of our fans in Rome's Olympic Stadium with that sea of red and white chequered flags.

"When the players came out, they walked in silence across the pitch. No-one could believe it. So many supporters had travelled so far and the lads produced the goods to make it so very special."

Phil saw the club go from strength to strength. He said: "Liverpool developed into a great team in the Seventies, playing with flair, concentration and determination.

"Some people said we were robotic because of the way we steamrollered teams, but I would prefer to describe us as world class. We had a steely determination, great understanding and we also possessed the best goalkeeper in the country. People outside of Liverpool might talk about Peter Shilton, but Ray Clemence was magnificent for me."

As a member of the Hall of Fame panel, Phil was able to consider the powerful claims of Clem, although he couldn't vote because he was on the 1970s shortlist himself and this ruled him out when it came to the final show of hands. The same applied to Ian Callaghan.

It didn't stop Thommo from expressing his own feelings ahead of the vote. He said: "I spent some time getting my own thoughts together about the Seventies because I wanted my nominations to be absolutely right.

"When the panel met, I was quick to point out that the beginning of the Seventies belonged to Kevin Keegan. He was young, enthusiastic and a brilliant footballer.

"He looked the part with his long hair and the fans related to his passion for the club. The arrival of Keegan and the impact he made was what everyone needed. Later in the Seventies, Kenny Dalglish swept onto the scene.

"Kevin was all-action, but Kenny had a skill and vision that raised him to a different level. This pair jump >

out as the central figures of the era, but as soon as I found myself saying that, I looked at the Scroll Of Fame for this decade featuring every player who was involved and a host of players jumped out as legends in their own right. This is why it was such a fascinating debate.

"There were many unsung heroes, like Phil Neal, who was top-class for club and country.

"You forget that the Tommy Smiths and Ian Callaghans starred in the Sixties and were still influential late in the Seventies.

"I've mentioned Keegan and Dalglish, but Cally played 857 top-class games and epitomised everything that was good about our club. It was a red-hot debate.

"Liverpool was the centre of the universe in the Sixties and Seventies for football, music, fashion, hairstyles - everything. Now I'm not going to dwell on the hairstyle theme, but I will say that the Seventies were special, for me and hopefully for you. I wasn't able to vote in the final reckoning on the Seventies because I was amongst the candidates. As it turned out, I didn't get in, but to be on the shortlist alongside men like Cally, Clem, Tommy Smith, Emlyn Hughes, Kevin Keegan, Ray Kennedy, Steve Heighway, Phil Neal and John Toshack was an honour in itself.

'We needed to listen to **the fans.** Then we had to use our **experience** and the statistics to make a final decision. Many people may **disagree** with our final verdicts. Others will say we **got it right'**

"Finally, Chief Executive Rick Parry played his part. The mix was perfect for me, because of the different experiences.

"One thing I must say about Rick is that while he is the club's Chief Executive and in the boardroom, he retains that fierce passion of being a Liverpudlian man and boy.

"His views were interesting and it was a nice balance of thoughts when we got down to the selection process."

Rick Parry said: "One thing is for certain. One of the beauties of football is that 45,000 people can

Hall Of
FAME

We're there! Panel have final say

for Liverpool was such a
ful experience - Hansen

assemble for a match and disagree on a whole range of issues. They discuss the game in the street, the shops, the offices and the pubs and there is still wide-ranging opinions. It's what football is all about. It's what makes the game so fascinating.

"Hall of Fame is part of this process. I saw our role as a panel in a simple way.

"We needed to listen to the fans. Then we had to use our experience and the statistical support we were given to make a final decision.

"Many people may disagree with our final verdicts. Many others will argue that we got it exactly right.

I don't think the ultimate player nominations will cause controversy because of the sheer quality and character of the people we have selected.

"I'm sure it will cause debate. That is what supporting football is all about. But equally I'm sure that our knowledgeable fans will recognise that Hall of Fame is a symbol of everything that is great about Liverpool Football Club.

"It will throw up some exciting possibilities both now and when we eventually move to our new stadium. It will highlight how important Anfield is to all of us and it will enable us to leave something tangible behind for everyone to revel in and remember."

Over to you: Rick Parry involves the fans. Above: LFC magazine carried the debate

Making a shortlist

The panel's first task was to select the players from each decade in the running for the Hall of Fame. Then the final 22 selections could be made . . .

The Liverpool FC Hall of Fame panel met for the first time charged with the task of forming a shortlist of players for the official Liverpool Football Club Hall of Fame.

Phil Thompson, Alan Hansen, Ian Callaghan, Brian Hall and Rick Parry gathered at Anfield to get to grips with the hottest player debate in the club's history.

They assessed the emotional claims of a host of super heroes. They looked at the statistical breakdown, honours won in the relevant decades and international caps gained. They also studied your valued views.

At the end of this all-important first session, a consensus was reached on the shortlist of magnificent individuals who moved through to the final selection stage.

Panel AND fans alike automatically put a tick by three truly outstanding names. Clearly, no debate was needed when it came to legends:

ELISHA SCOTT, BILLY LIDDELL and KENNY DALGLISH.

Undisputed legends: Elisha Scott, Billy Liddell and Kenny Dalglish . . .

They researched all 11 qualifying decades carefully and presented readers of the official LFC weekly club magazine with a complete history of the Reds to inspire debate. Hall of Fame updates were provided in the matchday programme and local press and fanzines were encouraged to play their part.

A formal presentation was then made to the Official Liverpool Supporters' Club, aiming to cover all the angles and take on board the respected views of the fans.

This was always going to be a mammoth exercise. It was never going to be as simple as looking at the stats because many players bridged the decades. You also have to take other key factors into account. For instance, to have made 300 to 400 appearances prior to the Sixties was the equivalent to making 600 to 800 appearances now.

In the early pioneering years, football was based on the league and the FA Cup. Early on, the league season was much shorter. For instance, Liverpool's first league campaign in 1893-94 consisted of just 28 games. This increased to 30 in 1894-95 and this remained the standard until 1898-99 when it became 34 and then 38 in 1905. The 42-game standard was invoked in 1919 and this was the norm right up until the Nineties. Now, of course, it has been reduced to 38 games because of other commitments.

Prior to the Sixties there was no serious European action and no League Cup. Equally, international caps were truly precious in those days with games few and far between, the main action being the now defunct Home International

'The panel **researched** all 11 qualifying decades carefully and presented readers of the official **LFC magazine** with a complete history of the club to assist their **decision-making**'

Fans interaction

Liverpool FC was determined that the fans would be central to the Hall of Fame debate and convened a meeting very early on with the Official Liverpool Supporters' Club to gauge reaction.

Chief executive Rick Parry, Ian Callaghan and Brian Hall were centre stage in terms of the top table, but the night was all about the fans.

They fired one question after another at the panel, made some fascinating recommendations and demonstrated that Liverpudlians have a passion and a knowledge for their club that is second to none.

As Rick Parry reflected: "Our meeting with the fans demonstrated clearly that this is genuinely an interactive process. We stated on day one that we wanted the fans to be involved and we had already been listening to their views and opinions.

"Now this was an opportunity to talk to them face-to-face. They clearly had strong views on who should be included and what the criteria should be. They also had a vision about how the Hall of Fame should ultimately manifest itself and be displayed."

One key question asked by the fans was whether or not the club could consider more than two nominees per decade because spells such as the 1970s and 1980s were so successful.

Passionate: Liverpool fans love their team

Mr Parry's view was straightforward. He said: "I don't think we should change the criteria between the decades. It suggests players in one era are more special than those from another.

"The fact that we are only choosing two from each era will actually make entry into the Hall of Fame very special indeed. Those nominated will be true Liverpool FC legends."

Championships.

The panel, at its first session, considered many things - like length of service, total games played outside the decade in question and a wider dedication to the club.

Every decade threw up a different dilemma when it comes to narrowing down a formidable list to just two final super heroes.

For instance, let's consider the panel's challenge in two contrasting eras - the 1890s, when Liverpool Football Club came into being and the 1980s, by which time the club was sweeping all before it

The 1890s had the panel considering 10 outstanding candidates.

An interesting argument unfolded regarding two in particular, one who made more appearances than any other in that first qualifying era and another who played fewer games, but was one of the most remarkable characters the club has ever had.

'In restricting each decade to just **two giants,** the Hall of Fame will be very **special** indeed. Those who are honoured will be **genuine legends** in every way'

John McCartney played in 165 games over five seasons including 18 Lancashire League, a real Anfield pioneer and a Scot who soon established himself on the right-hand side of the half-back line. He was described as having a fierce tackle and elegant distribution. McCartney won two Division Two titles, as did Matt McQueen, another key member of the original Scottish 'Team of Macs.'

If you were simply basing your judgement on total appearances in the decade, the excellent McCartney would clearly overshadow team mate McQueen.

But Matt was possibly Liverpool's most versatile player ever, playing in goal on many occasions as well as at centre-forward, outside-right, inside-right, inside-left and right-back.

This remarkable character would later serve Liverpool as player, director and manager and even had a spell as a Football League referee.

He had a leg amputated in 1924, but he was indomitable and returned to manage the club for a further four years, reflecting his exceptional resilience.

So you see, the selection process was tough.

Would you back McCartney or McQueen if you had a straight vote?

Others compete with both of them, like goalscoring hero of the day Harry Bradshaw, who could play right across the front line and free-scoring centre-forward George Allan.

Panel members Hansen, Callaghan, Hall, Thompson and Parry discovered from the word go that the selection process was difficult.

By the time they had reached the 1980s, they were really caught up in a massive challenge.

They were asked to consider the merit of 11 giants who contributed to the winning of six Championships ('80, '82, '83, '84, '86, and '88), two European Cups ('81, '84), two FA Cups ('86, '89) and four League Cups ('81, '82, '83, '84).

In coming to a final consensus and restricting each decade to just two giants, Hall of Fame is very special indeed. Those who are honoured are genuine legends in every way. Equally, every player to have worn the red shirt are featured in 11 definitive Scrolls of Fame.

Ian Callaghan, who wore the famous Red himself on over 800 occasions, summed things up on behalf of the panel.

He said: "Yes, it was a major challenge and a difficult one, but I found the whole process fascinating and extremely enjoyable.

"People ask why we were assessing the merits of people whose exploits were in the dim and distant past and who we can only judge through playing records, newspaper cuttings and pen pictures.

"The fact is, without these individuals we would not have been able to go on to become a world-famous organisation.

"It's great that we are recalling their achievements and salute them along with the modern greats.

"The selection process wasn't as straightforward as looking at statistics and putting a tick alongside names. But on a host of issues, the panel was clearly on the same wavelength."

Key panel members were then set to attended a meeting of the Official Liverpool Supporters Club at Anfield to bring fans up-to-date and to listen to their views.

The panel then had another exhaustive session to turn their shortlist into the first-ever Liverpool FC Hall of Fame, with two players saluted from every decade from 1892 up until 2000.

You may agree or disagree with the selections that were ultimately made. What is certain is that no stone was left unturned when it came to involving all the people with a knowledge and love of Liverpool Football Club.

What follows is a decade by decade excursion through the years, from 1892 to 2000, as the 22 Hall of Fame legends are revealed.

Each chapter highlights the famous deeds of the men who made that exclusive shortlist before we reveal the names of those who have actually secured a position of honour in the "Hall of Fame" and therefore a cherished place in the annals of Anfield history.

Enjoy the journey . . .

The fans' debate dealt with a whole host of issues. One fan asked if it was right that an era like the Forties should be considered because six war years disrupted Football League action, reducing the options when considering Hall of Fame nominees for that era. The same principle applies to the spell 1910-1920.

Rick Parry said: "I don't think it's fair to say that because the selection years in these decades were reduced, we should not feature them. There were still some terrific players around. Our panel discussions highlighted this. After all, Elisha Scott came to us before the First World War and the great Billy Liddell was a super hero in the Forties when Liverpool won a deserved League Championship, inspired by many excellent players."

Another key point made was that the Hall of Fame process had gone a long way to reviving memories of players whose achievements might otherwise have been forgotten or at least only remembered within yellowing newspaper cuttings or history books.

Hall of Fame allowed the club to focus on every decade in the club's history and ensure that, in a very high-profile way, the club's pioneers were elevated to the same importance as those heroes who have contributed so much in modern times.

Goalkeepers were very much in the mind of fans attending the Official Supporters' Club evening. We have already mentioned the great Elisha Scott, one of those whose achievements led to the club's old and famous telegraphic address being 'Goalkeeper.'

Ray Clemence was another whose exploits were noted on the night. The panel assured supporters that the former England star was one of those whose claims were under serious scrutiny.

Obviously, all the stars mentioned during the evening read like a 'Who's Who Of Football' with World Cup winner Roger Hunt and another record-breaking goalscorer Ian Rush earning their fair share of plaudits.

All in all, a fascinating meeting left the panel with a lot to think about as the selection process continued at that time.

Main image: Davie Hannah scores for Liverpool against Sunderland in a 3-0 win on November 7, 1896. The beaten goalkeeper - Teddy Doig - would go on to sign for Liverpool in 1904 and and became the oldest player ever to make his debut or play for Liverpool. Fittingly, he is the grandfather of Hall of Fame statistician Eric Doig

HAS ANY PLAYER IN HISTORY EVER SHOWN SUCH VERSATILITY?

1890s

LIVERPOOL
(ASSOCIATION)
Football Club.
GROUND—ANFIELD ROAD.

Season 1893-94.

This Ticket is issued subject to Rule VI., and admits to all League and Ordinary Matches, but is NOT available for Cup Ties, Benefit or Charity Matches.

J. J. RAMSAY, Hon. Treas.,
7, Hawkesworth Street, Everton.

10/-

SUBSCRIBER'S TICKET
Not Transferable.
ADMIT
Name

The Kop pioneers

A row over rent put paid to the original inhabitants of Anfield, paving the way for the birth of a new set of footballing heroes on Merseyside

When you talk about a Liverpool Football Club Hall of Fame, you instinctively think about great footballers and legendary games.

However, there are many individuals who have served Liverpool magnificently down the years to whom the club owes a remarkable debt of gratitude.

It could be argued that the most important of these was effectively the founding father of Liverpool FC - John Houlding.

The history books remind us that there was a time when the two big clubs in these parts were Everton and...BOOTLE!

Everton, of course, played at Anfield, having migrated there from Stanley Park. Houlding had become a real power broker in the Everton camp. Born close to Scotland Road, his father was a cowkeeper, but the young Houlding was determined to spread his wings and by the mid-1850s he was working for a local brewery and clearly destined for bigger things.

He would buy two pubs of his own - and a brewery - and one of his premises was the Sandon Hotel in Oakfield Road, where the Everton players (and the opposition) originally changed before trecking through the streets to Anfield itself. The Sandon, of course, still stands and remains a major meeting point for football fans.

Houlding would eventually become Lord Mayor of Liverpool. However, all was not well within the ranks of Everton Football Club and it was about money and power. Houlding had become president of the club and it clearly suited both his sporting and business ambitions. The Sandon Hotel, just as it does today, benefited greatly from the nearby presence of the football ground. Houlding, or "King John" as he was known, was capitalising on the rising interest in the game. He had also become Everton's representative tenant at Anfield, but the power game changed when he actually became the club's landlord.

It was in his power to put up the

rent which he duly did, arguing that it should be linked with Everton's ever-increasing profits. The turmoil within the Blues' committee would begin to reach a peak in January, 1892 when Houlding's biggest rival, local accountant George Mahon, declared at a special general meeting that he had found a new ground on the other side of Stanley Park. By mid-March it was becoming clear that Houlding was losing his battle.

The vote for the move was ratified, but Houlding and his right-hand men William Barclay and John McKenna resolved to stay at Anfield and actually launched a battle with the FA to retain the "Everton" name. When it became clear that he had no legal hold on it, he made the obvious decision. Rather than head a team with a district name, he would call his new club "Liverpool". The rest is history.

Barclay and McKenna were called directors, but were actually joint managers of the club. Barclay initially looked after administration and McKenna team affairs.

John Houlding, the overlord, lived in Stanley House on Anfield Road which still stands, opposite the gates into the Centenary Stand car park. From his small balcony, he could actually see into Anfield itself. The brewer who caused a football revolution would no doubt smile that the modern Liverpool has had, as its main sponsor, a world drinks brand - *Carlsberg*!

LFC spent its first season (1892-93) in the Lancashire League, which was promptly won. **Andrew Hannah** and **Duncan McLean** had refused to go with Everton to Goodison and formed the backbone of the first LFC team. Ironically, Liverpool continued to play in blue and white and would do so for a further six years.

'There are many **individuals** who have served Liverpool magnificently down the **years** to whom the club owes a remarkable debt of gratitude, not least founding father **John Houlding**'

We salute the first 11 men who turned out as Liverpool FC: *Ross, Hannah, McLean, Pearson, McQue, McBride, Wyllie, Smith, McVean, Cameron, Kelvin.*

Another former Everton player, **Pat Gordon,** would be a regular as Liverpool secured their place in the Second Division of the Football League in 1893-94 along with Woolwich Arsenal. What a rivalry that would develop into! Ironically, Liverpool gained league status at the expense of their more well-known local rivals - Bootle!

The club stormed to promotion at the first time of asking after finishing top and winning a Test Match against bottom Division One team Newton Heath (now Manchester United). However, relegation followed immediately, then promotion again as Second Division champions in 1895-96 after the compulsory Test Matches.

Star players at this time included forward **Harry Bradshaw,** whose first-half goal in the Newton Heath >

Hall of Fame

1890s

SCROLL OF FAME

1892-1899: Men who made a first team appearance, players in gold shortlisted for Hall of Fame

ALLAN George
BATTLES Ben
BECTON Frank
BRADSHAW Harry
BULL Ben
CAMERON J
CAMERON James
CLEGHORN Thomas
CLELAND James
COLVIN Robert
COX Jack
CUNLIFFE Daniel
CURRAN John
DEWHURST Gerald
DICK Douglas
DONNELLY William
DRUMMOND John
DUNLOP Billy
FINNERHAN Patrick
FOXALL Abraham
GEARY Fred
GIVENS John
GOLDIE Archie
GOLDIE Bill
GORDON Patrick
HANNAH Andrew
HANNAH Davy
HARTLEY Abraham
HENDERSON David
HENDERSON James
HENDERSON Hugh
HOLMES John
HOWELL Raby
HUGHES William
HUNTER 'Sailor'
HUNTER Thomas
JOWITT Charles
KEECH William
KELLY P
KELSO J
KELVIN Andrew
KERR Neil
KYLE Peter
LUMSDEN Joe
MARSHALL Bobby
McBRIDE James
McCANN William
McCARTNEY John
McCOWIE Andrew
McLEAN Duncan
McLEAN John
McOWEN William
McQUE Joe
McQUEEN Hugh
McQUEEN Matthew
McVEAN Malcolm
MICHAEL William
MILLER John
MORGAN Hugh
NEILL Robert
PARKINSON John
PEARSON
PERKINS William
RICHARDSON
RAISBECK Alex
ROBERTSON Tommy
ROSS Jimmy
ROSS Sydney
SATTERTHWAITE Charles
SMITH Jock
STEVENSON 'General'
STORER Harry
STOTT James
WALKER John
WALKER William
WHITEHEAD John
WILKIE Thomas
WILSON Charlie
WILSON David
WORGAN Arthu
WYLLIE Thomas

LIVERPOOL FC'S OFFICIAL HALL OF FAME

Test Match secured promotion to the top flight for the first time. Harry played centre-forward and inside-left and was top scorer in that opening Division One season with 17 goals.

He won two Division Two Championship medals and in 1897 played for England. He left for Spurs in 1898, having figured in 138 games and scored 53 goals.

Billy Dunlop was a talented left-back who was one of a host of Scottish players who ended up at Anfield. He arrived via Kilmarnock and Paisley Abercorn in 1894-95. Dunlop would still be playing for Liverpool in 1908-09 and so bridges two decades. The club programme said of Billy:

"There are some men who perform brilliantly in their various positions on the field, but there was never one who year in, year out has given such wholehearted service as Dunlop to Liverpool."

Leading the way: Joe McQue, a Liverpool pioneer. Above right: An original Liverpool FC programme from November 1892 and match ticket for McQue's benefit game

He served the club for 15 seasons and while the first four were years of establishing himself, he then became a regular, playing 363 career games and scoring two goals.

Archie Goldie was another imported Scot, this time from Clyde. He was a dour defender and a powerful tackler with a strong right-foot shot. Archie played in 149 games between 1895 and the turn of the century.

LIVERPOOL FOOTBALL CLUB.
Ground: ANFIELD ROAD.
Authorized Programme and Fixtures.
ONE PENNY.] SATURDAY, 26th NOVEMBER, 1892. [ONE PENNY.

SMOKE "BOATS" 'BACCA. Sole Proprietor: WATTS-his-Name, Dale St.

BOOTLE ATHLETIC.
Referee—Mr. R. Stevenson.
Goal: Owens
Right Back: Caldwell
Left Back: Pollock
Half Backs: Grant, Marshall, McFarlane
Right Wing: Edgar, Hay
Left Wing: Halliday, L Higgins
Centre: Gillies

KICK-OFF AT 2-45 P.M. PROMPT.

Centre: Fenn
Left Wing: Kelvin, Clarke
Right Wing: Hurst, Hill
Half Backs: Farish, Swinton, Richardson
Left Back: Pearson
Right Back: McNally
Goal: McOwen
...OL. RESERVE

SUGG, 7, Whitechapel and 32, Lord Street, LIVERPOOL
FOOTBALL KING, ... 9/6
CENTRE-HALF, ... 7/6
JUNIOR LEAGUE, ... 4/11
...rseys, Shirts, Shin-guards, Boots and all Requisites at WHOLESALE Prices. Send for Catalogue, Post Free.
THE PRACTICAL MAN.
...per cent cheaper than other houses.

ALEXANDRA HOTEL, DALE ST., LIVERPOOL.
Newly Decorated and Re-Furnished throughout.
Luncheons, 2/-; Table d'hote 3/6
A Cut off the Joint, with Cheese, 1/6.
Neptune Hotel, CLAYTON SQUARE, LIVERPOOL.
Proprietor of both Hotels: H. HEARD.

NOTICE! NOTICE! NOTICE!
CAIN is Able
To supply a First-Class Scotch Tweed SUIT for —40/-— and TROUSERS, all latest designs from —11/6.—
Cycling Outfits a Speciality
Good, Honest English Workmanship.
A Perfect Fit Guaranteed.
29, Kirkdale Rd.

For Latest Styles, Best Value, and Reliable Goods Only
HOBBS & Co., HATTERS AND UMBRELLA MAKERS
Are the Foremost.
—50 Years Reputation—
Hobbs & Co., 9 LONDON RD., LIVERPOOL.

...RUISEN & SON,
over 2,000 INSTRUMENTS In Stock TO SELECT FROM
...ST., LIVERPOOL.

Telegraphic Address—"Serviceable! Liverpool." Telephone No. 5048.
JNO. A. TURNER & Co.
THE BEST OUTFITTERS, HATTERS & HOSIERS,
41 GT. CHARLOTTE ST., And 18 & 20, ELLIOT ST., LIVERPOOL.
Opposite ST. JOHN'S MARKET.

A GRAND Football Match AT ANFIELD.
JOE McQUE'S BENEFIT.
BURNLEY v. LIVERPOOL.
Easter Monday, April 6th, 1896.
KICK-OFF 11-30 A.M.
Admission to Ground and Stands 6d.

His brother Bill was also a faithful Liverpool servant. **Bill Goldie** switched from full-back to wing-half with great success. He joined Liverpool in 1897-98, also from Clyde and was renowned for his penetrating passes. He was solid and dependable and finished with Liverpool career statistics of 174 games and six goals.

One of Liverpool's pioneer players was **Andrew Hannah,** who had been one of Everton's most powerful full-backs before joining the Houlding revolution. He had appeared in three Scottish Cup finals for Renton and won a Scottish cap in 1888 before he joined Everton, where he won a Championship medal before having two seasons with Liverpool, between 1893-95. He captained the club as a mature and experienced 28-year-old and gave a young team poise. His commitment to Liverpool was crucial in those early years.

John McCartney joined Liverpool in 1892-93, an accomplished wing-half whose fierce tackling and elegant distribution made him a favourite. He figured in 165 games, scoring six goals.

Liverpool were called the team of Macs at this time and **Joe McQue** was one of them. He was a commanding centre-half who came down from Celtic in 1893 and played for five seasons (scoring 12 goals in 122 games). It was said that 1895-96 was his finest season and he was granted a benefit game by the club.

Matt McQueen joined Liverpool with his brother Hugh from Leith Athletic in 1892. Matt was versatile enough to appear at centre-forward, outside-right, inside-right, inside-left - and even goalkeeper - during his league first season. He

Liverpool Football Club.
No. 137
Liverpool, March 1897
Received from M. B. Halhed
the sum of Ten Shillings, being the amount of his Subscription for the Season 1896 1897
£0 : 10 : 0
A. Grueller
Hon. Treasurer.

kept goal on five occasions and was unbeaten in four of them.

Malcom McVean came from Third Lanark in 1892-93. He was a speedy inside forward and has the distinction of having scored Liverpool's first-ever Football League goal against Middlesbrough on September 2, 1893. He also scored Liverpool's first FA Cup goal in October, 1892. He played in all the forward positions except inside-left and scored 29 goals in 105 appearances, leaving for Burnley in 1897.

Alex Raisbeck played for Liverpool for 11 seasons between 1898-99 and 1908-09 and would ultimately win two Championship medals and a Second Division winners' medal, but his glory days were arguably in the 1900-1910 decade.

Tommy Robertson came from Hearts in 1898. He scored 34 goals in 141 games over five seasons from the left wing and was second top scorer in 1899-1900 when he was ever-present. He would win a Championship medal in 1900-01.

Jimmy Ross was one of the League's early stars and had three seasons with Liverpool between 1894 and 1897. He was a clever ball player with an eye for goal, finishing with 40 in 85 games for Liverpool. His best Anfield season was 1895-96 when he was top scorer with 23 goals in 25 games. **Harry Storer** made his debut in goal on New Year's Day 1896 and made 121 appearances in five seasons, also playing cricket for Derbyshire while **John Walker** was a Scotland international when he came to Anfield in 1898 He had the knack of scoring crucial goals, 31 in 120 appearances.

Above: Early 'season tickets' - a receipt given for payment of 10 shillings for the 1986-97 season

Below: The Liverpool team in 1892

How the panel called it:

Bradshaw was the acknowledged hero of the decade as a great goalscorer. His goal in the Test Match against Newton Heath (Manchester United) in 1894 gained Liverpool promotion to the top flight for the first time. The panel settled on him and then had a fascinating debate between half-back John McCartney (who played more games than any of his rivals in this decade) and Matt McQueen, who was, as we've said, one of the great characters of the day (a man who successfully played in goal for Liverpool as well as centre-forward and who later became manager and a league referee!). McQueen, possibly the most versatile LFC player of all time, finally got the vote as a remarkable Anfield servant (still being involved at the club in 1928).

McQue. J McCartney. A. Hannah. S. H. Ross. M. McQueen. D. McLean. J. McBride A. Dick (*Trainer*).
T. Wyllie. J. Smith. J. Miller. M. McVean. H. McQueen

Anfield **giant** and first **England** star

No. 1: **HARRY BRADSHAW**

Thomas Henry Bradshaw - known to everyone as Harry - is the first giant to take his place in the official Liverpool Hall of Fame. He would play a massive part in supporting John Houlding's bold ambitions for the new Merseyside club.

A forward, who operated on the left wing, at centre-forward or in either of the two inside-forward positions, Harry had a real eye for goal and he would have the distinction of becoming the first Liverpool player to star for England.

If you took the first 10 years of Liverpool's existence, only George Allan would score more goals than Harry, 58 to 53. But Allan operated mainly at centre-forward while many of Bradshaw's games were on the left wing.

Born in Liverpool on August 24, 1873, Harry first made a name for himself with Northwich Victoria, who he played for between 1892-93.

Said to be strong and courageous, the talented Bradshaw would serve Liverpool for five seasons after making his debut in October 1893.

That first major game was a memorable experience for him. Bradshaw, wearing the No 9 shirt, scored in a 5-0 hammering of Arsenal in front of 7,000 fans. These were exciting times for the fledgling Liverpool FC.

The club had been forced to play its inaugural season in the Lancashire League (1892-93) after failing to gain entry to the Football League at the first time of asking.

Liverpool stormed to the championship and were well placed to seize their opportunity when the Football League increased the size of the First Division to 16 clubs, therefore creating the need for more clubs to play in the Second Division.

Ironically, Woolwich Arsenal were also admitted alongside the Merseysiders, becoming the first London team to play in the Football League.

Liverpool kicked off with Bradshaw still at Northwich. It was a storming start: 2-0 v Middlesbrough (a), 4-0 v Lincoln (h), 1-0 v Ardwick (a), 3-1 v Small Heath (h), 1-1 v Notts County (a), 6-0 v Middlesbrough (h), 4-3 v Small Heath (a) and then 1-1 v Burton Swifts (a). Determined to build on this start, Bradshaw was signed and drafted in for the trip to Arsenal.

Even then, the rivalry was fierce. Liverpool wanted to show the capital's fans that the north still possessed the best professional football teams, despite Arsenal's emergence on the Football League scene.

The 5-0 success for the visitors confirmed the lighthearted 'Southern Softies' theory, which still exists today! Bradshaw scored on his debut along with three Macs - McLean, Matt McQueen and McCartney. Stott was the other goal hero.

Harry then scored on his Anfield home debut, a 5-1 drubbing of Newcastle.

He would finish the season with eight goals in 14 league games, his greatest moment of that first eventful campaign coming on April 28, 1894, when Liverpool found themselves, as champions, still having to play in a Test Match against Newton Heath (later Manchester United) for the honour of gaining entry to the top flight. >

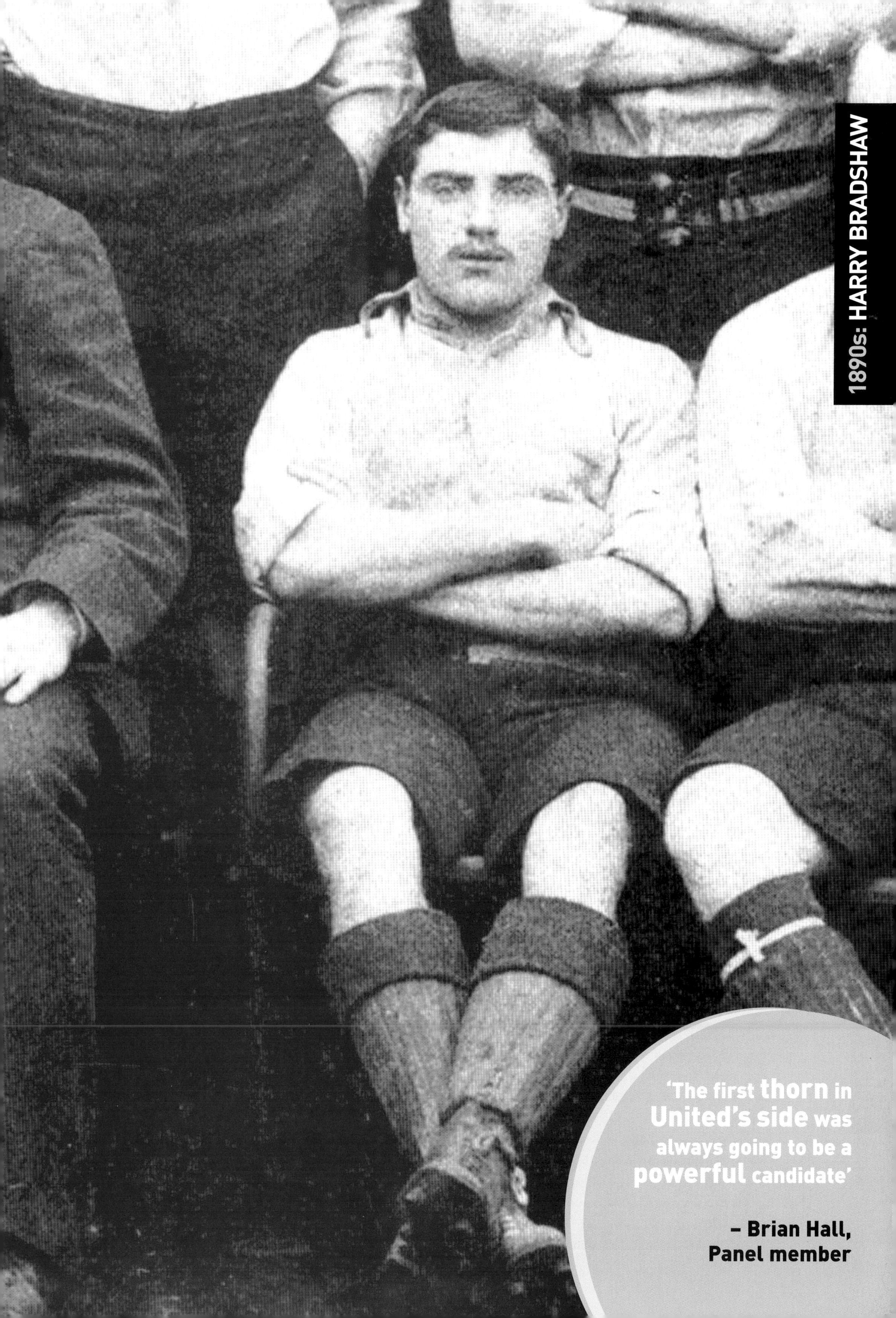

'The first **thorn** in **United's side** was always going to be a **powerful** candidate'

– Brian Hall, Panel member

In those days the top team in the Second faced the bottom team in the First in a play-off. Bradshaw and Patrick Gordon scored the goals that would finally elevate the club to the top flight, a sweet moment for president John Houlding as he savoured potential games against rivals Everton.

Harry would top the Liverpool scoring charts in that first Division One campaign with 17 goals in 30 ever-present league games.

By now the Anfield crowds were beginning to build. In the Second Division, the top home gate had been in the region of 8,000 (the journalists were adept at predicting the crowds in those days).

In the First Division, Liverpool actually drew 30,000 fans for their first ever top flight home game against Everton, a 2-2 draw. Weeks before, 44,000 had packed the new Goodison Park for the first ever league derby match, unhappily a losing experience for Bradshaw and Co. Indeed, apart from Harry's scoring exploits, the Liverpudlians would have to endure a frustrating first year at the highest level, at the end of which the club went back down to the Second Division. Bury would replace them after another Test Match.

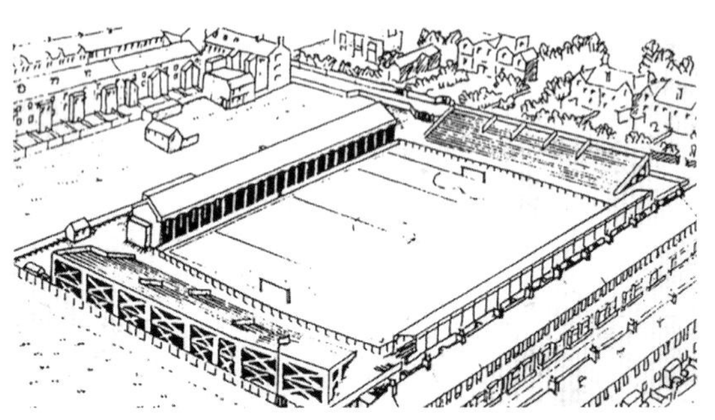

Anfield in 1894-5, when Harry Bradshaw starred for Liverpool

Liverpool, having tasted the big time, were determined to bounce straight back. The club went in search of more stars to support men like Bradshaw and captured Leith's George Allan, who would become the club's first Scottish international.

Another Scot, Archie Goldie came from Clyde. England international Francis Becton followed Jimmy Ross from Preston, the league's first champions. Liverpool would prove unmatchable in an attacking sense in that 1895-96 campaign. Allan grabbed 25 goals, Ross 23, Becton 18 and Bradshaw, now operating at outside-left, 11. Harry would therefore secure his second Division Two championship medal.

The first game of 1896/97 was away against the Wednesday in Sheffield, won 2-1. This was a match in which a local newspaper reported that Liverpool had turned out in red shirts and white pants, believed to be the first time ever they had changed from the original blue and white quarters.

Bradshaw therefore had the honour with the rest of the team of playing in the first red shirt.

This season would be one of consolidation with one of the country's top coaches Tom Watson brought from Sunderland to lead the team. Allan got the bulk of the goals once more with Bradshaw a provider and third top scorer with four.

By 1897, Bradshaw's qualities were being tracked by the England selectors. No other Liverpool player had won an England cap while playing for the club. Harry made history when that honour fell to him on February 20, 1897, when he turned out for his country at Nottingham against Ireland in a 6-0 winning experience.

Remarkably, it would be his one and only international appearance. This was a different world in terms of media coverage. We tried to gain an insight into Harry's moment of glory with England by studying the Liverpool Football Echo report of the day.

For starters, most of that 'specialised' paper in those days was devoted to general news.

We seemed more preoccupied with international news affairs, reflecting the fact, possibly, that reading newspapers in Victorian England was an upper class exercise. Football was very much a working class game. Indeed, the Football Echo seemed to have as much material about the local theatre as the local football scene.

It was nothing like its modern equivalent. The England report, on page five, carried the simple tiny headline: ENGLAND v IRELAND. A sub-head said: 'Association International At Nottingham.'

The teams showed Harry Bradshaw at outside-left, but he was only mentioned once in the body of the report when it was stated: "Wheldon twice shot when he should have passed to Bradshaw."

The sub-editors chose not to write in the historic local fact that Harry had become the first Liverpool

'By 1897, Bradshaw's qualities were being tracked by the England selectors. **No other player** had won an England cap while playing for Liverpool. Harry **made history** when that honour fell to him'

star to turn out for England. Soon after it was reported that Scottish champions Hearts were on Merseyside for a challenge match. Liverpool won 2-1.

Harry was prominent in the game. The Football Echo reported: 'Pressure came from the Liverpool forwards, whose work showed more combination than that of the visitors. Some smart play by Bradshaw and Becton deserved better success.'

It wasn't the style of newspapers to go over the top in those days. Indeed, after Liverpool's famous Test Match victories over Small Heath and West Brom in 1896 - games in which Bradshaw scored crucial goals as the club gained promotion back to the First Division - there was no follow-up report in the local papers. However, there was a lengthy report of the professional wrestling at Hengler's Circus (near to the Grafton in West Derby Road). In nearby Anfield, the flexing of some famous football muscles was much more relevant to the mass of the working class population.

Harry Bradshaw was amongst those pioneers who put in the strong foundations on which Liverpool FC was built. He signed for Southern League Spurs for the 1898-1899 season, making 66 appearances and scoring 17 goals. Within a year he had moved on to another London outfit, Thames Ironworks (later West Ham), playing just 12 games for them in 1899.

Harry died suddenly on Christmas Day 1899 of consumption, more commonly known these days as tuberculosis. A benefit game was played between Spurs and Thames Ironworks on April 2, 1900, for his dependants. He was just 26.

THOMAS HENRY 'HARRY' BRADSHAW

Born 24.08.1873 in Liverpool. Known as 'Harry'.

Career: Northwich Victoria 1892-93 to 1893-94, 22 appearances, 8 goals.

Signed for Liverpool on 14.10.1893.
Position: Outside-left or all three inside-forward positions.
League: 118 appearances, 45 goals.
FA Cup: 14 appearances, 5 goals.
Test matches: 6 appearances, 3 goals.
Totals: 138 appearances, 53 goals.
Also 29 friendly games, 17 goals.
Club honours: Second Division championship 1893-94; 1895-96.
First Liverpool player to win England cap, v. Ireland 20.02.1897 at Nottingham. Won 6-0.
Football League representative games: v. Irish League, 7.11.1896, won 2-0; v. Scottish League 24.04.1897, lost 0-3.

Signed for Tottenham Hotspur in 1898-1899.
Southern League: 24 appearances, 5 goals.
United League: 19 appearances 3 goals.
Thames & Med. League: 14 appearances, 4 goals.
FA Cup: 9 appearances, 5 goals.
Total: 66 appearances, 17 goals.
Representative game: South v North, 1.02.1899, lost 1-3.
Played for Thames Ironworks 1899 (later West Ham United).
FA Cup: 7 appearances, 2 goals.
Southern League: 5 appearances.
Total: 12 appearances, 2 goals.
Died on 25.12.1899 at Tottenham, aged 26.
A benefit game was played on 2.04.1900, Thames Ironworks v Tottenham Hotspur, score 0-3.

Liverpool appearances and goals:

	League		Other	
	App	Gls	App	Gls
1893-94	14	8	4	3
1894-95	30	17	4	1
1895-96	26	11	6	3
1896-97	25	4	3	0
1897-98	23	5	3	1
Total	**118**	**45**	**20**	**8**

Overall: 138 appearances and 53 goals.

LIVERPOOL
(ASSOCIATION)
Football Club.
GROUND—ANFIELD ROAD.

Season 1893-94.

This Ticket is issued subject to Rule VI., and admits to all League and Ordinary Matches, but is NOT available for Cup Ties, Benefit or Charity Matches.

J. J. RAMSAY, Hon. Treas.,
7, Hawkesworth Street, Everton.

10/- SUBSCRIBER'S TICKET.
Not Transferable.
Admit
Name...
Address...
To Ground and Covered Stands.
...Hon. Treas.

Super Mac at the back and **in attack**

No. 2: **MATTHEW McQUEEN**

Matthew McQueen was one of those remarkable characters who simply could not get enough of Liverpool FC.

Like many great Scots, he understood the passion of the Merseyside football scene and was at ease in the city of Liverpool, where he enjoyed the company of the increasing number of people who were captivated by the rising interest in the professional game.

Other players made more appearances than Matt, but few showed his versatility.

He is unique in that he was a player who would operate in goal one week and then star in an outfield position the next!

Matt was a great goalkeeper, just as he was a top-class defender and a more than capable centre-forward. Here was the complete all-round footballer.

In his first Football League season with Liverpool he started at right-half before operating for two games at centre-forward. He then returned to right-half for five games before switching to centre-back, scoring in a 5-0 thrashing of Woolwich Arsenal.

Fittingly, one of his team mates and fellow goalscorers that day was Harry Bradshaw, the man he now stands alongside in the Hall of Fame.

Matt then played at right and left half before accepting the goalkeeper's jersey for two matches against Newcastle United and Ardwick (later Manchester City) - keeping a clean sheet in both of these clashes. The first was a goalless draw and the second a 3-0 victory.

Incredibly, it was then back to half-back before accepting another new position, left-back, in a 2-0 win against Grimsby Town.

The more familiar half-back was then his for six games before he went back in goal for three matches, keeping clean sheets against Crewe and Grimsby.

A brand new role, at right-back, completely unfazed the remarkable Matt McQueen who finished the season back at half-back with 27 contrasting appearances to his name.

Matt's brother Hugh, who also joined Liverpool from Scottish club Leith Athletic, was often in the same team.

Hugh, a left-winger, would actually finish that 1893-94 season with 9 goals in 27 league appearances. Clearly the McQueen family were a potent football force for Liverpool.

In Matt, the Anfield fans knew they had a special character on their hands.

This 1893-94 campaign was the club's first in the Football League.

As a highly dependable goalkeeper during that campaign, Matt would enjoy four shut-outs in his five games between the posts.

Technically, the regular keeper at the time was William 'Bill' McOwen who figured in 23 of the 28 matches that secured promotion to the top flight at the first time of asking. But many fans wondered if Matt McQueen was not at least his equal, judging by the 'goals against' column.

Bill stepped back in goal for the final two eventful matches of that watershed season – back-to-back games against Burslem Port Vale. Liverpool drew the first away 2-2 and finished the season on

Matt McQueen served the club with distinction as both player and manager

'He could be the most **versatile** Liverpool figure of all time so he had a **strong claim**'

– Brian Hall, Panel member

> a high note, winning 2-1.

Matt had figured in seven different roles as the season unfolded with this incredible ability to look equally confident in goal, in the heart of defence as a wing half or centre-half, or at centre-forward.

Matt had played in 27 of the 28 championship games, scoring two goals. However, his all-round input would have won him any Footballer of the Year award, if such an accolade had existed at that time.

Of course, you didn't go up just because you won the title.

Liverpool had to face a Test Match against the bottom team in Division One, Newton Heath. Both McQueen brothers were in the thick of the action. In fairytale fashion, Matt was selected in goal - a challenge which he wholeheartedly accepted.

Yes, you've guessed it, he kept another clean sheet which meant five out of six! Liverpool won 2-0 and their Manchester rivals were consigned to the drop while the Merseysiders moved into football's top flight for the first time.

Has any player in the history of league football ever shown such all-round dedication, versatility and complete unselfishness as was displayed by Matt McQueen in his first and most famous season as a Liverpool player?

The two-footed (and two-handed) Matt, with his drooping moustache and his liking for any football challenge, had endeared himself to the Anfield faithful in that title-winning year.

He had already won two Scottish caps playing at right half against Wales in 1890 and 1891 before arriving at Anfield. Liverpool had remarkable links with the Scots at that time.

Indeed, they were known as the team of Macs. There was McLean (D), McOwen, McCartney, McQue, McQueen (M. and H.), McVean and McBride. Other Macs would follow.

Liverpool's elevation to the top flight in 1894-95 proved a tough experience. Regular goalkeeper McOwen left the scene to be replaced by W. McCann (it had to be another Mac!).

But the Reds failed to secure a victory until the 10th game of the season when they won 2-0 at Stoke and included in the reversals was a 3-0 defeat at the new Goodison Park in the first ever League derby game against Everton.

The Liverpool management instinctively turned to Matt McQueen for some respite. He had started the season at half-back, only to be left out for six consecutive matches. Now Liverpool asked Matt to reclaim the goalkeeper's jersey - for the Anfield return against Everton. What a request. What a challenge. The previous home game against Burnley had attracted just 8,000 fans. This blockbuster drew 30,000 - an amazing gate at that time.

Liverpool were determined not to go under as Everton returned to their former Anfield ground, determined to claim the double and assert their Merseyside authority. The game was eventful to say the least and Everton led 2-1 with just a minute to go. Liverpool refused to give up and Anfield exploded as they gained a penalty. Jimmy Ross stepped forward to slot home the equaliser.

'Matt had played in 27 of the 28 championship games, **scoring one goal.** However, his all-round input would have won him any **Footballer of the Year** award, if such an accolade had existed **at that time'**

Matt would play in all of the remaining games in goal except for two when he operated at left-back. The records show that he conceded fewer goals than 'regular' keeper McCann in an equal number of appearances.

The agony for all concerned at Anfield was that Liverpool went down after losing a Test Match to Bury 1-0.

The club's faith in McQueen the goalkeeper was highlighted in 1895-96 as Liverpool looked to bounce straight back up.

Matt was between the posts in 17 of the opening 19 games, missing one match and playing the other at half-back. Liverpool's solid start meant they were on course for promotion, but it was clear that a 'full-time' goalkeeper would be required if they were ultimately to return to the top flight and stay there.

Eleven games from the end of the season, the outstanding Harry Storer was signed from Woolwich Arsenal and Matt found himself battling for an outfield place, although his second Division Two championship medal was secured.

Three seasons later Matt retired as a player, but this is not the end of the Matt McQueen story.

This remarkable character decided to qualify as a Football League referee.

Towards the end of the First World War in 1918 he became a Liverpool director.

In February 1923, he was appointed team manager in succession to David Ashworth, who had guided the Reds to the league championship in 1921-22. Ashworth's decision to leave his Anfield champions for Oldham Athletic while on course for a second successive title was bemusing to say the least and left Liverpool in a difficult situation.

It was no surprise that they turned to Matt McQueen, who was at the helm as the club held its nerve to win its fourth championship.

McQueen, who was in charge for five years, was the man who signed striker Gordon Hodgson, who would become a true Anfield great in his own right.

Tragically, McQueen lost a leg in a road accident while returning from a scouting mission to Sheffield. After continuing ill health, he retired in 1928, but always retained his connections with the club he had served so magnificently.

Matt lived in the shadow of the Anfield stadium at 32 Kemlyn Road in his later years.

This site is now enclosed inside the ground boundaries within the Centenary Stand car park. The houses were knocked down when that side of the stadium was further developed.

Not many people can reflect on such a remarkable football career.

Matt McQueen fully deserves to be in the official Liverpool Hall of Fame.

Many of his modern successors would be absolutely stunned if asked to take on his many different roles. people complain about rotation and different modern tactics, but Matt is the kind of player every manager would dearly want in his squad.

MATTHEW McQUEEN

Born Harthill 18.05.1863

Career: Leith Athletic, Heart of Midlothian 1887, Leith Athletic 1889.
Signed for Liverpool in November, 1892 and was Football League registered on 14.08.1893.
16 Lancashire League appearances, 5 goals.
77 league appearances, 2 goals.
FA Cup: 8 appearances + 1 abandoned
2 Test Match appearances.
7 Lancashire Cup appearances.
5 Liverpool Senior Cup appearances.
Also 42 friendly games.
Honours: Two Second Division titles.
Granted a benefit match 23.09.1895. Liverpool v England XI - lost 0-3.
Total official games: 114 appearances, 6 goals. Played in goal in 51 games and the rest were played in all other positions except outside-right.
Listed with Liverpool for 1899-1900 season as third choice goalkeeper.
Qualified as a referee and frequently officiated in pre-season public practice games.
Director of Liverpool: 1919-1922
Manager of Liverpool: February 1922 to 15.02.1928.
Died 29.09.1944.

Liverpool appearances and goals:

	League		FAC/ Tests	
	App	Gls	App	App
1892-93*	16	5	1	
1893-94	27	2	3	1
1894-95	23	0	3	1
1895-96	22	0	0	0
1896-97	1	0	0	0
1897-98	2	0	0	0
1898-99	2	0	1	0
Total	**93**	**7**	**8**	**2**

* First season in Lancashire League.
Overall (including Lancs Lg, Lancs Cup, Liverpool Senior Cup) 115 games, 7 goals

‘RAISBECK IS FULLY WOUND UP AND READY TO LAST THE LONGEST GAME ON RECORD’

1900s

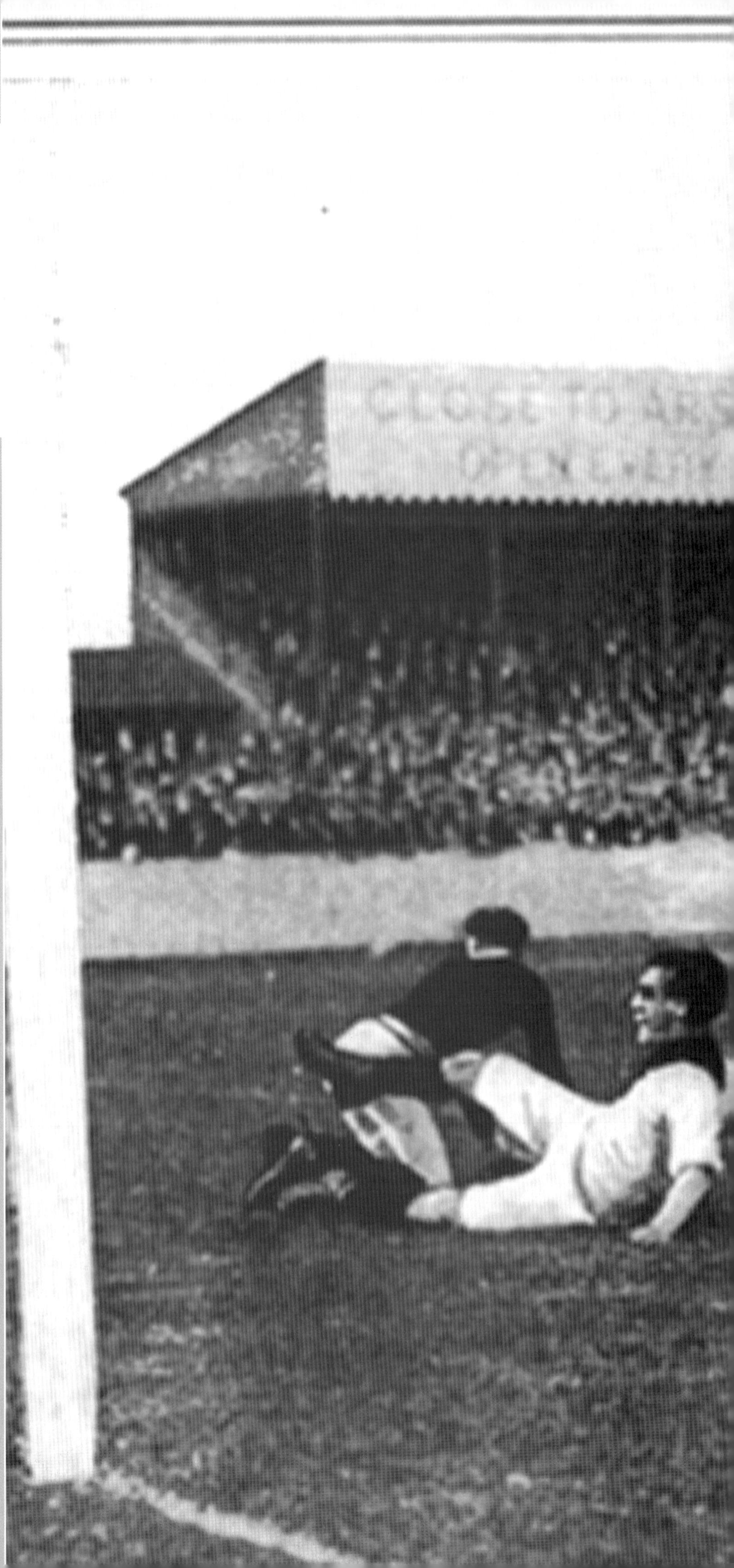

* Cartoon (above): Liverpool were champions in 1905-6 – the same season Everton won the FA Cup

Forging reputations

The 1900s witnessed the emergence of some talented performers as the Reds bounced back from disappointment to establish themselves as a rising force

Liverpool Football Club strode into the 20th century full of hope for the future, but with that elusive first League Championship success still to be achieved. The Reds, formed in 1892, were forced to play their first season in the Lancashire League after their application to join the newly-formed Second Division of the Football League was rejected.

The club gained admission to an extended Second Division the following season, 1893-94, after winning the Lancashire title and the Liverpool Senior Cup. They immediately gained promotion to the top flight as Second Division champions, but only after being forced to play a Test Match against the bottom team in Division One, Newton Heath (Manchester United).

Sadly, the reverse then happened and a Liverpool side that was not yet fully equipped for the top flight was immediately relegated in another Test Match, this time against Bury.

This rollercoaster era saw the Reds power straight back up with another Second Division Championship success in 1895-96. Clearly, there was a need to achieve more consistency to become established at the highest level. Subsequently, league placings of fifth, ninth and then second (in 1898-99) demonstrated that the new Liverpool could head into the first decade of the 20th century with renewed optimism and a determination to claim that first major honour.

There was disappointment when that runners-up slot was not improved on. Indeed, the club had to settle for 10th place in 1899-1900. But the following year the whole of Merseyside, indeed the whole of football, was forced to salute the arrival of Liverpool as giants of the game.

The 1900-1901 season would end with the Reds as undisputed champions, the side finishing with a run of nine wins and three draws in their final 12 matches.

Incredibly, the elation of the fans was short-lived. Liverpool would then slip to 11th, escaping the drop by just two points. The forwards managed just 42 goals and seven of these came in a January fixture against a Stoke team ravaged by food poisoning, who were down to seven men at one stage.

This fixture, not surprisingly, produced a five-goal scoring feat from **Andy McGuigan** that would not be matched for over 50 years.

But it painted a false picture and there was clearly a need to produce some firepower up front in time for the 1902-03 campaign. A hero stepped forward by the name of **Sam Raybould** who scored 31 goals in 33 appearances that season. This record would stand for 28 years before being beaten by another goalscoring hero, **Gordon Hodgson**.

Raybould had scored after only 30 seconds of his second league game for the Reds, a derby clash with Everton. Even though the Blues went on to win this Goodison clash 3-1, it earned the centre-forward a special place in the hearts of the Liverpudlians. He had finished top of the Anfield scoring charts in the 1900-01 title campaign with 17 goals and would be the main man in attack for three out of the next six years.

His best return was in that 1902-03 season when the club finished fifth. Sadly, with Raybould often sidelined through injury, Liverpool would be relegated again in 1903-04 with crowds down to 10,000 from an opening high of 18,000.

It was a case of starting again and in typical fashion the club responded with its third Second Division title. Raybould was fit and rejuvenated and plundered 19 league goals in 32 games. Indeed two Liverpool strikers would each get over 20 goals. Raybould was partnered superbly by Bootle-born **Jack Parkinson** and also **Robert Robinson** who, like goalkeeper Ted Doig, was captured from Sunderland.

Doig was the oldest to make a debut, at 38, and the oldest to have ever played for Liverpool.

Parkinson had joined the club in 1902, but had been forced to play in Raybould's shadow. But as the Reds powered back to the top flight, the Reds found a place for Parkinson at inside-left and the goals flowed, 21 in just 21 games.

But it was Robinson who actually finished as top scorer with 23 goals from 32 games, including four against Leicester in October, 1904.

The Reds secured a record 10 successive victories and from Boxing Day lost only once in 18 games. The 27 league victories secured remained a record until the arrival of Bill Shankly's revolution.

The stage was now set for another concerted attack on the First Division title and success was immediate in 1905-06. Nine wins and two draws mid-season inspired that second Championship success for the Reds. Preston North End provided the biggest threat, but a 2-1 win at Deepdale effectively settled things in Liverpool's favour.

Highly-rated goalkeeper **Sam** >

'The following year the **whole of Merseyside,** indeed the whole of football, was forced to **salute** the arrival of Liverpool as **giants**'

Hall of Fame

1900s

SCROLL OF FAME

1900-1909: Men who made a first team appearance, players in gold shortlisted for Hall of Fame

ALLMAN 'Dick'
BEEBY Augustus
BERRY Arthur
BLANTHORNE Robert
BOWEN George
BOWYER Sam
BRADLEY James
BUCK Fred
CARLIN John
CHADBURN John
CHADWICK Edgar
CHORLTON Tom
COTTON Charles
COX Jack
CRAIK Herbert
CRAWFORD Robert
DAVIES John
DOIG Teddy
DUNLOP Billy
FITZPATRICK Harry
FLEMING George
GARSIDE James
GLOVER John
GODDARD Arthur
GOLDIE Archie
GOLDIE Bill
GOODE Bertram
GORMAN James
GREEN Thomas
GRIFFIN Michael
GRIFFITHS Harry
HARDY Sam
HARROP James
HEWITT Charlie
HEWITT Joe
HIGNETT Samuel
HOARE Joseph
HOWELL 'Raby'
HUGHES James
HUGHES John
HUNTER 'Sailor'
HUNTER Thomas
HUNTER William
KYLE Peter
LATHAM George
LIPSHAM John
LIVINGSTONE George
MARSHALL William
McCALLUM Donald
McCONNELL John
McDONALD John
McGUIGAN Andy
McKENNA John
McLEAN James
McPHERSON William
MORGAN Hugh
MORRIS Richard
MURRAY David
ORR Ronald
PARKINSON Jack
PARRY Maurice
PEAKE Ernest
PERKINS William
PLATT Peter
RAISBECK Alex
RAYBOULD Sam
ROBERTSON John
ROBERTSON Tommy
ROBINSON Robert
ROGERS Thomas
SATTERTHWAITE Charlie
SAUL Percy
SLOAN Donald
SMITH Sydney
SPEAKMAN James
STEWART James
STORER Harry
UREN Harold
WALKER John
WEST Alfred
WHITE William
WILSON Charlie

Hardy had been signed from Chesterfield in time for that Championship year, the £500 investment, small change now, was significant then. Sam went on to become one of England's finest goalkeepers with 21 international caps. He would amass a total of 552 league appearances, 240 of them for Liverpool.

Hardy was safe rather than spectacular with tremendous anticipation. He really did make the job look easy, hence his 13-year England career. After making his debut in the Reds' goal against Nottingham Forest in October, 1905, Hardy remained a virtual ever-present in the side for the remainder of that decade.

Solid at the back in that championship year, the Reds produced another excellent striker who would grab 24 goals in 37 games. **Joe Hewitt** was a dedicated Red and during his lifetime would serve the club for 60 years, first as a centre-forward and later as a coach and handyman. The fans never forgot the part he played in 1905-06 and were always quick to talk about the double he struck in the famous 7-4 defeat of Manchester United at Anfield in March, 1908.

The Reds finished that opening decade of the century finishing eighth, 16th and then runners-up in 1909-10.

Other Hall of Fame candidates for that era would include **James Bradley**, who arrived from Stoke in time for the 1905-06 season. He provided stability and imagination in the centre of the field, was renowned for his passing and had a powerful left-foot shot. He was a title winner in 1906.

Tremendously consistent, he missed only 10 games over the following three years. He finally left Anfield for Reading in 1910 with a record of 185 appearances and eight goals.

Jack Cox was a flying winger who conjured up 81 goals in 361 games, having joined the club in 1898. Jack wore the Red throughout the opening decade of the 20th century, making and taking goals. He missed only two games in the championship season of 1900-01, scoring 10 goals. He repeated his success in the promotion year of 1904-05 and scored nine goals from the flanks as Liverpool claimed their second Championship crown in 1905-06. His final average for the Reds was one goal every four-and-a-half matches, an extremely respectable return for a winger. Cox won three England caps and played three times for the Football League.

On the other flank, **Arthur Goddard** also scored a career total 77 goals for the Reds in 415 appearances. In eight seasons he missed only 19 games. He played in 23 consecutive FA Cup ties between 1903 and 1912 and his loyal service earned him a benefit game.

When left-back **Billy Dunlop** earned a benefit match in 1906, the Liverpool programme said: "There are some men who perform brilliantly in their various positions on the field, but there was never one who, year in, year out, has given such wholehearted service as Dunlop." He made 363 appearances and won two league titles and a Second Division championship medal.

'Alex [Raisbeck] seemed to inspire **poetic tributes.** Another writer described him as 'an **intelligent** automaton, pulsating to his finger-tips with the **joy of life'**

A real star of this period was **Alex Raisbeck**, one of seven brothers born in the Scottish village of Polmont. A winger and half-back, he came to Anfield in 1898-99. Alex seemed to inspire poetic tributes.

One writer described him as "an intelligent automaton, pulsating to his finger-tips with the joy of life."

Raisbeck remained at Anfield for 11 seasons, scoring 20 goals in 341 games. He was still scouting for Liverpool in 1949 when he died.

Bowden Bros.]

WOOLWICH ARSENAL v. LIVERPOOL AT PLUMSTEAD, SEPTEMBER 2, 1905.

If a forward is allowed to break through the defence the position is well nigh hopeless. Yet on this occasion Parkinson, of Liverpool, perhaps the fastest forward playing League football, fell at the critical moment as he was about to net the ball. The result was a fractured wrist, which kept the gallant fellow out of the field a number of weeks. The ball went just wide of the post, and Ashcroft is seen watching its course with some concern. Woolwich won the match by 3 goals to 1.

How the panel called it:

Raisbeck, with his career total of 341 games, was the undisputed star of this period and the panel had no problem in naming him.

Two others bridged two decades and finished with 300-plus games, a tremendous total at this time (Jack Cox 361, Billy Dunlop 363). Cox played the most games of any player in this decade (313) and scored an astonishing number of goals for a winger (72).

Like Raisbeck, both Cox and Dunlop won two Division One titles and one Division Two title. Cox finally edged it.

Reds **unearth** a **superstar** skipper

No. 3: **ALEX RAISBECK**

World class footballers captivate the imagination of fans in many ways. When assessing the adulation heaped on Liverpool FC pioneer Alex Raisbeck it is clear that here was a man whose performances were electric in every game.

It's not very often that hardened sports writers purr about the qualities of a centre-half and defender. They normally reserve their flowery prose for classy midfielders, skilful wingers and match-winning strikers.

But in an era when defenders were renowned for being big, brutal and uncompromising, Raisbeck's style clearly struck a chord with journalists and fans alike. This is the story of the famous Scot who would be revealed as the third super hero to take his place in the official Liverpool Hall of Fame.

Having named Harry Bradshaw and Matt McQueen as the two giants elected into Hall of Fame for the period 1892-1900, it was straight on into the 1900-1910 era in which Raisbeck was undoubtedly one of the superstars of the great game. This was a spell in which Liverpool won its first league championship. It was also an era in which the club suffered the pain of relegation from the top flight for the third time. But Raisbeck rallied the team immediately for an instant return and a second league championship would follow in what was clearly a golden age for everyone who visited Anfield.

Something else locked this era firmly in the minds of Liverpudlians. In 1906 the goal terracing on Walton Breck Road was redeveloped. The Spion Kop, as it would come to be known, was part of an ambitious plan to help turn the old stadium into a fortress. It would become the home of the most passionate, noisy and partisan fans in the English game and these supporters never forgot the input of the heroes who finally put Liverpool FC on the map.

One of these legends, of course, was Raisbeck - truly one of the great names in the history of the club. He was a larger-than-life character who dominated the Anfield scene at this time, skippering the club for many years. A contemporary writer once summed Alex up beautifully. He said: "Raisbeck is fully wound up and ready to last through the longest game on record...swift, rapid movement, fierce electrical rushes are to him an everlasting delight."

The image is of a player with the energy of a Steven Gerrard allied to the defensive class of an Alan Hansen. Raisbeck stood less than 5 feet 10" tall, which was unusual for a centre-half, but few people could outjump him. Those who did would find themselves on the receiving end of a swift recovery as the Scot used his power and mobility to retrieve the situation.

Raisbeck was one of seven brothers born in the Stirlingshire village of Polmont. His first club was Blantyre Brigade and then Larkhill Thistle, where he operated at outside-right. The big city scene beckoned when Edinburgh Hibernian spotted his tremendous potential. It was here that he developed his game to become a quality half-back.

At the youthful age of 18 he was selected to >

'Alex Raisbeck was a real leader who loved playing for Liverpool'

– Phil Thompson, Panel member

represent the Scottish League against the Football League in 1897. The English scouts, who saw Scotland as a source of rich talent, were out in force. You did not need to be a football genius to recognise the emerging talent that was young Alex Raisbeck.

Within a year he would be playing in the English top flight, but it was struggling Stoke City who had taken the plunge and persuaded the rising star to join them. He helped them to stay up and Liverpool, amongst many clubs, began to cast envious eyes towards the Potteries. John McKenna, an Irishman who had come to Liverpool from Ulster and become a prominent businessman, was now the major powerbroker at Anfield in succession to founder father John Houlding. 'Honest John' as he was called, would also become a leading figure in the English game. He discussed Raisbeck's potential and ability with manager Tom Watson who had left Sunderland's 'Team of all the Talents' to become Liverpool secretary-manager in 1896.

It was Watson who insisted that Liverpool should sign the Stoke player although it is acknowledged that McKenna, a shrewd judge, had first spotted and identified the talent.

McKenna put Watson on an express train to Stoke with a firm instruction. "Don't come back without Raisbeck!"

It was said that Alex was full of restless energy, which he channelled against the opposition on a football pitch. He was aggressive but fair, and a dedicated professional. Again, the newspapers of the day reported the qualities that made him stand head and shoulders above most of his rivals. One said: 'Raisbeck is an intelligent automaton, pulsating to his finger tips with the joy of life.'

Here was clearly a man who loved and revelled in his football existence. Liverpool had used various players at centre-half in 1897-98 including McQue, Holmes and Cleghorn. Watson wanted consistency and Raisbeck would immediately provide it, playing in 32 of the 34 league games in 1898-99, a season in which Liverpool would go desperately close to securing an historic league and cup double. As it turned out, they finished with nothing but the improvement in the side was immense as the club improved from ninth the previous year to championship runners-up.

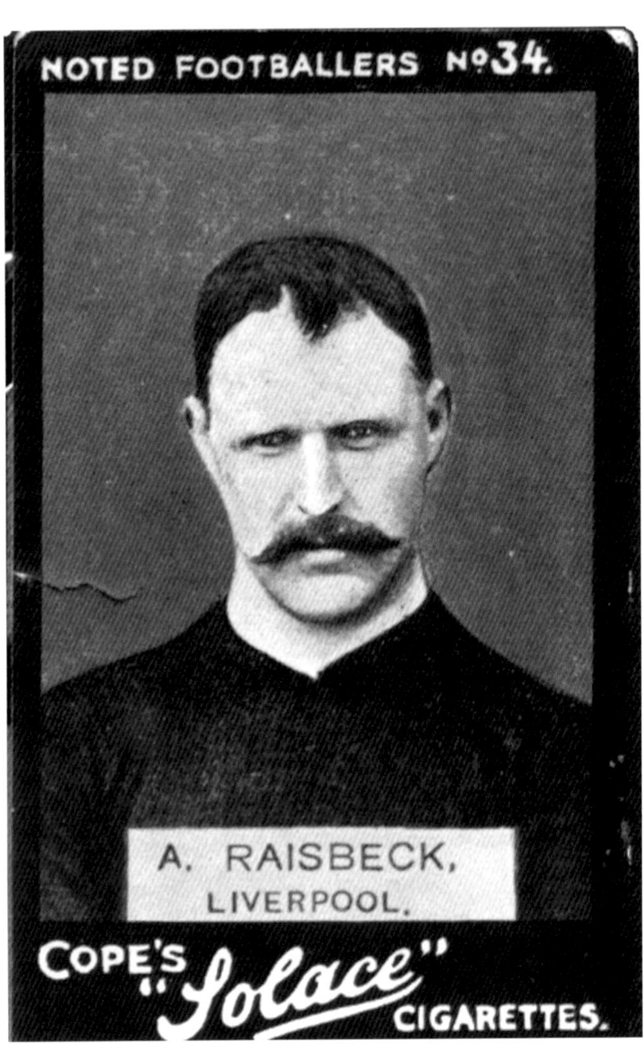

'In an era when **defenders** were renowned for being big, brutal and **uncompromising,** Raisbeck's style clearly **struck a chord** with journalists and fans alike'

The real heartbreak was in the FA Cup. Liverpool beat Blackburn, Newcastle and West Brom to reach the semi-final against Sheffield United. A 2-2 draw unfolded on neutral territory in Nottingham. The team then fought out a sensational 4-4 draw at Bolton. They were leading a third game 1-0 at Fallowfield when it was abandoned. The fourth replay, at Derby, resulted in a painful lone-goal reversal. It was a particularly bitter blow for Raisbeck, who had shunned the opportunity to secure his first full Scottish cap to concentrate on Liverpool's double challenge.

The disappointment felt at Anfield was immense. However, Liverpudlians recognised the qualities of a smaller, leaner squad inspired by men like Raisbeck, his Scottish partner Archie Goldie, flying winger Jack Cox and dedicated left-back Billy Dunlop.

This was a side with real potential and while the team could only finish the following season in 10th position, there was a feeling of real optimism at Anfield.

The 1900-01 campaign would see Raisbeck and Co. driving forward to secure the club's first league championship.

Raisbeck would remain at Anfield for 11 seasons. Despite shock relegation in 1903-04, the Reds would bounce straight back as Second Division champions and then power through the next year, 1905-06, to win the top flight title for a second time.

Raisbeck's international ambitions would be recognised with eight Scottish caps, seven of them against England. The Anfield career that started in 1898 would finally draw to a close in 1909 when Alex moved back to Scotland with 341 Liverpool games under his belt, 20 goals, two championship medals, one Second Division championship medal and a host of wonderful Merseyside memories to savour.

He was arguably Liverpool's first superstar with his Hollywood looks and powerful physique. Sporting journalists had waxed lyrical about him throughout his career.

Raisbeck was regularly described as the best defender in Britain and one sports journalist declared: "A man of Raisbeck's proportions, style and carriage would rivet attention anywhere. He is a fine and beautifully balanced figure."

Need we say more. Alex Raisbeck fully deserves to become the third member of the prestigious official Liverpool Hall of Fame.

ALEXANDER GALLOWAY RAISBECK

Born 26.12.1878 at Wallacestone, near Polmont, Stirlingshire.

Career: Blantyre Boys Brigade as a junior, Larkhill Thistle, Royal Albert, Hibernian 1896.
Representative game: Scottish League v Irish League, 30.01.1897 (2-0).
Stoke City: March 1898; 4 appearances 1897-98 in Division 1; 4 Test Match appearances, 1 goal.

Signed for Liverpool on 6.05.1898 for £350.
Position: Mainly centre-half.
Club captain: 1900-01 to 1908-09.
First Division championship winner: 1900-01 and 1905-06.
Second Division championship winner: 1904-05.
Sheriff of London's Charity Shield winner: 1906.
Liverpool Senior Cup winner: 1904-05; 1908-09.
Lancashire Cup finalist: 1906-07.
Caps for Scotland, 8: 1900, 1901, 1902, 1903*, 1904, 1906*, 1907* v England; 1903 v Wales* (* denotes captain).
Awarded a benefit game in 1904. Along with John Cox, given a further benefit, 17.04.1909 v Bury (h).
Signed for Partick Thistle in 16.08.1909 for £500.
Other representative games: Scotland B v Scotland A 21.02.1910. Scottish League v Football League 4.03.1911.
Awarded a benefit game: Scotland v World Team, January 1914.
Played for Hamilton Academicals from April 1914 to 1917. Director 1917. Manager 1918.
Bristol City: Secretary/manager 28.12.1921 to 29.06.1929
Halifax Town: Manager July 1930 to May 1936.
Chester City: Manager 1.06.1936 to 12.04.1938.
Bath City: Manager 1938 to 1939.
Liverpool Football Club scout: 1939 to 1949.
Died 12.03.1949 in a Liverpool hospital.

Liverpool appearances and goals:

	League		**FA Cup**	
	App	Gls	App	Gls
1898-99	32	1	6	1
1899-00	32	3	4	0
1900-01	31	1	2	0
1901-02	26	0	3	1
1902-03	27	1	1	0
1903-04	30	1	1	0
1904-05	33	2	2	0
1905-06	36	1	4	0
1906-07	27	4	1	0
1907-08	23	2	3	0
1908-09	15	2	1	0
Total	**312**	**18**	**28**	**2**

Also 1 appearance in Sheriff of London Charity Shield.
Overall: 341 games, 20 goals.

14 appearances in Lancashire Senior Cup, at least 6 in Liverpool Senior Cup and 18 friendly games.

* Liverpool had 2 A. Raisbecks, both centre-halves, on their books at the same time. Andrew Raisbeck was signed from Queens Park Rangers on 29.08.1902. Andrew played at No. 5 in the reserves in 1902-03 and 1903-04. Andrew Raisbeck was transferred to Hull City later in 1904 and played in 47 games for them, with 5 goals. There is no evidence they were related.

The **original** goal king from the **wing**

No. 4: **JACK COX**

In the world of football, wingers have traditionally been heroes in the minds of fans because of their adventure, skill and pace.

The truly great wingers have been revered, not just at club level by their own fans, but on an international stage.

It is why the mesmerising dribbling style of Sir Stanley Matthews earned him worldwide acclaim during his days with Blackpool and Stoke City. It's why the pace and penetrative ability of Sir Tom Finney made him a superstar at Preston North End.

At Anfield, Liverpool have had some great wingers down the years - people who have helped to light up the famous stadium with their magic. Liverpudlians think instinctively about the pace, power and skill of Billy Liddell. The fans roared to the tricky, intricate ball skills of Peter Thompson in the Sixties with Ian Callaghan a different, but equally effective wide man in the same era.

The two 'Bambers' came from university with degrees in effective wing play - Messrs Heighway and Hall. 'Little Bamber' Brian and 'Big Bamber' Steve - nicknamed after University Challenge host Bamber Gascoigne - highlighted the importance of stretching the opposition down the flanks.

John Barnes and Craig Johnston maintained the Liverpool tradition for star quality in this area, but the game has gradually changed and genuine wingers are now few and far between.

Whether wing play ever becomes totally extinct is highly unlikely. There will always be a need for individuals who can get in behind defenders by exploiting the full width of the pitch. Certainly, if the young up-and-coming stars of today need any role models in this area, they only have to study the record books. It is fitting that wingers will figure prominently in the official Liverpool Hall of Fame. The panel simply could not ignore this aspect of the great game, highlighted in the announcement concerning the fifth giant to be elected to this very exclusive club.

John 'Jack' Cox became the second individual named for the 1900-1910 era, following in the illustrious footsteps of team-mate and centre-half Alex Raisbeck.

Cox was an extremely talented winger. Indeed, he won England caps in this position, always playing on the left for the Reds with Tommy Robertson on the right.

Jack secured his Championship medals for the Reds in 1900-01 and 1905-06.

He was a flying winger in every sense, earning rave reviews with his first club Blackpool before joining Liverpool in 1897. The greatest winger of the day was England's Billy Meredith and when people began to say that Cox had many of the same attributes, it was the definitive tribute to the new Anfield star.

Ian Callaghan, himself a great Liverpool winger and a key member of the Hall of Fame panel, highlighted the importance of effective and entertaining wide play. He said: "Nothing is more exciting for a supporter than seeing a winger surge past a full-back. From the team perspective, it puts that person in the most dangerous place on the pitch from which to cross the ball. Strikers love it when

>

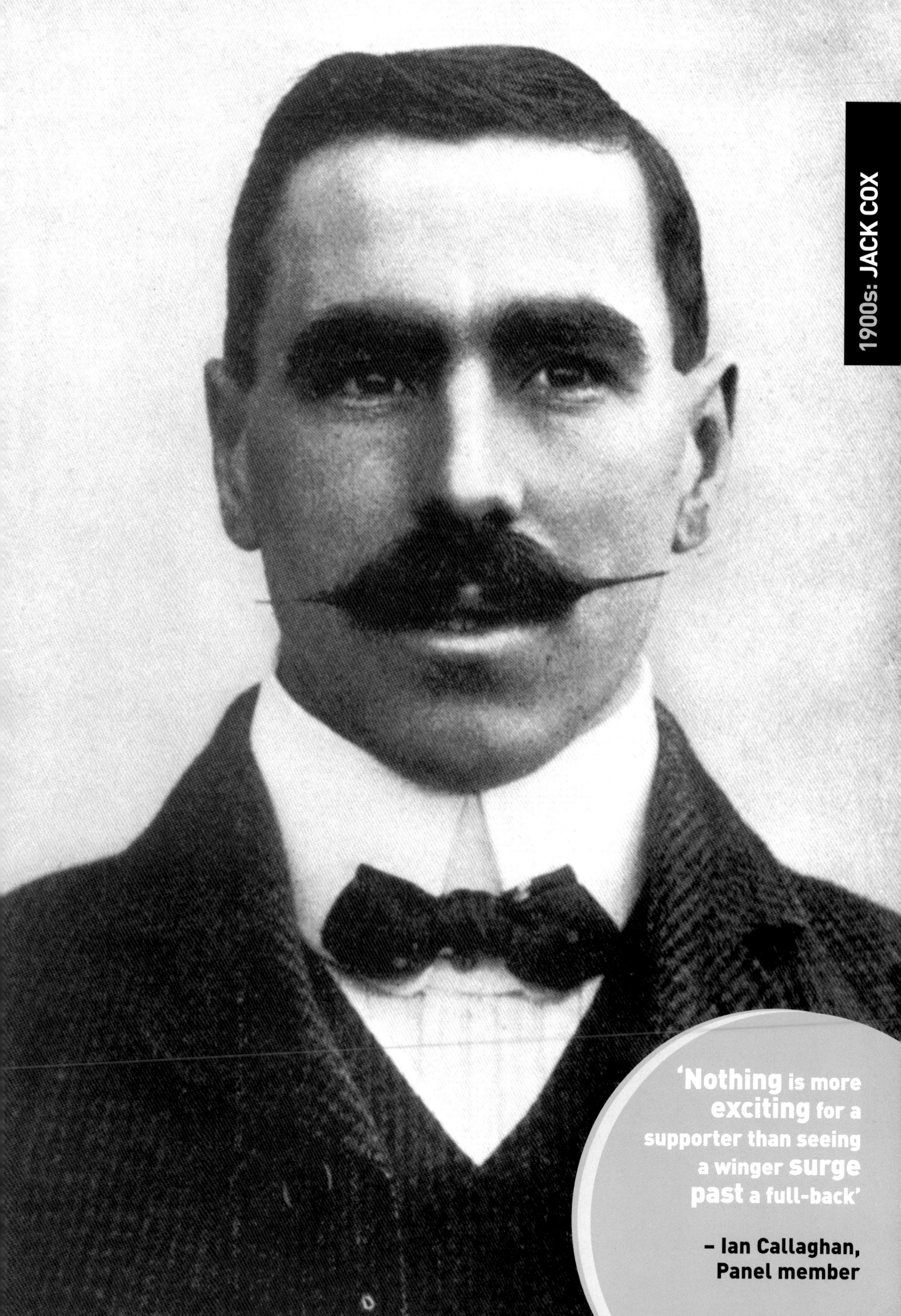

'**Nothing** is more **exciting** for a supporter than seeing a winger **surge past** a full-back'

– Ian Callaghan, Panel member

Class on the grass: Jack Cox (middle row, fourth from right) with the 1905-6 championship winning team

> the ball is pulled back to them from the by-line, but you don't see too much of that in the modern game.

"The most exciting time for me as a player was when I was on the wing. Of course, I later enjoyed my game in centre midfield, but playing wide was special because of the reaction of the fans. They lift you and you lift them.

"Wing play was a vital part of football then. It is less so now, but the best way to open up a game is still by stretching the play and asking your wide men to go past their markers. You think about people like George Best from the Sixties, although he could go past defenders anywhere on the field, often right down the middle! Liverpool had Peter Thompson showing flashes of real skill on the left flank and John Barnes years later.

"As a member of the panel I recognised that Jack Cox also scored a goal every four-and-a-half games. That is a heck of a record for a winger and it makes him stand out from his rivals. It indicates that he was different class."

Cox won over the fans because he was a taker of goals as well as a provider. He would finish his Liverpool career with 81 goals in 361 games over 12 seasons, which gave him a magnificent return for a winger.

'Jack Cox scored a goal every four-and-a-half games. That is a **heck of a record** for a winger and it makes him stand out from his rivals. It indicates that he was **different class'**

Of course, his prime role was skipping down the flanks and sending in crosses for men like Sam Raybould and Joe Hewitt to convert.

Cox missed just two games during the 1900-01 championship-winning season, scoring 10 goals for good measure. He repeated that tally in the promotion-winning season of 1904-05 to ensure that the Reds bounced straight back to the top flight after the shock of relegation in 1903-04. Jack had been one of the few to acquit himself during that disastrous drop year, playing in 33 of the 34 games and finishing as top scorer. He plundered another nine goals in just 28 matches as Liverpool stormed to another championship success in 1905-06.

That was a great team with loyal servant Bill Dunlop at left-back. England's Sam Hardy came in after eight games to finally replace the veteran Teddy Doig in goal. Doig had become he club's oldest debutant at 38 the previous year and a key player in the promotion campaign. Arthur Goddard complemented Cox with some great play on the right flank. Centre-forward Hewitt thrived off the quality wing play to bag 24 goals.

Cox had been rewarded for his quality with three England caps, against Northern Ireland in 1901 and Scotland in 1902 and 1903. Jack also played three times for the Football League.

He finally left Liverpool in 1909, returning to Blackpool where he became player-manager. His long and illustrious career ended two years later when he retired.

Liverpudlians always remembered the cut and thrust of his play, the crucial goals and the loyalty he showed to the Reds. He deserved to become the fourth hero to be elected into the official Liverpool Hall of Fame.

JOHN 'JACK' COX

Born 21.11.1876 in Blackpool.

Career:
Southshore Standard (Blackpool). Southshore, Blackpool 1897 (Second Division), 17 appearances, 12 goals 1897-98.

Signed for Liverpool on 24.12.1898.
Position: outside left/outside right.
Club vice-captain: 1907-08.
First Division championship winner: 1900-01 and 1905-06.
Second Division championship winner: 1904-05.
Sheriff of London's Charity Shield winner: 1906.
Liverpool Senior Cup winner: 1904-05.
Lancashire Cup: Finalist 1906-07.
3 caps for England: v Ireland 1901, v Scotland 1902 and 1903.
Representative games:
English League v Scottish League 8.03.1900. (6-3 - 1 goal)
English League v Irish League 10.11.1900. (4-2).
North v South 25.02.1901. (3-3 - 1 goal).
English League v Scottish League 4.04.1904 (2-1).
Awarded a benefit game (with Raisbeck) 17.04.1909 v Bury (h).
Moved to Blackpool as player/manager May 1909-1912. Second Division. 68 appearances, 6 goals.
Date of death - unknown.

Liverpool appearances and goals:

	League		FAC	
	App	Gls	App	Gls
1897-98	2	1	0	0
1898-99	27	5	6	2
1899-1900	25	5	4	1
1900-01	32	10	2	0
1901-02	31	4	3	0
1902-03	29	9	1	0
1903-04	33	9	1	0
1904-05	32	10	2	0
1905-06	28	9	4	0
1906-07	25	7	4	1
1907-08	35	2	4	3
1908-09	28	2	2	1
Total	**327**	**73**	**33**	**8**

Also 1 appearance in Sheriff of London's Charity Shield

Overall: 361 games, 81 goals.

Plus 13 games in Lancashire Senior Cup, 3 in Liverpool Senior Cup and 22 friendly games.

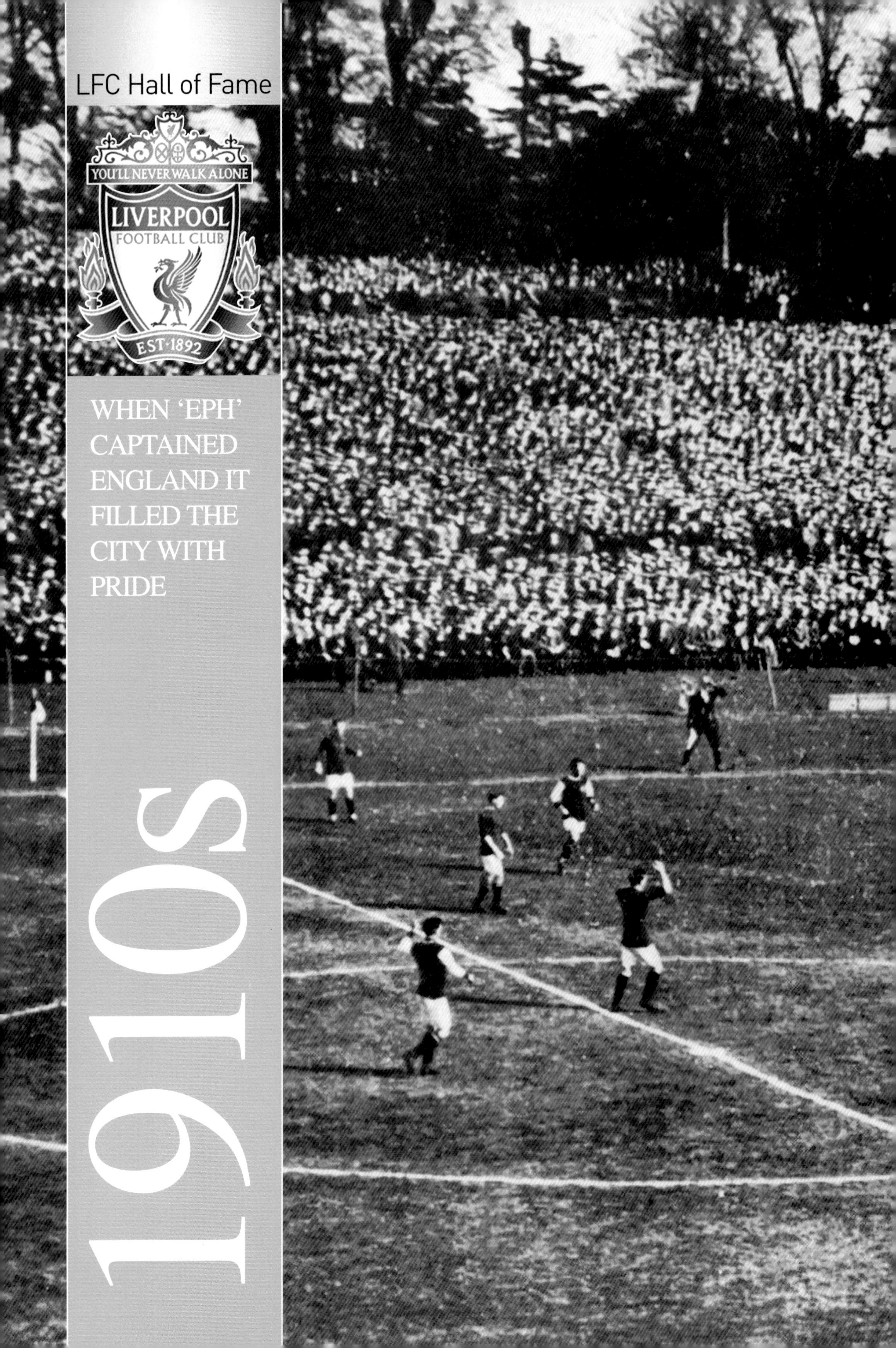

LFC Hall of Fame

WHEN 'EPH' CAPTAINED ENGLAND IT FILLED THE CITY WITH PRIDE

1910s

Main image: Action from the 1914 FA Cup final at Crystal Palace which saw Liverpool lose 1-0 to Burnley

Top-class servants

An FA Cup final appearance brightened the gloom at Anfield - although matchfixing and the onset of the First World War would overshadow the period

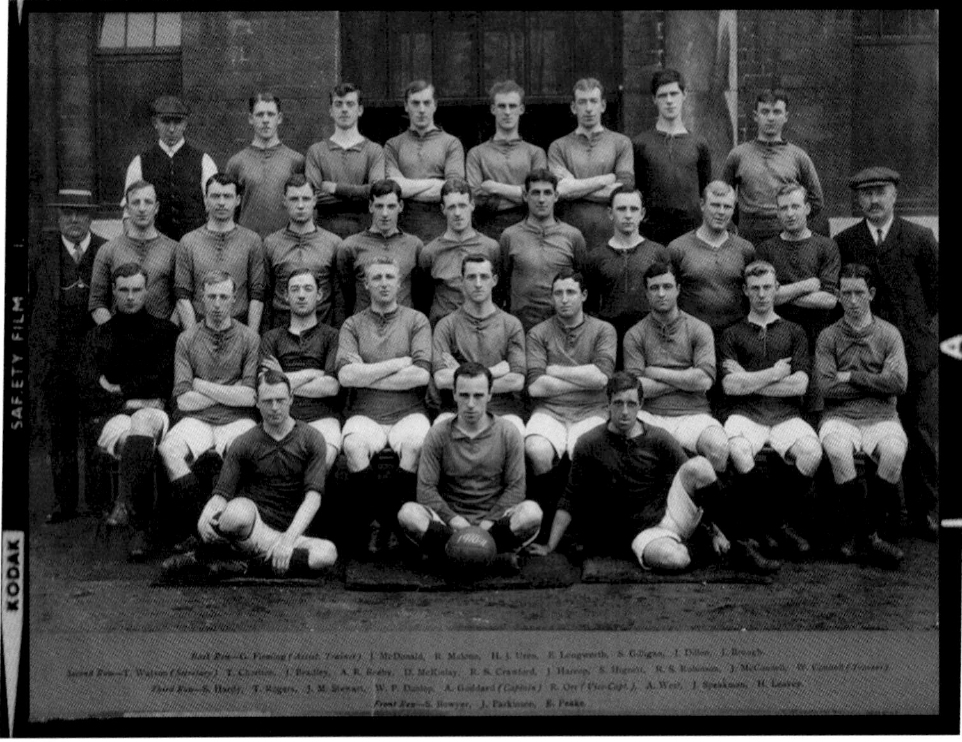

After the league championship triumph of 1905-06, Liverpool endured a tough period up to the First World War.

The club ironically found itself in a relegation fight just a year after winning the title and survived again in the nail-biting 1908-09 campaign when a final-day victory over Newcastle United enabled the team to miss the drop by just two points.

The elation lifted everyone at the club and in 1909-10 the Reds actually finished championship runners-up.

It suggested that the 1910-1920 decade might hold real promise. However, by 1911-12 they were back in trouble and only victory in the final two games saved them from the Second Division. Liverpool would make a bit of club history in this era, reaching their first FA Cup final in 1914, but it would be a losing experience at the old Crystal Palace against Burnley.

The fans returned from London bitterly disappointed that day because the team had dominated for much of the game, losing to a fine individual goal.

Burnley would point to an early Lindley shot that thudded against the Liverpool crossbar with goalkeeper **Kenny Campbell** beaten, but with **Ephraim Longworth** and **Bob Pursell** beginning to have a major impact, the Reds were soon on top.

They had the ball in the back of the net after 20 minutes through **Tom Miller** from a **Jackie Sheldon** cross, but it was ruled offside.

When **Jimmy Nicholl** hit the crossbar, the Merseyside fans were beginning to fear it was not going to be their day.

Liverpool were totally dominant after the break, only for Burnley to break away and score through Freeman with a magnificent shot.

Burnley had the cup and the Merseysiders would have to wait until 1965 before a Liverpool captain, Ron Yeats, was able to hold the famous trophy aloft.

The First World War would naturally force a halt to serious football after the 1914-15 campaign in which Liverpool finished 14th in the top flight. It was a season to forget, not least because four of their players and four Manchester United players were suspended for fixing a

'It would be 1919-20 before the **League** started up in earnest again with the Reds finishing **fourth.** The club would now be heading into a **golden period'**

Above: A 'Liverton' Merseyside team join forces for a charity match in 1912 - hence the stripes!

Good Friday game at Old Trafford. Liverpool lost 2-0.

The war meant people had other things on their minds, but Liverpudlians nevertheless reflected angrily on the episode in which Bob Pursell, Jackie Sheldon (who contrived to miss a penalty), Tommy Miller and Tommy Fairfoul were in the headlines for all the wrong reasons.

It would be 1919-20 before the Football League started up in earnest again with the Reds finishing fourth.

We would now be heading into a golden period at Anfield, the "Roaring Twenties", when two championships would be won in quick succession. But, as in all eras, the decade still had its super heroes.

Liverpool have always had good goalkeepers. The club's old telegraphic address was 'Goalkeeper'.

Kenny Campbell was one of these traditionally excellent custodians. He joined the Reds in May 1911, arriving as understudy to the great Sam Hardy.

When Hardy moved to Villa, Campbell seized his chance. >

Hall of Fame

1910s

SCROLL OF FAME

1910-1919: Men who made a first team appearance, players in gold shortlisted for Hall of Fame

BAMBER John
BANKS William
BARTROP Wilf
BEEBY Augustus
BENNETT Thomas
BERRY Arthur
BOVILL John
BOWYER Sam
BRADLEY James
BRATLEY Philip
BROMILOW Tom
BROUGH Joseph
CAMPBELL Kenneth
CHAMBERS Harry
CHORLTON Tom
CRAWFORD Robert
DAWSON James
DINES Joseph
FAIRFOUL Thomas
FERGUSON Robert
FORSHAW Dick
GILLIGAN Sam
GODDARD Arthur
GRACIE Tommy
GRAYER Frank
HAFEKOST Charles
HARDY Sam
HARROP James
HEWITT Joseph
HIGNETT Samuel
HOLDEN Ralph
JENKINSON William
LACEY Billy
LEAVEY Herbert
LESTER Henry
LEWIS Henry
LONGWORTH Ephraim
LOWE Henry
LUCAS Tommy
MACKINLAY Donald
McCONNELL John
McDONALD John
McDOUGALL Robert
METCALFE Arthur
MILLER John
MILLER Tom
NICHOLL Jimmy
ORR Ronald
PAGNAM Frederick
PARKINSON Jack
PEAKE Ernest
PEARSON Albert
PURSELL Bob
ROBINSON Robert
ROGERS Thomas
SCOTT Elisha
SCOTT James
SHELDON Jackie
SPEAKMAN James
SPEAKMAN Samuel
STANIFORTH Frederick
STEWART James
STUART William
TOSSWILL John
UREN Harold
WADSWORTH Harold
WADSWORTH Walter
WELFARE J
WEST Alfred

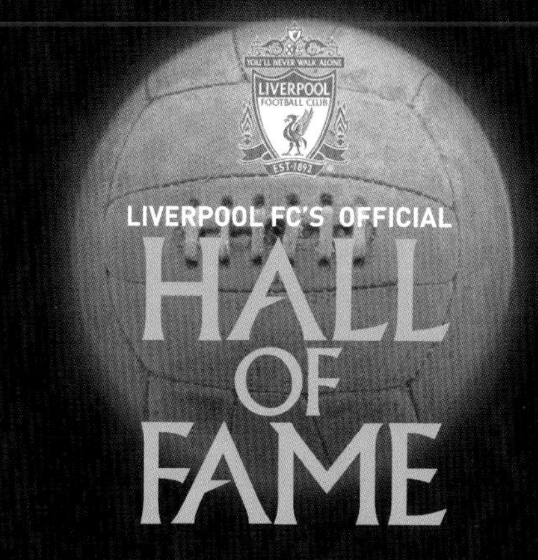

> In 1912-13 he missed just one league game and only four the following season. Things looked bright for Campbell, but having stepped up from understudy, he found another talented young keeper waiting in the wings trying to usurp him.

It was, of course, **Elisha Scott** who would ultimately become an Anfield legend.

Nevertheless, Campbell was good enough in his own right to win eight Scotland caps, three of them during his Anfield days.

He played in the 1914 FA Cup final and was a hero that day, despite the defeat. The war would interrupt his career and while he would return for one more campaign, Scott would finally oust him.

Irishman Elisha played in an astonishing 468 games between 1912 and 1935.

The superstar keeper bridged three decades, 1910-1920 being just one of them.

Above: The FA Cup final squad of 1914. Left: Official match programmes from 1919

He won two Championship medals and 31 Irish caps. A contemporary said he had the eye of an eagle and the clutch of a panther (see 1920s).

He was nearly 42 when he finished at Anfield, having arrived as a 17-year-old.

Arthur Goddard was a speedy and skilful winger who joined Liverpool as early as 1902. He quickly became a regular and was still going strong when the 1910-20 decade began when he skippered the side from outside-right.

He played through to season 1913-14 and clocked up 415 appearances with 77 goals.

Arthur was selected three times by the Football League and played in 23 consecutive FA Cup ties between 1903 and 1912.

The club gave him a benefit game in 1914 which earned him the princely sum in those days of £250.

Ephraim Longworth was another marathon man, described as the prince of full-backs and a proud Liverpool captain. Liverpool signed him from Leyton in 1910-11 and he was still on the books in 1927-28. His 371 appearances would have been substantially more but for the war. Longworth won five England caps, four at right-back.

He could kick with either foot and had good vision for a full-back. He made 197 appearances in this decade.

Billy Lacey is one of the few players to have crossed the park from Goodison to Anfield. He was involved in a swap deal in February, 1912.

Lacey would remain a Liverpool player for 12 years, clocking up over 250 appearances. He prospered at Anfield and occupied numerous positions during his career. His best role, however, was on the wing where his ball skills came into their own.

He appeared in the losing 1914 FA Cup final, but won Championship medals in 1922 and 1923. Lacey won 23 Ireland caps.

Donald Mackinlay was one of the great players of this era (and the Twenties). His 19 years with the club says it all.

He joined Liverpool in 1909-10 from Glasgow junior football and was still playing in 1928-29.

He won two Scotland caps and skippered the Reds in their two Twenties title-winning seasons. Don was therefore a Hall of Fame candidate in two separate decades.

Jack Parkinson's Anfield career stretched to 220 games and 130 goals between 1899 and 1914. Ironically, he did not become an Anfield regular until 1908-09, scoring 30 league goals the following season and then 19, 12 and 12 in the following three campaigns to show his consistency and quality.

'Billy Lacey is one of the **few players** to have **crossed** the park from Goodison to Anfield. He was involved in a **swap deal** in February, 1912. Lacey would remain a Liverpool player for **12 years**'

Walter Wadsworth is a centre-half worthy of mention, playing 241 times for the Reds.

He was rock solid at the back and could also steal into opposing territory to grab a crucial goal, scoring eight goals.

Walter's brother **Harold** also played for Liverpool, as a winger.

The era was not memorable, but it generated more than its share of top-class servants who served Liverpool magnificently.

How the panel called it:
Again, one man stood out - right-back Eph Longworth who was the first Liverpool player to captain England. A skilful defender, he amassed 197 games in this decade, more than any of his rivals. He played on into the Twenties when he would secure two Championship medals, but never scored a goal!

Statistically, a handful of games separated other candidates in the decade like Lacey, Lowe, Miller, Parkinson and Goddard, but Goddard served the club for 14 years and was a club captain from outside-right. His ultimate 415-game tally had to be recognised, an immense total at this time.

Top: Jack Parkinson played 222 games for the Reds. Above: 'Billy' Lacey swapped Everton for Liverpool

'Graceful Arthur' led from the wing

No. 5: ARTHUR GODDARD

Captains normally come from the heart of defence or the midfield engine room. It's a tradition that is only occasionally broken. Robbie Fowler has skippered the Reds from the main striking position while Michael Owen had the same honour bestowed on him for his country. Managers sometimes look to inspirational, highly-respected goalscorers who are prepared to lead from the front. Alan Shearer is a typical example, handed the armband by Newcastle United and England.

But you rarely get a skipper nominated from the wing fraternity. There is no logical reason why it should not happen, but is normally the exception rather than the rule.

When it happens you instinctively feel that the individual concerned is a very special character, possessing more than silky skills and a burst of pace. Arthur Goddard might have been dubbed 'Graceful Arthur' by the Anfield fans who admired his qualities for over 12 years. But don't think for one minute that this individual was a pushover for the teak-tough defenders of the day who would kick anything that moved - especially anyone showing what might be described as a 'Fancy Dan' streak.

Operating down the right wing, Goddard was skilful, no doubt about that. But he was also extremely durable and a virtual ever-present during his marathon Anfield career. You had to be top quality to survive as a winger in his era, which was 1902-1914. Full-backs didn't take any prisoners in those days and Liverpool had a variety of Anfield Irons before Smithy finally came on the scene!

Goddard had one operating behind him in Alf West as the Reds powered to the championship. The other full-back berth was occupied by one of Liverpool's greatest servants, another fearsome tackler in Billy Dunlop.

Players like these would tackle a 26 bus as it headed up Everton Valley towards Anfield. Referees would applaud the scything tackle and smile at the juddering shoulder charge. You had to get out a gun and shoot someone before the man in the middle even considered a sending off.

And so 'Graceful Arthur' was clearly a special talent to have survived and prospered across two separate decades for the Reds. This 'Captain Fantastic' deservedly became the fifth player to be named in the official Liverpool Hall of Fame - nominated for the war-interrupted 1910-1920 period alongside Ephraim Longworth, although both of these stars actually won their most significant domestic honours in the previous decade.

Goddard was very proud of the Second Division championship medal secured in 1904-05 as the Reds surged back to the top flight at the first time of asking after a frustrating relegation campaign. The league championship medal he secured the following year was the highlight of a great career. But the true measure of the man was that in 1914, a full eight years later, he was still cutting the mustard in a very exposed position. Sadly, he would miss out that season as the Reds surged to their first FA Cup final.

Arthur's demotion a dozen games into the 1913-14 campaign, his 12th in a Liverpool shirt, opened the door for a highly-rated younger player in Jackie >

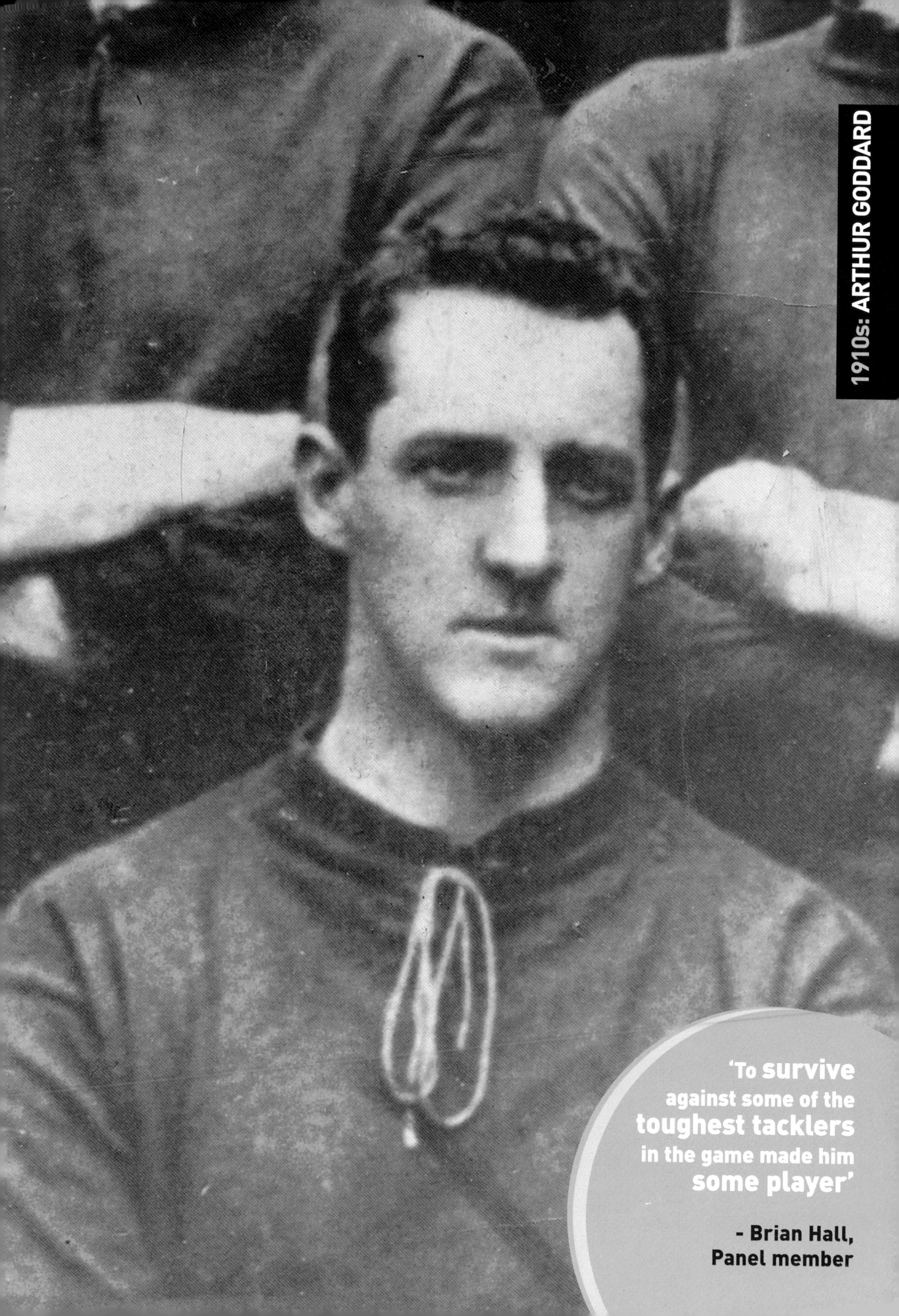
1910s: ARTHUR GODDARD
'To survive
against some of the
toughest tacklers
in the game made him
some player'
- Brian Hall,
Panel member

Sheldon, one of the few individuals Liverpool have signed from Manchester United. But Sheldon would disgrace the shirt that Arthur had graced for so long. On Good Friday - or should it be Black Friday - in 1915 Sheldon contrived to help fix a game against his former club by missing a penalty. He was suspended, although the ban was subsequently lifted as war forced the abandonment of the league.

The No. 7 shirt, even then, stood for skill, vision and determination. Goddard was the real spirit of Liverpool. He arrived in 1901-02 and missed just one match the following season. During the next eight, he would be absent on just 20 occasions. If he could be criticised for anything it was his lack of goals. Only twice did he reach double figures, although the 77 he did manage to plunder in his 414 games would be rated as highly credible today.

Arthur more than made up for this so-called weakness with his ability to create goals from the flank. It is a credit to him that he seemed to become even more influential the older he got. His first serious representative honours were secured in 1900-01 when he appeared in an eventful 4-4 draw playing for the North against the South. Even more astonishing was the 9-0 Football League win over the Irish League at Oldham's Boundary Park. Goddard was playing for Glossop North End at that time and it was no surprise when Liverpool offered him terms the following year, 1902, paying a fee of £460. Yes, that's right, £460!

It was substantial then, but nevertheless it was still a coup for an individual who would be supremely consistent for over 12 years. The fans are grateful to 'Graceful Arthur.'

'The **No. 7 shirt,** even then, stood for skill, vision and determination. Goddard was the real **spirit of Liverpool.** If he could be criticised for anything it was **lack of goals'**

ARTHUR M. GODDARD

Born at Heaton Norris, Stockport, date unknown.

Career: Heaton Norris Albion, Stockport County 1897 (appearances 35, goals 1.) Glossop North End, November 1899, fee £250 (appearances 77, goals 20). Representative games: North v South, 7.03.1900, 4-4. Football League v Irish League, 9.11.1901, 9-0 at Boundary Park.

Signed for Liverpool on 24.02.1902. Fee £460.
Position: Right-wing.
Club honours: Club captain 1909-10, 1910-11, 1911-12.
First Division championship winner: 1905-06.
Second Division championship winner: 1904-05.
League: 387 appearances, 72 goals.
FA Cup: 27 appearances, 5 goals.
Sheriff of London's Charity Shield winner: 1906.
Liverpool Senior Cup winner: 1904-05, 1908-09, 1912-13, shared 1911-12.
Lancashire Cup finalist: 1906-07.

Representative games: North v South, 26.01.1903, 2-1. Football League v Irish League, 9.10.1909, 8-1. Football League v Southern League, 11.04.1910, 2-2 at Stamford Bridge. Football League v Southern League, 30.09.1912, 2-1 at Old Trafford.
Benefit games (league games): Bolton Wanderers, 18.01.1908, won 1-0. Preston North End, 21.03.1914, won 3-1 (shared with Parkinson - neither played.)
Cardiff City. Transferred September 1914, 1914-15 appearances 31, 8 goals and 1 FA Cup.
Barnsley (WWI guest) 1918/19, 5 appearances, 3 goals.
Liverpool FC (WWI guest) 1915-16 to 1917-18, 49 appearances, 7 goals.

Post football: Had business in Liverpool. Died in Liverpool, date unknown.

Liverpool appearances:

	League		FAC	
	App	Gls	App	Gls
1901-02	11	2	0	0
1902-03	33	11	1	0
1903-04	33	6	1	0
1904-05	28	7	2	1
1905-06	38	6	5	2
1906-07	35	3	4	0
1907-08	35	4	4	0
1908-09	36	4	2	0
1909-10	35	12	1	0
1910-11	31	8	2	1
1911-12	28	2	1	0
1912-13	33	7	4	1
1913-14	11	0	0	0
Total	**387**	**72**	**27**	**5**

WWI Guest	App	Gls
1915-16	26	3
1916-17	22	3
1917-18	1	1
Total	**49**	**7**

1890s - Matt McQueen and Harry Bradshaw: McQueen was the club's most versatile player. Between 1892 and 1899 he played in EVERY position including 44 in goal out of a total of 103 appearances.

Bradshaw was a versatile forward making 138 appearances with 53 goals between 1893-94 and 1897-98.

1900s – Alex Raisbeck and Sam Raybould: Raisbeck made 284 appearances and was club captain from 1900 to 1909. He led his sides to two First Division titles and one Second Division championship.

Raybould played in 226 games, scoring 128 goals in his eight seasons. He was leading scorer in four seasons.

1910s – Ephraim Longworth and Arthur Goddard: Longworth was a right-back with immense talent, amassing 197 games in this decade. A club captain, he was also the first Liverpool player to captain England.

Goddard was club captain from outside-right and was a fluent, fast forward with an accurate centre.

1920s – Elisha Scott and Donald Mackinlay: Scott was a goalkeeper of superb judgement who played 339 times in th decade and was the rock at the back of the double-title side.

Mackinlay operated at left-back during the two championship years and was captain for several seasons.

1930s - Gordon Hodgson and Jimmy McDougall: Hodgson was a free-scoring forward scoring an incredible 241 goals in 377 games.

McDougall was a cultured left-half playing in 296 games. Partenered Matt Busby and Tom Bradshaw.

Bundle of energy: Kevin Keegan

ERIC DOIG'S official statistics helped guide and inform the **Hall of Fame** panel. Figures apart, who would this dedicated Red have voted for himself, based on the heart as well as straight facts

1940s - Albert Stubbins and Jackie Balmer: Stubbins led the attack in the 1947 title winning team. He scored 66 goals in 118 games.

Balmer scored 61 goals in 138 post-war games and is best remembered for his record feat of three hat-tricks (10 goals) in three consecutive games.

1950s – Billy Liddell and Laurie Hughes: What more can be said about 'King' Billy? 310 goals in 686 games says it all.

Hughes was a consistent centre-half clocking up 439 games.

1960s – Ron Yeats and Ian Callaghan: Yeats was the rock that promotion, the first FA Cup win and two First Division titles were built on. Skipper throughout most of the Sixties.

Callaghan made the record number of appearances.

1970s – Kevin Keegan and Ray Clemence: Keegan was a bundle of energy who inspired the Seventies sides.

Clemence was the best ever Anfield goalkeeper. Missed only 15 games out of a possible 584 in this decade.

1980s – Kenny Dalglish and Ian Rush: The stature of Dalglish must put him at the top of all the lists.

Rush was the goalscorer extraordinaire.

1990s – Robbie Fowler and Steve McManaman: Fowler's scoring feats promised to eclipse all others. Scored 151 goals in 258 games.

McManaman was an exciting talent whose skill was always evident.

NOTE: Five of Eric's personal favourites - Raybould, Laurie Hughes, Keegan, Fowler and McManaman - were amongst the stars who did not make it, highlighting how tough it was to ultimately make the official Hall of Fame.

Top **full-back** for club and **country**

No. 6: EPHRAIM LONGWORTH

The search to find the 22 players who would initially form Liverpool's first-ever official Hall of Fame set the panel an almost impossible challenge.

In any given decade, particularly those in which major honours were secured, how can you narrow your selection down to just two players from an all-star cast consisting of a host of legendary names?

It wasn't easy, but usually one or two traits or achievements were highlighted that separated giants from legends and legends from immortals.

This was certainly the case in the era 1910 to 1920, a spell in which the Reds reached the FA Cup final for the first time, but failed to follow up on the two Championship successes that had made the previous decade shine like a beacon.

The fans, looking for something to feel especially proud of, revelled in the quality of a man who was described as the prince of full-backs, not just for his club but also for his country.

Ephraim Longworth, known simply as Eph to the Anfield faithful, became the first player on Liverpool's books to captain England, fitting for a man who was described as one of the most stylish and accomplished defenders in Britain.

His England honour set Longworth apart from many equally fine club servants at this time. But there was more to it than that. Many things made Eph stand out. Firstly, there was his appearance. He was easily recognised on the field of play in his early days because of a lock of hair that always seemed to hang down over his forehead. Distinctive in looks, he was also distinctive in terms of his playing style.

Longworth had a tremendous positional sense and was able to play on the right or left with equal fluency. He would use these natural instincts to great effect during a remarkable Liverpool career that stretched over 18 years, helping him to fight off the challenge of many younger rivals.

We have already revealed the names of the first five individuals who will take their place in the Hall of Fame. The panel named star striker Harry Bradshaw and the supremely versatile Matt McQueen for decade number one, 1892-1900. Then they saluted sensational captain and defender Alex Raisbeck and flying winger Jack Cox for the period 1900-1910 before inducting winger Arthur Goddard for 1910-1920.

Now they had to complete this era as they continued to assess the heroes who would have to put their famous careers on hold to fight for their country as the First World War brought football to a halt.

Eph Longworth had been a Liverpool giant for five years by the time war hostilities put football on hold between 1915 and 1918. Born at Halliwell, near Bolton, he joined the local Wanderers in 1906, but arrived at Anfield via Leyton, then in the Southern League, in 1910.

If the war years had not intervened, Eph would have played many more games than the 370 that he is credited with.

He was bitterly disappointed to be on the losing side on the day Liverpool played in their first FA Cup final in 1914. Opponents Burnley snatched the >

1910s: EPHRAIM LONGWORTH
'A class defender
who won two titles
and was our first
England captain'
Panel member,
Ian Callaghan

> trophy with the only goal of the game at the old Crystal Palace in front of 72,778 supporters. The match was significant for many reasons. Burnley captain Tommy Boyle became the first player to receive the cup from a reigning monarch - the last formal act of the last and 20th final to be played at the giant bowl that was the Crystal Palace. King George V sported a Red Rose for an all-Lancashire occasion. The entry for the tournament had been a record 476 teams, but just four months later war was declared.

When peace finally returned after four long and painful years, football was seen as a way of helping the nation to get back to normal. Liverpudlians welcomed back their heroes, including former captain Longworth. The years had not diminished their memories of his stylish play from full-back. He was a scheming, clever player who could strike the ball superbly with either foot. Eph was as likely to start an attack as end one and he would remain a dominant figure at the club for a further 10 years until his retirement in 1928.

While he gets his Hall of Fame place for the era 1910-1920, the panel naturally noted that he won his two League Championships in 1922 and 1923, regaining the club captaincy to play a supremely influential role in those successes.

He was just one of those individuals whose brilliance spanned the decades, often as a partner for fellow Anfield defensive giants like Don Mackinlay and Tommy Lucas. It was Longworth's stamina and supreme fitness, backed up by his technical ability, that enabled him to go on and on as a quality Liverpool player.

Eph's five England caps came against Scotland in 1920, Belgium in 1921 and Scotland, Wales and Belgium in 1923. His achievement in becoming England captain filled the whole city with pride, but it was particularly significant in that it was a first for a Liverpool player.

His international debut game against the Scots was sensational to say the least. England came from 4-2 down to beat their old rivals 5-4. It was the following year that he skippered his country, against the Belgians.

Eph continued playing until the age of 40. When he finally hung up his boots, the fans had much to look back on. The defender had given 18 years service and 14 playing seasons, sadly interrupted by the war.

The trouble with all of these things is that, on a given day, supporters usually have no perception that it might be a hero's last. Having been rock solid

'He was one of those individuals whose brilliance **spanned the decades,** often as a partner for fellow defensive giants like Don MacKinlay and Tommy Lucas. It was Longworth's **supreme fitness** that enabled him to go on and on'

1910s

Hall of Fame

for so long, Eph managed just one appearance in 1927-28, sadly away at Birmingham three games before the end of the season. He operated at left-back in a 2-0 defeat. The fans were therefore denied the opportunity of a proper Anfield league farewell, but that did not lessen their admiration and respect for one of the club's greatest-ever players.

It should be noted that he was one of those who refused to take part in a notorious match-fixing scandal in 1915. The League inquiry that followed indicated clearly that he had desperately tried to persuade some guilty team-mates to scrap the idea.

This honesty would add to his powerful reputation. When his great playing days were over the famous link would not be totally broken.

The club recognised his vast experience and Eph was offered a coaching role, a position he held for many years.

He truly gave a wonderful service to Liverpool and, indeed, was still at Anfield when the Championship returned again in 1947, which truly is a lifetime's commitment.

It was fitting that the man who played in Liverpool first-ever FA Cup final in 1914 lived long enough to see his beloved Reds win that most famous of trophies for the first time in 1965 against Leeds. It made him very proud.

EPHRAIM LONGWORTH

Born 2.10.1887 at Halliwell near Bolton, Lancs.

Career : Bolton St. Lukes. Junior for 3 seasons.
Chorley Road Congregationals. Junior for 2 seasons.
Bolton St. Lukes. Lancashire Combination. Amateur.
Halliwell Rovers. Amateur.
Hyde St. George. Amateur.
Bolton Wanderers. June 1907. Professional - no appearances.
Leyton. 1908.
Southern League appearances - 67 in 1908-09 and 1909-10.

Signed for Liverpool on 09.06.1910.
Position: Mainly right back. Left back from 1924-25
Club vice- captain 1911-12, 1924-25; Captain 1912-13, 1919-20.
First Division Championship winner: 1921-22 and 1922-23.
FA Cup: Finalist 1913-14.
28 appearances, no goals.
League: 342 appearances, no goals.
W.W.I: 120 appearances, 1 goal.
Lancashire Senior Cup winner: 1918-19, 1923-24 and finalist 1922-23.
Liverpool Senior Cup winner (shared): 1911-12. (Proceeds donated to Titanic Disaster Fund).
Five England caps. 1920, 1923 v Scotland, 1921, 1923 v Belgium, 1923 v Wales.
First L.F.C. player to captain England - v Belgium 21.05.1921.
Representative games for Football League:
v Southern League 30.09.1912, 2-1.
v Scottish League 20.03.1915, 4-1 at Celtic Park.
v Scottish League 5.04.1919, 2-3 at Ibrox Park. Victory Match.
v Irish League 19.11.1919, 2-2 at Anfield.
v Scottish League 20.03.1920 4-0 at Celtic Park.
Retired from playing in May 1928 and appointed reserve team trainer until 1939 and then on ground staff. Died 7.01.1968 in Liverpool.

Liverpool appearances:

	League	FAC
1910-11	33	1
1911-12	37	2
1912-13	36	3
1913-14	27	7
1914-15	35	2
1919-20	27	5
1920-21	24	0
1921-22	26	0
1922-23	41	4
1923-24	14	0
1924-25	22	2
1925-26	4	2
1926-27	15	0
1927-28	1	0
Total	**342**	**28**

War games

1915-16	32	
1916-17	34	
1917-18	32	
1918-19	22	1 goal

Overall: 490 games 1 goal

* Also 1 appearance in Charity Shield, 9+ appearances in Lancashire and Liverpool Senior Cups, and many friendly games including tours to Sweden and Denmark (May 1914, France 1923.

Notes. As captain he was presented to King George V at Manchester City in a league game 27.03.1920. 1918/19 Lancashire Senior Cup win was the first time that LFC won this competition. Four days after losing the cup final to Burnley on 25.04.1912, the same teams met in a charity game at Anfield. This time the Reds won 1 - 0. Longworth's only recorded goals :- one in WWI on 29.03.1919 v Stockport and in a public practice game for Stripes v Reds 16.08.1924.

THE KOP ROOF WOULD LIFT OFF AS FANS ROARED 'LISHA, LISHA'

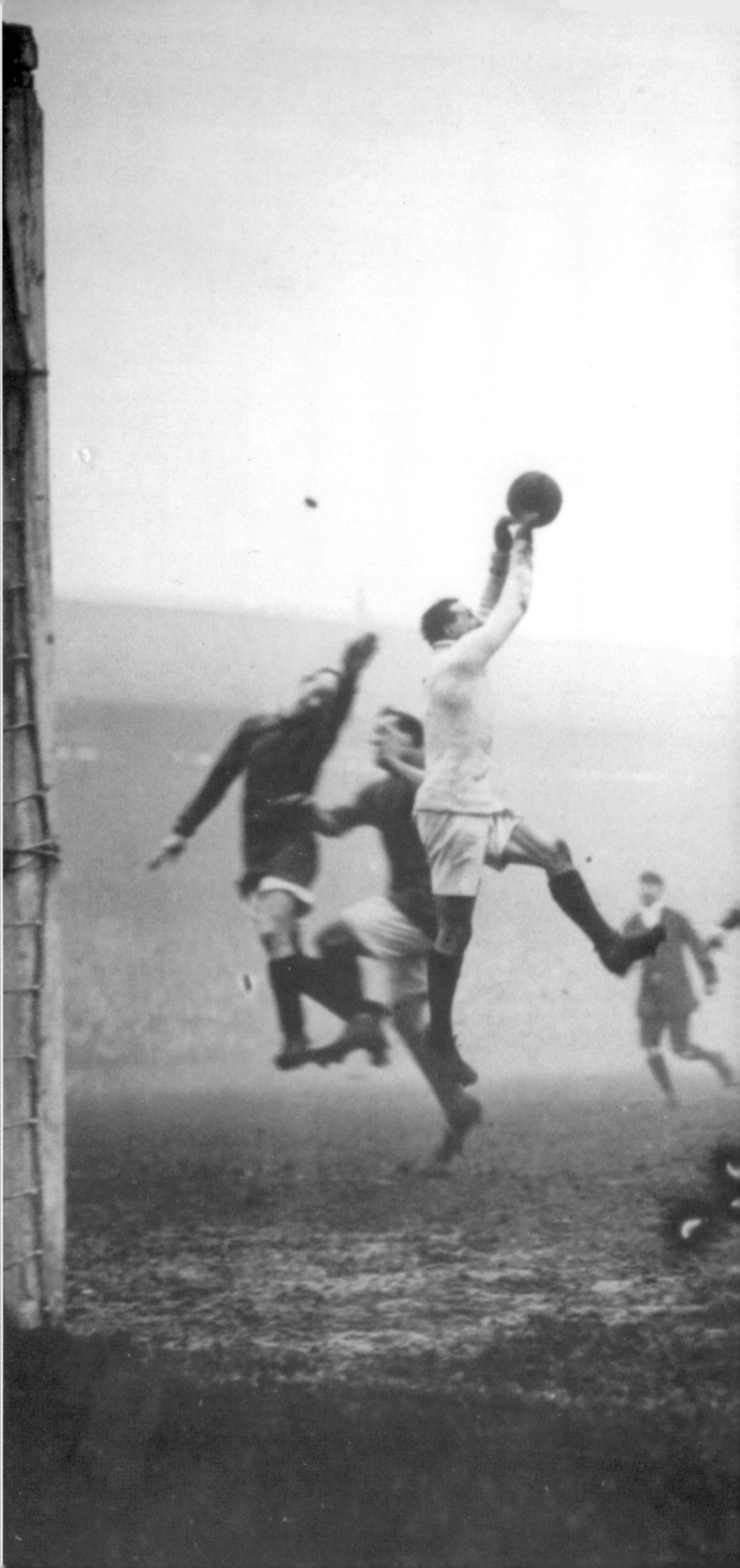

1920s

Liverpool Association
Football Club
English League Champions
Division I. Season 1922-23.
Commemoration Dinner
Held at the
Midland Adelphi Hotel
Liverpool
Chairman — W. R. Williams Esq
27th. June, 1923.

The 'untouchables'

Liverpool secured consecutive titles as the era yielded a number of players who would secure their place in Anfield history - and also a shock departure . . .

The Roaring Twenties seemed a perfect way to describe Anfield as an exciting new decade dawned and the fans of the early 20th century began to put behind them the devastation of the First World War that had raged between 1914 and 1918.

Sport was important as young men began to build a new life away from the dreaded trenches. Here on Merseyside, Liverpool named a new manager in 1920, former referee David Ashworth. Excellent players like **Harold Beadles**, **Danny Shone** and **Fred Hopkin** came to the club and under Ashworth's leadership, the Championship was won in 1921-22. This was Liverpool's third title success.

1922 THESE NAMES MADE NEWS

Standing — Mr. W. Harvey Webb (director), Freddie Hopkin, A. G. Whitehurst, Gordon Hodgson, Charlie Wilson, Elisha Scott, Jimmy McDougall, W. Miller, the late Mr. W. H. Cartwright (director).
Sitting — Dave Davidson, Dick Edmed, James Jackson, Donald McKinlay (captain), Tom Morrison, Tom Bromilow

Down the decades, the club's senior supporters would argue that this team was Liverpool's greatest. The fact that the debate raged for so long highlights that this era featured some very special players, men like **Tommy Bromilow**, **Harry Chambers**, **Dick Forshaw**, **Dick Johnson**, **Billy Lacey**, **Ephraim Longworth**, **Donald Mackinlay** and legendary goalkeeper **Elisha Scott**.

Incredibly, manager Ashworth would part company with the club in February 1923, leaving players behind who were on course for a second successive title success. He joined Oldham who were at the foot of the top flight. It was a puzzling move that was not properly explained in the newspapers of the day.

In 1920-21, Liverpool finished fourth in the table. Chambers had plundered 22 league goals and Johnson 13. Chambers was at it again a year later, top scoring in the championship side with 19 goals. Harry's consistency was remarkable and another 22 goals in 1922-23 ensured the championship crown would be retained.

Chambers, born near Newcastle and nicknamed "Smiler", had a ferocious left-foot shot. His career total of 151 for the Reds worked out at almost a goal every other game. He would top the Anfield scoring charts in the first four post-war seasons and his record of a goal every other game was mirrored with England (five in eight appearances). The determined inside-forward was finally transferred to West Bromwich

Shock departure: David Ashworth

Albion in 1927-28 and he was still playing at 52 for Shropshire side Oakengates!

Throughout the Twenties, the name of **Tommy Bromilow** was usually one of the first on the team sheet. Small and slim, he was a highly constructive left-half, said to be the brains behind the double championship winners. His defence-splitting passes would send a mighty roar around Anfield and he would win five England caps while clocking up 375 Liverpool appearances.

Tommy actually had the distinction of managing in Dutch football when his career ended. Perhaps that's where their tradition for "Total Football" started! He also managed Crystal Palace, Newport County, Burnley and Leicester City and the football world was stunned when he died suddenly on a train after a scouting mission to watch Wrexham play Merthyr Tydfil in a cup tie.

Dick Forshaw was ever-present in the title seasons. He had arrived from Middlesbrough in 1919, a tall and skilful inside-forward whose creativity was the perfect foil for the less complicated goal machine, Chambers. There was consternation amongst many Liverpudlians when Dick crossed the park to join Everton in 1927 where he linked up with that legendary Blue, Dixie Dean. At Goodison, Forshaw would win a third championship medal and Liverpool's loss was Everton's gain.

But Reds fans never forgot Dick, who was at his potent best in 1925-26 when he grabbed 27 goals in 32 league matches. His final Liverpool total was an excellent 124 goals in 288 games.

Transfers between Merseyside's "Big Two" were as talked about at the start of the 20th century as they are now. Liverpool got the better of the deal when they exchanged **Billy Lacey** for Gracie and Uren in 1912. The latter made only 13 and 24 appearances respectively for the Blues, but Lacey would figure in 259 Liverpool matches in a near 12-year Anfield career.

Lacey occupied numerous positions at Anfield, but was at his best as a winger. He appeared in the 1914 FA Cup final, a losing >

'**Incredibly**, manager Ashworth would **part company** with the club in February 1923, leaving players behind who were on course for a **second successive** title'

Hall of Fame

1920s

SCROLL OF FAME

1920-1929: Men who made a first team appearance, players in gold shortlisted for Hall of Fame

ARMSTRONG Thomas
BAMBER John
BARON Frederick
BARTON Harold
BEADLES George
BROMILOW Tom
CAMPBELL Kenneth
CHALMERS William
CHAMBERS Harry
CHECKLAND Francis
CLARK John
COCKBURN Bill
CUNNINGHAM W
DAVIDSON David
DEVLIN William
DONE Robert
EDMED Dick
FORSHAW Dick
GARDNER Tom
GARNER James
GILHESPY Cyril
GRAY William
HARRINGTON James
HODGSON Gordon
HOPKIN Fred
JACKSON James
JENKINSON William
JOHNSON Dick
JONES John
KEETLEY Joseph
LACEY Billy
LAWSON Hector
LEWIS Harry
LINDSAY John
LONGWORTH Ephraim
LUCAS Tommy
MACKINLAY Donald
MATTHEWS Bill
McBAIN Neil
McDEVITT William
McDOUGALL Jimmy
McFARLANE John
McKINNEY Peter
McMULLAN David
McNAB John
McNAUGHTON Harold
McPHERSON Archie
MILLAR William
MILLER John
MILLER Tom
MITCHELL Frank
MORRISON Tom
MURRAY William
OXLEY Cyril
PARRY Edward
PEARSON Albert
PENMAN James
PITHER George
PRATT David
RACE Henry
RAWLINGS Archie
REID Tom
RILEY Arthur
SALISBURY William
SAMBROOK John
SCOTT Alan
SCOTT Elisha
SCOTT Tom
SHEARS Albert
SHELDON Jackie
SHONE Danny
SMITH Jimmy
WADSWORTH Harold
WADSWORTH Walter
WALSH Jimmy
WHITEHURST Albert

LIVERPOOL FOOTBALL CLUB 1924-5

Carbonora Co. Lpool.

experience against Burnley at the Crystal Palace. But his longevity as a Red was rewarded with championship medals in 1922 and 1923 when he figured in 69 of the triumphant league games. Billy played 23 times for Ireland and finished his career with New Brighton.

This was a difficult era to name just two Hall of Fame candidates. **Ephraim Longworth** had already been named by the panel for the era 1910-20, but was still going strong in the Twenties.

Donald Mackinlay was another Anfield marathon man. His career actually extended to 19 years and 434 games with the bonus of 34 goals. The Scot was a fierce tackler who was one of the first full-backs to employ the over-lapping manoeuvre down the flanks in an age when players in that position usually held their ground to deal with tricky wingers. Perhaps it was no surprise that this exciting left-back plundered all those goals.

He captained Liverpool in both of their title seasons at the start of the Twenties and won two Scottish caps.

Having spoken about two men who played for 18 and 19 years respectively for the Reds, it seems incredible that we can now talk about a team-mate who actually played for the club for 22 years, but that was the achievement of legendary goalkeeper **Elisha Scott**. Even though his career was interrupted by the First World War, he still achieved 468 games for the Reds between 1912 and 1934. A Belfast boy, Scott's elder brother Billy was Everton's Irish international goalkeeper. The Blues could have used the family connection to get 17-year-old Elisha, but they thought he was too young for them. Liverpool snapped him up and he made his debut at Newcastle United in January, 1913. Incredibly, he might have signed for the Geordies that day!

They had offered £1,000 for the youngster who was being kept out of the Liverpool team by the excellent **Kenny Campbell**. The Reds chose instead to give Scott his debut and he kept a clean sheet, the start of a lifetime's love affair with the Liverpudlians.

Everton, having missed out on the "Boy Wonder", actually tried to sign him in the twilight of his career in 1934 for just £250, but the controversy was too great and ultimately he moved back to Ireland as manager of Belfast Celtic.

On May 2, 1934, at Liverpool's last home match of the season, Elisha addressed the fans at Anfield and thanked them for their support. There wasn't a dry eye in the house. He made his last international appearance at the age of 39 and was truly a football legend.

How the panel called it:

The powerful list of candidates reflects this golden era for the Reds with two titles won at the start of the decade. Legendary goalkeeper Elisha Scott, who played in three separate decades, effectively picked himself. Golden boy Gordon Hodgson was more relevant to the Thirties. Having named Scott, the panel assessed the other '300-plus' appearance brigade for this decade (Bromilow, Chambers, Hopkin, Mackinlay). Mackinlay was captain for several years, a class defender, an ever-present in the second Championship year of that decade and a man who ultimately clocked up a career total that surpassed any of his rivals (434 games). His Anfield career stretched between 1909 and 1929 and he finally got the vote. Mackinlay's name is erroniously shown as McKinlay in modern record books, but he clearly signs his name Mackinlay on an autograph sheetstill held by the club from the title years.

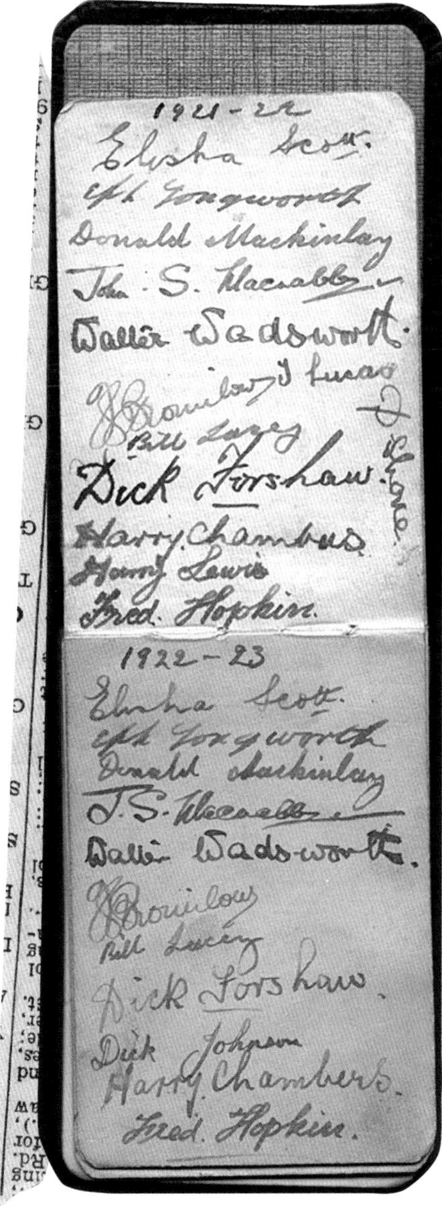

Left: Elisha Scott in action, and (above) autographs from the legendary sides of 1921-23, including 'Donald Mackinlay'. Right: A cartoon from the era

The eye of **an eagle, the clutch** of a vice

No. 7: **ELISHA SCOTT**

The prestigious Hall of Fame panel that spent months studying the credentials of hundreds of outstanding Hall of Fame candidates realised very early on that there are top class players, true greats - and then a very exclusive band of legends.

To understand the boundaries between the good, the very good and the creme de la creme is to have a complete grasp of the illustrious history of the famous organisation that is Liverpool Football Club.

The Hall of Fame panel were not presumptuous enough to claim that they had all the answers as they tried to separate the quality from the star quality. The trick was to listen to the voice of the fans; spend genuine time assessing the statistical claims of an army of red heroes; study contemporary books, newspapers and journals and try and put things into context linked with the 11 decades under review.

There were times when the panel struggled to eliminate a hero from a particular era. The Seventies and the Eighties were clearly very difficult to call. Remember, the panel's challenge was to select just two players from each 10-year stretch.

However, there were moments - albeit few and far between - when a Hall of Fame nomination was beyond debate. Elisha Scott slotted comfortably into this category, immediately named as the first Hall of Fame inductee for the roaring 1920s.

Scott was a goalkeeper whose remarkable Liverpool career would begin as a boy and end as a man. The young Irishman from Belfast was just 18 when he came to Anfield as a total unknown. He was 40 and one of the most famous characters in the game by the time he left.

Sometimes it doesn't take a book full of tributes and accolades to sum up the man. You can often do it in one sentence. I hand you over to a newspaper scribe who regularly reported on Liverpool during this famous spell. He wrote: "Elisha Scott had the eye of an eagle, the swift movement of a panther when flinging himself at a shot, and the clutch of a vice when gripping the ball."

Sadly, the man who penned the words is anonymous, otherwise he would be selected for a journalistic Hall of Fame. The colour of the writing matched the drama of the period, days of war and peace, pain and supreme elation. Elisha's career stretched out either side of the First World War.

Scott came from a famous football family. His elder brother Billy actually played for Everton, appearing in the victorious team that won the FA Cup in 1906, a year in which Liverpool won the League Championship.

As we've already heard, Everton looked at the promising young Elisha but felt the boy was too young and inexperienced for their needs at that time. Billy therefore made contact with the hierarchy across the park and suggested to John McKenna and Tom Watson that they should take a serious look at the up-and-coming stopper playing for his hometown club, Belfast Celtic.

The Reds didn't need to look twice, viewing the player as a long-term investment. It would turn out to be more of a marathon marriage. Elisha initially found himself kept out by the excellent Kenny >

1920s: ELISHA SCOTT
'He had to be in our Hall of Fame. He must have been a phenomenal player'
– Ian Callaghan, Panel member

> Campbell, but when the senior keeper was injured on New Year's Day, 1913, the young pretender seized his chance. He was so impressive that straight after the final whistle opponents Newcastle United immediately offered £1,000 to take him to the North East.

Scott knew that Campbell would quickly regain his place, but the youngster was persuaded that he was the future of Liverpool.

A great debt is owed to Tom Watson for keeping this Irish gem. The manager predicted that Elisha would be undisputed first choice within two years and he kept his word, although the war years then put many a budding football career on hold. When the hostilities finally ended, the supremacy of Scott was never in question. He remained No. 1 for another 16 years and it was no surprise that Liverpool's telegraphic address was 'Goalkeeper.'

Scott cut an unlikely image for a custodian. He was just over 5ft 9ins tall, but his agility meant he could stretch to reach balls others would simply give up on. With his brushed-back hair, long shorts, woollen gloves and distinctive knee pads, Elisha was a character and a half. It is said that he was obsessive about his training, working on after others had left and keeping himself tremendously fit.

The late Leslie Edwards, a sports editor of both the Liverpool Echo and Daily Post, knew Scott well. Leslie claimed: "He believed in taking total control of his defence, and was murder on the men in front of him." Edwards recalled another side of the Irishman. He said: "Elisha was notoriously tight-fisted about money. I remember one midweek match at West Bromwich when he took a nasty knock on

'Whenever Elisha stepped out in front of the Kop, the roar would lift the roof. **'Lisha, Lisha.'** During the action, Scott would keep the crowd entertained with his **industrial language,** which was famous'

the ankle and had to come off. We travelled home on the Great Western Railway and when we pulled into Woodside in Birkenhead it was nearly midnight. All the buses had gone and the obvious thing was for Scott to hire a taxi back to his home in Wallasey. Instead he walked four miles and was then out of the game for three weeks with a damaged ankle."

I like the matter-of-fact way in which Edwards suggests that there were 'no buses' and so the star should get a taxi. It sums up an age when the game's great playing heroes stood alongside the fans who supported them in every way, travelled to matches on the trams or other public transport and had no high expectations about owning a car themselves. It's a wonderful though that Scott chose to save a few bob that night rather than waste it on a cab!

Elisha had some tremendous duels with Everton centre-forward Dixie Dean. It was jokingly said that they were passing each other on opposite sides of Everton Valley one morning when Dean gave Scott a nod of acknowledgement. Scott automatically threw his hands in the air to make a save!

Whenever Elisha stepped out in front of the Kop, the roar would lift the roof. 'Lisha, Lisha.' During the action, Scott would keep the crowd entertained with his industrial language, which was famous. It is said that his distinctive Belfast brogue could cut through any sustained football roar.

Scott would win two Championship medals in 1922 and 1923 and repelled countless claims to his famous jersey. Finally, after 21 years service the unthinkable happened and the great man finally began to struggle for his place in 1933/34.

Ironically, Everton had come in three years earlier, cursing their reticence from all those years before. This move was highlighted in a minute of the Liverpool FC board on 7 January, 1930 when the Reds actually agreed to transfer their hero across the Park for £5,000. Scott subsequently had an x-Ray on his ankle and Everton's interest faded. However, they came in again in 1934 and there was a major row in the local press with Liverpudlians demanding that their hero should not be sold to their arch-rivals.

Finally, Elisha's original club Belfast Celtic solved matters by tempting him back across the Irish Sea.

His final game for the Reds came at Chelsea in 1934. Three months later he bid his Anfield farewell with an emotional and tearful speech from the directors' box.

The silent crowd listened in awe of a legend, shared his tears and then roared one last time. 'LISHA. LISHA!'

What a relationship it had been. The great goalkeeper continued to play at the highest level in Belfast and two years later won his 31st Irish cap.

He remained as manager of the Belfast club until 1949 and was always welcome on Merseyside - a true super hero and a most deserving member of the official Hall of Fame.

ELISHA SCOTT

Born 24.08.1894 in Belfast, Northern Ireland.

Career :
Belfast Boys Brigade as a junior, Linfield, Broadway United.
Signed for Liverpool FC 3.09.1912.
Position: Goalkeeper.
First Division championship winner: 1921-22 and 1922-23
During W.W.I: 15 appearances
27 International caps: 1920 Ireland v Scotland* & England; 1921 Northern Ireland v Scotland, Wales & England; 1925 v Wales & England; 1926 v Wales, Scotland & England; 1927 v Scotland, Wales & England; 1928 v Wales, Scotland & England; 1929 v Wales, Scotland & England; 1930 v England; 1931 v Wales; 1932 v Scotland, England & Wales; 1933 v Scotland, England & Wales.
Representative games: Irish League v Football League 25.09.1935 (won 2-1).
v Scottish League 23.10.1935 (lost 2-3).
Captain for Central League v Lancashire Combination, 25.04.1921 (won 2-0).
Lancashire Cup winner - 1918-19, 1919-20 (shared), 1930-31.
Liverpool Senior Cup winner 1914-15.

Belfast Celtic as player/manager 25.06.1934 to 1936
Died 16.05.1959

Liverpool Appearances

	League	FAC
1912-13	1	0
1913-14	4	0
1914-15	23	2
1919-20	9	0
1920-21	26	3
1921-22	39	3
1922-23	42	4
1923-24	42	5
1924-25	38	4
1925-26	39	3
1926-27	32	4
1927-28	17	0
1928-29	22	0
1929-30	8	0
1930-31	14	0
1931-32	37	4
1932-33	27	1
1933-34	10	4
Total	**430**	**37**
plus 1915/16 W.W.I		15

SCOTT ECHO

'THE EYE OF AN EAGLE—SPEED OF A PANTHER AND CLUTCH OF A VICE'

KEN ROGERS LOOKS AT THE CAREER OF A GOALKEEPING SUPERSTAR

Overall: 482 games
Also 1 Charity Shield appearance, 25 Lancashire Cup, 10 Liverpool Senior Cup and 7+ friendly games including tour of Sweden and Denmark.

*13.03.1920 E. Scott and K. Campbell of Liverpool both selected for the international game Scotland v Ireland at Parkhead, Glasgow. It was the first time keepers from one club were chosen for the same game.
Elder brother William played 27 games in goal during W.W.I (1918-19) and younger brother J. Scott, also a goalkeeper, played in pre-season trial 1920-21.

Versatile skipper ahead of **his time**

No. 8: DON MACKINLAY

When Liverpool's Hall of Fame panel took residence in the Anfield boardroom to assess the claims of players from 11 different decades, many eras proved almost impossible to call.

The Twenties came into this category, an era when the club stormed to two championships in quick-fire succession, inspired by an army of magnificent servants.

In later years senior Liverpudlians would argue that this was possibly the greatest Reds team of all time.

Of course, the emergence of Bill Shankly and the exploits of his 'Sons Of Liverpool' made the Sixties and Seventies rather tasty.

The great Bob Paisley maintained this never-ending success story and Joe Fagan and Kenny Dalglish also earned glory during the supremely successful Eighties.

The panel had to dwell on these decades and pay due respect to the tremendous number of outstanding candidates vying for that Hall of Fame accolade - with just two legends ultimately selected from each 10-year stretch.

In the Twenties Liverpool celebrated two titles, the same as the Sixties. They had their hands on that famous trophy four times in the Seventies and six times in the Eighties.

Yes, those who claimed that the Twenties team were the 'Untouchables' of English football and the greatest Liverpool unit ever to take the field might have to bow to their modern successors in the final reckoning.

But that does not diminish the special qualities of this side - the steadfast team spirit, the loyalty of individuals who dedicated their entire careers to this club and the individual talent that captivated the imagination of the crowd week in, week out.

Amongst these, goalkeeper Elisha Scott was a legend in his own lifetime. We have already paid tribute to him as Liverpool's first Hall of Fame giant for the Twenties.

Elisha selected himself for the Hall of Fame, as he did every week for Liverpool during his great career. But having named Scott, the panel then had to assess the other '300-plus' appearance brigade for this decade - men like Tom Bromilow, Harry Chambers, Fred Hopkin and Don Mackinlay.

Mackinlay was captain for several years, a class defender, an ever-present in the second championship year of that decade and a man who ultimately clocked up a games total that surpassed any of his rivals (434).

His Anfield career stretched between 1909 and 1929. When the panel finally gave him their vote it was richly deserved.

Don's marathon service with Liverpool is said to be one of the longest career spans of a Scottish footballer with one English club.

His natural position was left-back and he was soon attracting the scouts while playing for Glasgow junior sides Newton Swifts and Newton Villa. He came to Anfield in 1909-10.

Mackinlay was only 5ft 9ins tall but he was 11st 9lbs and put himself about with a determination that provided balance when set against the poise and

>

'Don Mackinlay achieved **433 games** and was a captain, which caught my **attention**'

– Phil Thompson, Panel member

> power of his defensive partner (and Hall of Fame giant for 1910-1920) Eph Longworth.

Mackinlay's special talent was in his ability to go on the overlapping run, a tactic well known to modern fans but one that was revolutionary in those days.

This was an age when full-backs held their ground to mark tricky, speedy wingers. Don had the confidence and mobility to get forward himself, which is why he finished with a creditable 34 goals in his Liverpool career.

Having revealed that Mackinlay was mainly a left-back, he also operated in other positions, not least centre-half, outside-left and inside-left. Hall of Fame statistician Eric Doig's research indicated that in a friendly game at Anfield against Aberdeen in 1925, Mackinlay not only scored, but also later went in goal to replace the injured Scott. The subsequent newspaper report indicated that he had now played in every position for the Reds.

Don captained Liverpool and was proud to have held the league championship trophy above his head in that famous Twenties era. He was also a member of Liverpool's losing FA Cup final side in 1914. He won two Scotland caps - against Wales and Ireland. Sadly, Mackinlay's long and distinguished career was ended by injury. He was hurt playing in a 4-3 victory at Aston Villa in September 1928. The following year he joined Prescot Cables before retiring to become a licensee in Liverpool.

The pub locals revelled in his memories of that great double title-winning side. Mackinlay was one of Anfield's great Scots. The stories of one or two more would soon unfold as the official Liverpool Hall of Fame challenge began to gather pace.

'Mackinlay's **special talent** was in his ability to go on the **overlapping run,** a tactic well known to modern fans but one that was **revolutionary** in those days'

DONALD MACKINLAY

Born 25.07.1891, Newton Mearns, near Glasgow.

Career:
Newton Swifts and Newton Villa.

Signed for Liverpool Football Club on 27.01.1910.
Position: Left-back, left-half or outside-left mainly.
Club captain: 1922-23 to 1926.
First Division Championship winner: 1921-22, 1922-23.
FA Cup: Finalist 1913-14.
League: 393 appearances, 33 goals.
FA Cup: 40 appearances, 1 goal.
WWI: 134 appearances, 26 goals.
Lancashire Senior Cup winner: 1918-19, 1919-20 (shared), 1923-24.
Liverpool Senior Cup winner: 1911-12 (shared).
2 caps for Scotland at left-back:
4.02.1922 v Wales at Wrexham. Lost 1-2.
4.03.1922 v Ireland at Parkhead, Glasgow. Won 2-1.
Prescot Cables, July 1929.
Died 16.09.1959 in Liverpool.

Liverpool appearances and goals:

	League		**FAC**	
	App	Gls	App	Gls
1909-10	1	0	0	0
1910-11	2	0	0	0
1911-12	7	0	0	0
1912-13	22	6	1	0
1913-14	16	1	6	0
1914-15	20	1	2	0
1919-20	41	4	5	0
1920-21	35	2	3	0
1921-22	29	1	3	0
1922-23	42	5	4	1
1923-24	39	6	5	0
1924-25	28	4	2	0
1925-26	41	2	3	0
1926-27	28	1	4	0
1927-28	40	0	2	0
1928-29	2	0	0	0
Total	**393**	**33**	**40**	**1**

Overall 433 apps 34 goals.

WWI games	App	Gls
1915-16	29	4
1916-17	35	6
1917-18	35	5
1918-19	35	11
Total	**134**	**26**

* Also one appearance in Charity Shield, 18 Lancashire Senior Cup, 6 Liverpool Senior Cup, 13 friendly games including tours of Sweden & Denmark, France.
Note: In a friendly game at Anfield v Aberdeen on 22.04.1925, Mackinlay - after scoring - later went in goal in place of the injured Scott and helped the side to a 1-1 draw. It was reported that he had then played in every position for the team.

Throughout the Hall of Fame process, **the fans** had their say. Here's some of the letters and emails that were sent to **LFC Magazine** as the debate unfolded

'Elisha Scott gave us 23 years service and 457 appearances . . . amazing '

My nominations for the Liverpool Hall of Fame for the first decade of the twentieth century are Alex Raisbeck and Sam Raybould.

Raisbeck was the first star of Liverpool Football Club and earned a hero's stature among Kopites. The Scot was renowned as one of the greatest centre-halves of his time. As a captain he controlled Liverpool's defence in the championship sides of 1901 and 1906. I think it's fair to say he was the Ron Yeats, Alan Hansen or Sami Hyypia of his time.

Sam Raybould was the first Liverpool striker to score more than 30 league goals in one season. In season 1902-03 he scored 31 goals in 33 games.

That record stood until Gordon Hodgson scored 36 goals in 1930-31.

Sam was a great goalscorer and was top scorer for Liverpool in the league in four different seasons. All in all he scored 128 goals for Liverpool. Not bad in 225 games.

S. Guttormsson. Iceland.

My two nominations for the '70s are John Toshack and Ray Kennedy.

Although Kevin Keegan was seen as the superstar at the time, he would not have been the same player without

All-rounder: John Toshack was great on the ground and in the air, according to Steve Carey

Tosh's flick-ons and physical presence. Tosh was also no mug on the floor and scored some great goals with his head, most memorably against Everton soon after he joined in 1970.

That was one of the great fightbacks after being 2-0 down against the then champions, and winning 3-2.

Ray Kennedy was a powerful player who also had great touch on the ball and was one of Bob Paisley's masterstrokes when he was moved from centre-forward back into midfield, where he played the greatest football of his career.

Steve Carey, Liverpool.

My two greats for the 10 years between 1910-1920 when we played in our first FA Cup final are Donald Mackinlay for his 19 years' service to the Reds and, of course, Anfield legend Elisha Scott.

Scott gave us 23 years of service and 468 appearances. That is amazing.

Chris Harrison, Prenton.

For the 1990s there can only be two choices for the Hall of Fame - Robbie Fowler and Steve McManaman.

Both were shining lights in an otherwise disappointing decade during which the team promised much but failed to deliver. Both Robbie and Steve gave their all for us.

Andy Cochrane, Birkenhead.

What a great idea it was to embark on the challenge of putting together a Liverpool Hall of Fame.

My Sixties heroes? Ron Yeats and Ian St John. Two magnificent Scots who were both inspirational.

Alan Matthews, West Derby.

To pick just two players for the Hall of Fame from the 1980s is almost impossible. I hoped the rules might be changed to allow us to pick four?

There were so many good players and it's unfortunate to have to leave out the likes of Souness and Whelan, to name but two.

But, I've gone for Kenny - without doubt our greatest ever player - and Rushy the goal machine.

Paula Barratt, Merseyside.

GOAL RECORDS SMASHED BY HOTSHOT SOUTH AFRICAN

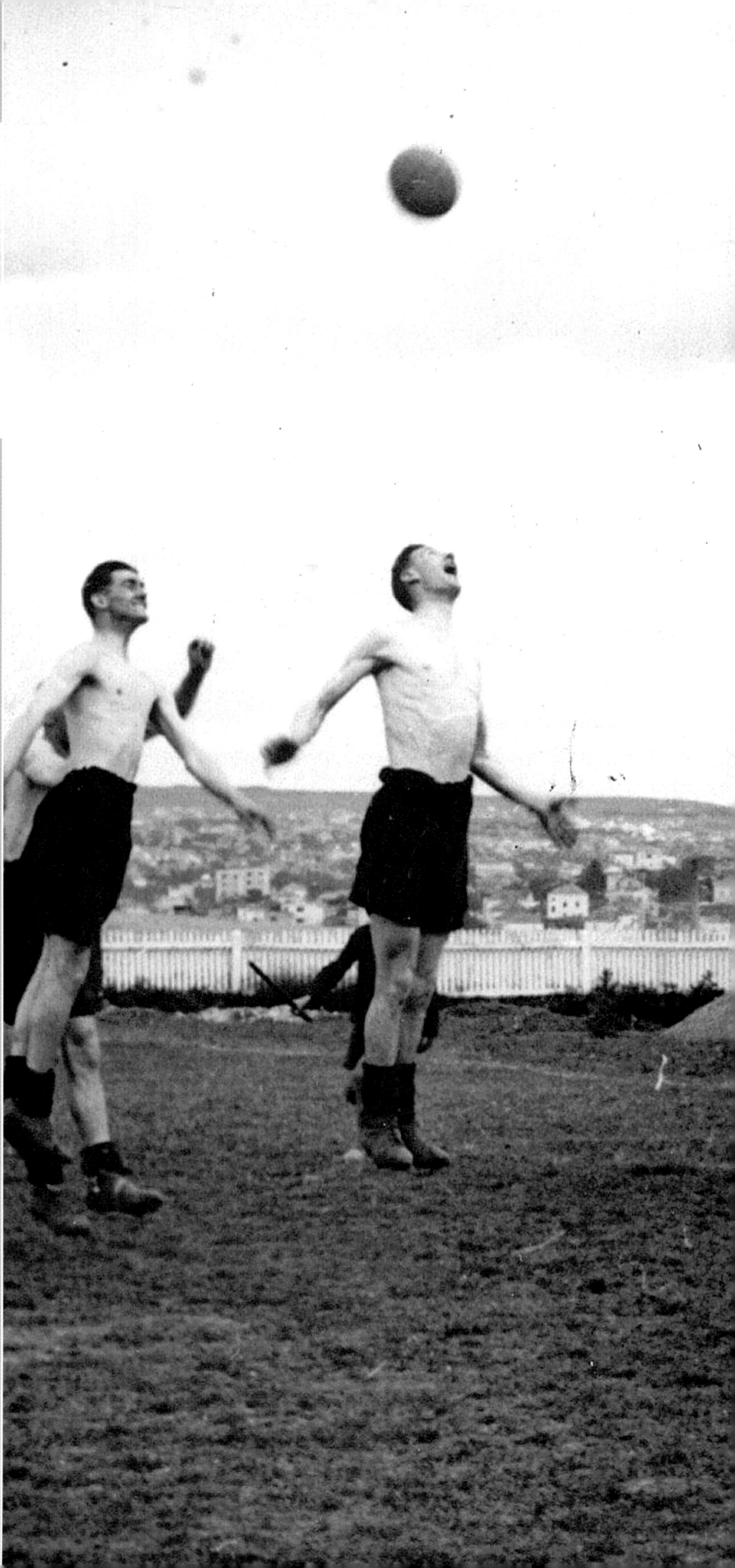

1930s

Friends and rivals

Inconsistency dogged the Reds in this decade, but several candidates made their mark for club and country as the pursuit of honours started to gather pace

The 1930s was an intriguing decade for Liverpool. No trophies were won and the club flirted with relegation on more than one occasion, but thankfully survived the experience.

But nevertheless some great players still wore the famous Red. Liverpool had a famous Scottish international half-back line that included a talented individual called **Matt Busby**.

Hall of Fame candidate Matt Busby. Recognise the name?

Recognise the name? Of course you do! He would later become the spiritual leader of the arch-enemy from down the East Lancs Road - Manchester United.

Many younger fans will not realise that Matt - or Sir Matt as he became - was once Liverpool captain and fiercely proud of the fact. But for fate, he could have actually become Liverpool manager and the pages of football history would have had to be re-written!

The Thirties were not the most glorious for the Reds, but the era conjured up many talking points. The previous decade had begun with two famous championship victories. It had ended with equal enthusiasm. For instance, in 1928-29 Liverpool powered from a near relegation position to fifth with a magnificent 90 goals, a tally that remained unequalled by the club until 1954-55.

Gordon Hodgson was the scoring sensation at this time and his 36 goals in 40 league games in 1930-31 would be his best return in 11 prolific seasons with the Reds. Therefore there was some room for optimism as the Thirties got underway.

Hodgson was a Lancashire cricketer as well as a formidable striker. He arrived in England with a South African touring soccer side and stayed behind when the team returned home, becoming a firm favourite at Anfield.

We have already mentioned Hodgson as a Twenties Hall of Fame candidate. Again, he was one of those whose career bridged two decades. He would be good enough to play for England three times and his finest season, without a doubt, was that free-scoring 1930-31 campaign when he set a club record with his 36 goals.

He bagged four hat-tricks and scored four goals in a 5-3 win at Sheffield Wednesday. Hodgson would hold the club scoring record with 233 league goals until Roger Hunt finally broke it 30 years later.

But despite the efforts of stars like Hodgson, Liverpool's inconsistency at this time meant that the club often struggled at the wrong end of the table.

In 1930, a 7-0 reversal at West Ham United remains one of the club's heaviest defeats, although Liverpool beat Bolton Wanderers 7-2 nine days later to emphasise some bizarre up-and-down form.

Everton, with legendary goalscorer Dixie Dean ruling the roost on Merseyside, stole much of the Mersey limelight at this time, but the Reds had their fair share of successes in the derby matches of the day. For instance, in the 1931-32 FA Cup, Liverpool recovered from a first minute Dean goal at Anfield to beat the eventual Division One champions 2-1 in front of 57,090 fans.

In 1932-33, the Reds actually beat their Mersey rivals 7-4 just nine weeks before Dean hoisted aloft the FA Cup for Everton. The following year it was three points taken off Everton (two for a win and one for a draw at that time) that helped Liverpool narrowly avoid the drop.

Hodgson moved to Aston Villa in 1935 for £4,000. It would be a long time before the club had a player to emulate his scoring feats.

Former West Ham star George Kay had become Liverpool boss in 1936. He would be the man who persuaded a young **Billy Liddell's** parents that his future lay in Liverpool - and what a future investment that would be. Liddell, of course, was the star all those years later when the Reds won the league in 1947 and reached the FA Cup final three years later with Kay still in charge.

'In 1930, a **7-0 reversal** at West Ham United remains one of the club's **heaviest defeats**, although the Reds beat Bolton Wanderers 7-2 **nine days later**...'

Many people often think that the great Joe Fagan played for Liverpool as well as coaching and managing them, but the famous Fagan who wore the Red was actually **Willie Fagan**, who arrived from Preston at the start of the 1937-38 campaign. The young Scottish inside-forward would finish the season with eight goals in 31 league games. The next year he was joint-top scorer with 14 >

Hall of Fame

1930s

SCROLL OF FAME

1930-1939: Men who made a first team appearance, players in gold shortlisted for Hall of Fame

AITKEN Andrew
BALMER Jack
BARKAS Harry
BARTON Harold
BLENKINSOP Ernie
BRADSHAW Tom
BROMILOW Tom
BROWNING John
BRUTON Les
BUSBY Matt
BUSH Tom
CARR Lance
CHARLTON John
CLARK John
COLLINS James
COOPER Tom
CRAWFORD Ted
DABBS Benjamin
DAVIDSON David
DONE Robert
EASTHAM Harry
EDMED Dick
ENGLISH Sam
FAGAN Willie
FITZSIMMONS M
GARDNER Tom
GLASSEY Robert
GUNSON Gordon
HANCOCK Ted
HANSON Alf
HARLEY Jim
HARSTON Ted
HARTHILL William
HENDERSON A
HOBSON Alfred
HODGSON Gordon
HOOD William
HOPKIN Fred
HOWE Fred
IRELAND Bob
JACKSON James
JAMES Norman
JOHNSON Tom
JONES Ron
KANE Stanley
KEMP Dirk
KINGHORN William
LOW Norman
LUCAS Tommy
McDOUGALL Jimmy
McINNES Jimmy
McPHERSON Archie
McRORIE Daniel
MORRISON Tom
NIEUWENHUYS B
PATERSON George
PETERS Keith
RACE Henry
RAMSDEN Bernard
RILEY Arthur
ROBERTS John
ROBERTS Syd
ROGERS Fred
SAVAGE Robert
SCOTT Alan
SCOTT Elisha
SHAFTO John
SHIELD John
SMITH Alex
SMITH Jimmy
STEELE William
TAYLOR Harold
TAYLOR Phil
TENNANT Jack
THOMPSON Charles
VAN DEN BERGH H
WRIGHT David
WRIGHT Vic

LIVERPOOL FC'S OFFICIAL
HALL OF FAME

> in 39 games. Willie's career would continue through the Forties, interrupted of course, by the Second World War. He would captain Liverpool and end his Anfield career in 1952 with 185 appearances and 57 goals to his name.

As highlighted, one of the most famous names that played for Liverpool in the Thirties was **Matt Busby**, who would, of course, go on to make his name with Manchester United.

Matt was a top quality wing-half who was signed by Kay for £8,000 in February, 1936. With **Tom Bradshaw** and **Jimmy McDougall**, he formed an all-Scottish half-back line at Anfield, one of the best the club has ever had. Busby was a Liverpool ever-present in 1938-39 and was actually offered a post on the Reds' backroom staff after the War, but he chose instead an offer to manage Manchester United. It is incredible to think what would have happened if he had taken the Anfield post. Would Bill Shankly have ever come to Liverpool in the passage of time if Busby had been able to weave his managerial magic at Anfield?

The Scots were great friends and while the rivalry between Liverpool and United would become intense in future years, senior Liverpudlians never forgot what a great player Matt had been for the club.

As it happened, another future managerial candidate arrived at this time. **Phil Taylor** arrived from Bristol Rovers in 1936, ironically signed as a possible successor for Busby. Another quality wing-half, he would later win a Championship medal in the first post-war campaign, win England caps, lead the club to Wembley in 1950 and later become Liverpool boss (1956) - the man who preceded Shanks!

Prolific striker **Jack Balmer** began his Liverpool career in the Thirties but his goalscoring exploits were at their peak in the Forties. Winger **Harold Barton** was a sight to behold, speeding down the wing at Anfield in the early Thirties, a real provider of goals for Hodgson. But he could score as well and netted all four in an FA Cup clash with Chesterfield in 1932. Barton also scored a hat-trick in the famous 7-4 win over Everton in 1933.

Scottish international centre-half **Tom Bradshaw** made 291 appearances. Ironically nicknamed 'Tiny' by the fans, the giant Bradshaw was a splendid servant to the club.

Full-back **Tom Cooper** won 15 England caps and captained his country as a Derby County player before moving to Liverpool in 1934 where he became skipper of the Reds. Sadly, while serving with the Military Police, he was killed in December, 1940, in a motorcycle accident. He played 160 times for Liverpool.

Alf Hanson, a Bootle boy, was a star winger in the Thirties. Again, Hodgson benefited from his quality wing play. Hanson also scored many great goals, 52 in 177 appearances, which was a great ratio for a winger.

The versatile **James Jackson**, mentioned amongst the Twenties Hall of Fame nominees, was still going strong at the start of the Thirties. He would later become an ordained priest. Not surprisingly, the fans nicknamed him **Jimmy 'The Parson' Jackson.**

Another Twenties star still making an impression at the start of the Thirties was **Tommy Lucas**, who played left and right-back.

Jimmy McDougall made 357 appearances for the Reds, most in the Thirties. He was a wing-half partner with Busby and Bradshaw. Jimmy was good enough to captain Scotland and rarely missed a game between 1928-29 and 1937-38.

'The **versatile** James Jackson would later become an ordained **priest**. Not surprisingly, the fans nicknamed him Jimmy **'The Parson'** Jackson'

Below: On tour in Las Palmas; meeting Miss Spain and sporting all rounder Gordon Hodgson! Opposite page: On a tour of Spain in 1935

Berry Nieuwenhuys was another South African recruited for the Reds. Marauding down the left, he scored some spectacular goals and when War interrupted in 1939, he could look back on 225 league appearances and 69 goals.

In 1939 a benefit match against Everton secured him a return of £658. He served in the RAF and returned to South Africa in 1949 with Liverpool his only league club.

South Africa seemed to be a breeding ground for Liverpool stars at this time. Another link was goalkeeper **Arthur Riley** who arrived in 1925-26 and was signed as an understudy to the ageing legend **Elisha Scott**. Arthur had to be patient, but he became a regular in 1929-30 and went on to play 338 times for the Reds.

How the panel called it:
Hodgson was the scoring sensation of this decade and five years of the previous decade. Again, he gave the panel a fairly easy choice. Looking at the others, the panel recognised the achievements of the famous Scottish half-back line of McDougall, Matt Busby (not enough career games to genuinely figure) and Bradshaw. There was little to choose between them (McDougall 297 appearances in this decade had the most games of any of the candidates, Bradshaw 291), both with four goals. Jimmy gave the club one extra year's service and his ultimate career record was superior (357 to Tom's 291). McDougall was given the vote.

'Red Dixie' heads African invasion

No. 9: GORDON HODGSON

Gordon Hodgson was Liverpool's answer to Everton's legendary Dixie Dean. He was idolised by Reds fans in an era when marauding centre-forwards were looked on as gods by football fans all over the country.

The Liverpool FC Official Hall of Fame panel - Rick Parry, Ian Callaghan, Phil Thompson, Alan Hansen and Brian Hall - were unanimous in naming Hodgson as the first of two individuals to be honoured for their exploits in the 1930s.

Indeed, the talented South African actually arrived at Anfield in December 1925 after impressing all and sundry the previous year during a Springbok tour of Britain. The visitors, an amateur set-up, would show tremendous potential in clashes against England, Ireland and Wales.

These games were played on club grounds, the two England matches taking place at Southampton and Tottenham. The clash with the Welsh actually took place at Colwyn Bay with the opening tour game against the Irish unfolding in Belfast.

The whole country was fascinated by the quality of the Springbok side, already well aware of their world class ability in other sports, not least cricket. Liverpool recognised the opportunity. By the end of the tour, they were showing interest in two of the South African stars - Hodgson and goalkeeper Arthur Riley, and both would be captured by the Reds and figure in that 1925-26 campaign.

Riley was initially seen as an understudy for the great, but ageing, Elisha Scott, although the legendary Irishman was not going to step aside without a fight. It took Arthur two years to get an extended run and he finally established himself as first choice in 1929-30. The remarkable Scott would then fight back to oust him, but Riley was a class act and in a 15-year stint at Anfield he would figure in 322 league games and 16 FA Cup matches.

Ironically it was another South African, his compatriot Dirk Kemp, who would challenge him, although the Second World War would soon put all football on hold.

Liverpool's Springbok link in the Thirties was very strong. We will return shortly to the exploits of Hall of Fame star Hodgson. But another talented South African forward would also earn respect in the shape of Berry Nieuwenhuys. Tall and slim with a powerful shot, the left-winger was recruited on the back of the success of Hodgson and demonstrated in five impressive reserve games that he was good enough for first team action.

Berry brought a new dimension to wing play. Many wingers at this time were small, but skilful - using their low centre of gravity to twist and turn away from powerful defenders. The tall Nieuwenhuys - or Nivvy as the fans called him - would lope up and down the line, but he had a deceptive turn of pace and would often cut in to unleash a powerful shot.

He could play on either wing and scored some spectacular goals. He would make 221 league appearances up to the war and score 69 times. So popular was he that the Reds gave him a benefit game in 1939, against Everton, which raised £658. Nivvy would serve in the RAF during the war and return to Anfield when hostilities ended, making 15 >

'Gordon Hodgson was the **scoring sensation** of his day and fans **love** their **strikers**'

– Phil Thompson, Panel member

appearances as the Reds claimed the first post-war league championship in 1946-47.

The exploits of these stars forged a strong link between Liverpool and South Africa - not least because of the strong trade links at that time.

Of course, the real gem was Gordon Hodgson. He was a powerful and free scoring inside-forward whose strength would drive huge gaps in opposing defences. Like most South Africans, Hodgson was as comfortable with a bat in his hand as he was with a ball at his feet. However, baseball was his other game, not cricket. It was said that he could strike a baseball as unerringly as legendary American superhero Babe Ruth - the definitive tribute.

It could be argued that he could also strike a football as powerfully and accurately as any of his contemporaries. Having impressed as a South African international, Gordon then qualified to play for England and was good enough to win three caps in an era when competition for places was fierce. He also played twice for the Football League.

In 1928-29, the year after centre-forward Dixie Dean scored his legendary 60 league goals for Everton, Hodgson plundered 30 league goals for Liverpool, including two hat-tricks from centre-forward.

One treble was plundered during a remarkable first half display against Arsenal.

Fittingly, in the light of his elevation to the Hall of Fame for the Thirties, his most productive season came in 1930-31 when he set a new club record with 36 league goals in 40 appearances.

These included four hat-tricks and a four-goal haul in a 5-3 win at Sheffield Wednesday's

'Like most South Africans, Hodgson was as comfortable with a **bat in his hand** as he was with a ball at his feet. It was said that he could **strike a baseball** as unerringly as legendary American Babe Ruth'

Hillsborough Stadium.

Hodgson would never score less than 23 league goals in his next four seasons and altogether he amassed 233 league strikes for the Reds, also a club record and one that would stand until World Cup hero Roger Hunt broke it some 30 years later.

He was transferred to Aston Villa in 1936 and later to Leeds United in 1937 for £1,500. He would later become a Leeds trainer and then manage Port Vale up until 1951 when he died of cancer in Stoke.

Liverpudlians mourned his passing and have never forgotten his scoring feats in the famous red. He symbolised the great links with South Africa, which would ultimately be sealed in the 1990s when the wheel turned full circle. Liverpool toured Hodgson's homeland and actually met up with President Nelson Mandela, who declared himself a Liverpudlian and an admirer of the club.

Later another Liverpool party would visit South Africa as part of the 'Tour of Hope' - a world charity fund-raising effort on behalf of the Roy Castle Cancer Appeal. The organisers took the FA Cup with them and again Mandela was happy to support the visit.

It reaffirmed the club's affinity with South Africa. Hodgson, Riley, Berry and the rest were truly great football ambassadors for their country.

GORDON HODGSON

Born 16.04.1904 in Johannesburg, South Africa.

Career: Benoni juniors, Rustenberg 1921, Transvaal 1924
Representative games during South African tour (with A.J.Riley):
v Ireland 24.09.1924 won 2-1 in Belfast.
v Wales 4.10.1924 lost 0-1 in Colwyn Bay.
v England 11.10.1924 lost 3-2 at The Dell, Southampton.
v England 26.11.1924 lost 3-2 at White Hart Lane.
In the 26-game tour Hodgson scored 15 goals.

Signed for Liverpool FC on 14.12.1925.
Position: Inside right.
Lancashire Senior Cup winner: 1930-31 (scored in 4-0 win v Manchester United); 1932-33 (won 2-1 v Bolton Wanderers)
Liverpool Senior Cup winner: 1926-27 v New Brighton (scored 1 goal in 8-2 win in final; 1928-29 v Tranmere Rovers (scored 1 goal in 9-0 win).
Three caps for England: 1930 v Northern Ireland and Wales.
1931 v Scotland.

Representative games:
Football League v Scottish League 5.11.1930, White Hart Lane (scored 1 goal in 7-3 win); England v Rest 4.03.1931, won 3-2.

Signed for Aston Villa on 8.01.1936. Fee reported to be between £3,000 and £4,000. Made 28 appearances, scoring 11 goals in 1935-36 & 1936-37
Signed for Leeds United in March 1937. Fee £1,500. Made 82 league appearances, scoring 51 goals.
Leeds United - junior trainer 1942 to October 1946,
Port Vale manager 1946 to 1951.
Died 14.06.1951 of cancer in Stoke-on-Trent.

Liverpool appearances:

	League		**FAC**	
	App	Gls	App	Gls
1925-26	12	4	0	0
1926-27	36	16	4	2
1927-28	32	23	0	0
1928-29	38	30	3	2
1929-30	36	14	1	0
1930-31	40	36	1	0
1931-32	39	26	4	1
1932-33	37	24	1	0
1933-34	37	24	3	1
1934-35	34	27	2	2
1935-36	17	9	0	0
Total	**358**	**233**	**19**	**8**

Overall **377 appearances, 241 goals.**

Battling Scot with real **staying** power

No. 10: **JIMMY McDOUGALL**

Soccer deals generate tremendous excitement among fans. They smack of glamour, excitement, change and challenge.

There's nothing the media like more than an exclusive transfer story and when they get one, the headlines explode all over the back pages.

Naturally, the truly big moves capture the imagination of the whole country. Liverpool's top three in terms of fees paid are reported to be Djibril Cisse (from Auxerre), Xabi Alonso (from Real Sociedad) and Emile Heskey, El-Hadji Diouf and Dirk Kuyt (from Leicester, Lens and Feyenoord respectively).

But the history books suggest that money isn't everything when it comes to signing players who might ultimately become household names - even legends.

Take two of the most important transfers ever conducted by the club for defenders. The selling outfit was not an Arsenal, Manchester United, Real Madrid or Juventus. Indeed few fans could actually pinpoint the club on a British map, even though it is smack in the middle of one of our biggest cities.

But mention its name and the link is obvious. So here we go...PARTICK THISTLE.

No prizes for immediately shouting out 'Alan Hansen'. But can you name the other Scottish international defender who gave a lifetime's service to the Reds after travelling south from Thistle's Firhill Stadium in Maryhill, which might not be as big as Celtic Park or Ibrox, but which is actually closer to Glasgow city centre than its rivals?

The answer is Jimmy McDougall, who would be revealed as the second player to stand in the official Liverpool Hall of Fame for the 1930s, following in the illustrious footsteps of striker Gordon Hodgson.

Ironically - but fittingly - one of the men who voted Jimmy into this exclusive 'club' was none other than Alan Hansen, who was an enthusiastic member of the Hall of Fame panel.

Jimmy actually arrived at Anfield in the summer of 1928, for £3,500. This was 49 years before his modern successor.

McDougall would take his place in a famous all-Scottish half-back line that also featured Matt Busby and Tom 'Tiny' Bradshaw. Fans would claim that this was one of the greatest units Liverpool have ever had.

Jimmy was originally an inside-forward, but skipper Don Mackinlay pulled him back to left-half in a match at Villa Park. It proved an inspirational move because McDougall would fill that role for the next 10 seasons.

It would also bring the solid and determined McDougall the captaincy of his country, although the Scots lost both of those games against Austria and Italy.

In the latter, in Rome, Jimmy had the dubious distinction of having to receive a bouquet from dictator Mussolini, although this was long before the Italians formed their Second World War alliance with the Germans.

McDougall was one of the most consistent players the Reds have ever had. He finished with a Liverpool career total of 356 games, scoring 12 goals. Apart from 1932-33, when he missed half >

McDougalls: Jimmy McDougall (right) with brother John, who was playing for Sunderland

'The **panel** took note of his games **tally**. We must have been hard to **break down** in those days'

– Ian Callaghan, Panel member

> the matches through injury, he was virtually an ever present. Totally dependable, he produced some magnificent displays in ten years with the Reds.

He retired from top flight football in 1938, joining non-League South Liverpool the following year shortly before war broke out. Jimmy never moved back to Scotland, looking on himself as an adopted Scouser. He lived in Allerton and always followed the Reds.

Alan Hansen said: "When we assessed Jimmy as a candidate for the Thirties, I was looking at his playing record, his consistency and the top class qualities he brought to the side. I knew he was a Scottish international, but I did not realise he was from my old club."

Hansen picked up on the fact that many of Liverpool's greatest signings have not been from the giants of the game, but from little set-ups like Partick Thistle. He said: "You think about Ray Clemence and Kevin Keegan from Scunthorpe and Steve Heighway from Skelmersdale United. It's one of the things that sets Liverpool apart - this great ability to spot talent.

"They've bought some tremendous players for virtually nothing and these individuals, like Jimmy McDougall in the Thirties, have become part and parcel of the Anfield success story.

"Liverpool have bought some all-time greats without necessarily paying outrageous transfer fees. Even when they have paid reasonable money, they have had this knack of getting real value for money. Just look at the John Barnes deal. I think we paid £900,000 for him from Watford.

"And when they have made a mistake, they have never been slow in putting it right. Sometimes you have to give players a chance to develop. Other times you can tell after 10 minutes on the training pitch that someone is never going to make it.

"When this happens, Liverpool have been very single-minded and shown no sentiment.

"We have had some true greats because we have done things correctly.

"This is why I have enjoyed being a member of the Hall of Fame panel. It has enabled me to look more closely at giants like Jimmy McDougall."

The Partick Thistle link adds to Alan's pride in being one of those who put this very special 'Mac' up there amongst the greats.

JIMMY McDOUGALL

Born 23.01.1904, Port Glasgow, Scotland.

Career:
Port of Glasgow Athletic, Partick Thistle (1925).

Signed for Liverpool on 23.04.1928.
Position: Left half /inside left.
Club vice-captain: 1931-32, 1932-33.
Lancashire Senior Cup winner: 1930-31.
(v Manchester United 4-0.)
2 International caps for Scotland on continental tour 1931:
v Austria 16.05.1931, lost 0-5 (at centre half).
v Italy 20.05.1931, lost 0-3 (captain and centre half).
Signed for South Liverpool as player/ junior trainer in May 1938.
He went on to have a successful chandlery business in Liverpool.
Elder brother John played for Airdrieonians, Sunderland and Leeds.
Died July 1984 in Liverpool.

Liverpool appearances and goals:

	League		FAC	
	App	Gls	App	Gls
1928-29	36	8	3	0
1929-30	34	1	1	0
1930-31	40	1	0	0
1931-32	39	0	4	0
1932-33	25	0	1	0
1933-34	32	0	4	0
1934-35	38	1	2	0
1935-36	38	1	2	0
1936-37	39	0	1	0
1937-38	17	0	0	0
Total	**338**	**12**	**18**	**0**

Overall: 356 appearances, 12 goals.

'I don't envy the panel but I know we'll end up with a list of special players'

I was thrilled to read about the club's Hall of Fame and the opportunity for the fans to revel in the memory of some legendary Reds.

I know that Kevin Keegan and Kenny Dalglish – two world class players – will get many plaudits for the Seventies era and rightly so. But one of my favourite players was Terry McDermott.

He had tremendous mobility and would surge forward from midfield, stunning opponents and inviting the long through ball.

Terry also had great skill and scored some crucial goals. It was fitting that he won two major Player of the Year awards, a reflection of the respect in which he was held all over the country.

Mike Thompson, Maghull.

Ask any Red and they'll say it's always difficult to choose their two favourite Liverpool players from the 1980s. Not for me though. Kenny Dalglish and John Barnes were outstanding.

Dalglish was, and still is, iconic. John Barnes at his Eighties peak was the best player of his era.

John Jones, Liverpool.

I have been watching the Reds since the mid-Seventies and we have had some great players down the years.

We shouldn't forget the early days though and for the period 1900-1910 I would have to nominate Sam Hardy and Alex Raisbeck for the Hall of Fame.

Ian Golder, Liverpool.

I was a kid in 1967 when my dad took me to my first match, so the Seventies were when I was in the park acting out the actions of my heroes. It's almost impossible to choose just two star names from that decade but for me Kevin Keegan was the first great superstar. What was great for kids as well was that he wasn't the most naturally gifted player, but he worked really hard and would have a go at anything.

The other player I'd choose is Ray Clemence. He played between the sticks throughout the Seventies and in his case he definitely had natural talent. He was the most gifted keeper of his era and was the foundation for the team in all their great triumphs.

Ashley Jones, North Wales.

Talented performer: Terry McDermott was an outstanding midfielder in his day

Here are my Hall of Fame candidates: 1890s - Jack Cox and Billy Dunlop, 1900s - Alex Raisbeck and Jack Cox, 1910s - Harry Chambers and Eph Longworth, 1920s - Elisha Scott and Richard Forshaw, 1930s - Gordon Hodgson and Willie Fagan, 1940s - Albert Stubbins and Jack Balmer, 1950s - Billy Liddell and Alan A'Court, 1960s - Roger Hunt and Tommy Smith, 1970s - Ray Clemence and Ian Callaghan, 1980s - Alan Hansen and Kenny Dalglish, 1990s - Ian Rush and Robbie Fowler.

As there were more excellent players from some of the decades, I hope there will be a chance to add one name from each decade again in the future.

R T Powell, Merthyr Tydfil.

For my money our great Scottish half-back line of Matt Busby, Tom Bradshaw and Jimmy McDougall would all have to be Hall of Fame candidates, along with striker Gordon Hodgson, who lifted our spirits through what was clearly a difficult period.

Generally though, I don't envy the panel who had to make some incredibly difficult decisions, although I know we will end up with a list of special players.

Mike Roberts, Wallasey.

My Fifties nominees are the legendary Billy Liddell and Bob Paisley.

Bob might not have been the most refined player, but his commitment to the club wins him my vote. And, of course, he would later become the greatest manager England has ever seen.

Alan Johnson, Aintree.

LFC Hall of Fame

YOU'LL NEVER WALK ALONE

LIVERPOOL

FOOTBALL CLUB

EST·1892

THE TOSS OF A COIN SAW GOAL HERO CHOOSE ANFIELD

1940s

16
9

Reds' silver service

Liverpool players did their bit to help during the War years, and on the resumption of League football, the club would yield further trophies

Football took on a whole new meaning in the Forties, a decade that began with the country embroiled in a war with Germany that would last for six years. Britain's national game would be used to help boost morale in all of the major towns and cities, including Liverpool which, as a large and influential port, was a natural target for enemy bombers.

While the nation fought for freedom, the government realised that entertainment was of paramount importance and the regional football that replaced official Football League action between 1940 and 1945 provided much-needed light relief.

Action at Anfield, circa 1947

During the 1938-39 season, with the clouds of war gathering, many professional footballers joined the volunteer Territorial Army or other national service organisations to spend their leisure time preparing for the inevitable. They were encouraged to do so by the Football Association which sent out a circular in April, 1939, encouraging players within the game to display a patriotic example to the youth of the country by signing up.

In the very well researched book *Soccer At War, 1939-45* by eminent football historian Jack Rollin, it is recalled that Liverpool FC became the first to join the Territorials as a club. Their entry included manager George Kay and assistant secretary Jack Rouse, but not all clubs had this collective desire to volunteer. Rollin reports that Manchester United's directors totally dismissed the idea, claiming that it was a matter for the individual to decide.

But Bolton Wanderers and West Ham United followed Liverpool's lead in virtually enlisting as a unit.

Despite the war fears, football had continued in 1938-39 with Everton crowned champions. In many respects, the certainty of war with Germany inspired typical British bravado and on the opening day of the 1939-40 season some 600,000 spectators saw 44 games played.

Even though children were evacuated from London on September 1, 1939, it was announced that the Saturday football fixtures would go ahead as planned. It was seen as getting on with business as usual and keeping spirits up. On the Saturday, Germany invaded Poland. Incredibly, the Home Office declared that it did not warrant the cancellation of matches.

However, Jack Rollin reveals that Liverpool only managed to field a full side thanks to the generosity of some of their Territorial Army friends, eight of whom volunteered for sentry duty to allow Kemp, Ramsden, Busby, Bush, McInnes, Fagan, Balmer and Done to turn out for the Reds.

The soldier stars were still forced to put in five hours on watch from 5am before reporting for football duty. Liverpool managed to beat Chelsea with a debut goal from **Cyril Done. Jim Harley** was sent off, but his case was never heard. The country suddenly had more important priorities and, with war declared, a ban was introduced on the assembly of crowds until further notice.

Official League action was suspended, but it would soon be realised that a nation under fire needed an entertainment outlet and regional football was introduced with many famous players guesting for the nearest club to their military headquarters. Hence, unfashionable Aldershot with its Army base found itself in the enviable position of being able to field 11 internationals!

Liverpool FC players would give exemplary military service. The early decision to support the Territorial Army meant that several of our players were promoted even before a shot was fired. Many had volunteered for the 9th King's Liverpool Battalion. **Arthur Riley** and **Dick Kemp** were made sergeants and **Tom Cooper, Willie Fagan, Bernard Ramsden** and **Tommy Bush** were promoted to Lance Corporals. Cooper would later lose his life in an accident.

Famous wing-half **Matt Busby** became a P.E. instructor and even though he was one of many selected for Army touring sides, he recalled: "Often we played matches only a few miles behind the front lines with the noise of gunfire sometimes drowning out the referee's whistle!"

Soccer had its war heroes and the Reds, as a club, had their share. Liverpool full-back **Eddie Spicer,** a Lieutenant in the Marines, actually captured a German NCO who turned out to be a soccer international. A commando, Spicer was commissioned in May, 1942, and later became a captain. He was wounded in the battle of Wesel in 1945.

Sadly, as mentioned, our England full-back **Tom Cooper** was killed on June 25, 1940, near Aldeburgh. A sergeant in the Military Police, he was killed when his motorcycle was involved in a head-on crash.

Another Kop star, defender **Bill Jones,** won the Military Medal for his war bravery. The 1939-40 season was only three matches old when hostilities were declared. Liverpool had begun to build a very good side with the acquisition of players like **Cyril Done, Willie Fagan, Jack Balmer and Billy Liddell.** Naturally, football ambitions would have to be put on hold although many of our players continued to >

'Liverpool FC players would give **exemplary** military service and several were even **promoted** before a shot was **fired**'

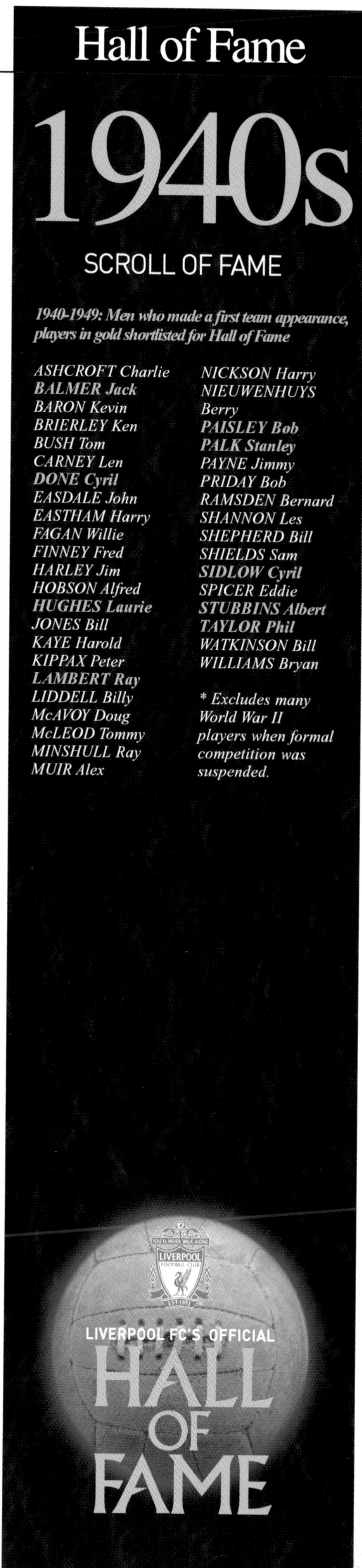

prosper in the regional game, not least the young Liddell who would go on to become one of Britain's greatest-ever players. He actually came to prominence in wartime football and was capped by Scotland in 1942, playing alongside Liverpool club-mate Matt Busby and another young player with powerful football ambitions, Bill Shankly.

Liverpool were beaten FA Cup semi-finalists in 1946-47 as official Football League action resumed. They lost in a Maine Road replay to Burnley after drawing at Ewood Park. More significantly, the Reds would win their fifth league championship title, becoming the first post-war champions and ironically taking the trophy off Everton who had become the last pre-war champions.

Jack Balmer and **Albert Stubbins** were joint-leading scorers and therefore natural Forties Hall of Fame candidates. Balmer made history as the first player to score League hat-tricks in three successive matches against Portsmouth, Derby County and Arsenal. Ironically, Jack began as an amateur with Everton, but he would serve Liverpool for more than 12 years.

Like many others, his career was interrupted by the War, but he won unofficial England recognition during this period. Balmer was a creator as well as a goal taker with skill and a tremendous shot. He was a Reds captain and left Anfield in 1952 after scoring 111 goals in 313 games.

Liverpool used an astonishing 26 players during the '47 championship season, particularly high for a title-winning side. One of them was Balmer's partner in goals Stubbins, who was one of the club's most popular stars, having been English football's top scorer in wartime football. Perhaps the fact that he chose the Reds ahead of the Mersey Blues endeared him to the Anfield fans.

Hall of Fame candidate Willie Fagan

Stubbins scored a famous horizontal diving header against Birmingham on an icy pitch that was talked about for years after. Albert's debut came in September 1946 when he scored a tremendous solo goal to get off to the perfect start. Stubbins was top scorer in 1947-48 and finished with career statistics of 83 goals in 178 games before his Anfield career ended in season 1952-53.

Another Kop favourite at this time was a young man from the North East, **Bob Paisley**. Between 1945-46 and 1953-54, wing-half Paisley played in 277 games, scoring 12 goals. A long throw expert, he was solid in the tackle and full of character. Bob made 33 appearances in the title-winning side of 1947. Of course, he would go on to become arguably Liverpool's greatest-ever servant as player, trainer, coach and supremely successful manager.

Liverpool's solid title-winning defence was based around Welsh international keeper **Cyril Sidlow,** full-back **Ray Lambert** and half-backs **Phil Taylor, Bill Jones** and **Laurie Hughes.**

Sidlow joined Liverpool for £4,000 from Wolves. He had won 11 wartime caps for Wales. One of his attributes was to be able to throw the ball out with accuracy, rather than kicking it. Cyril was brilliant in the final game of the 1947 Championship campaign, fittingly against his former club. He played for Liverpool 165 times.

In front of him, Lambert was another Welsh international. He signed in 1936 at just 13 years of age, but by the time he had developed into a player of size and stature the war intervened. It would be the first post-War season before he made his debut as a cool full-back with fine positional sense. Lambert could play on either flank and figured in 341 games before retiring in 1956.

Taylor was another splendid Liverpool servant who would serve the club as player, captain and manager. A classy wing-half, he won three England caps in 1947 against Wales, Northern Ireland and Sweden. Taylor was a great reader of the game, hence his extended career as a coach and manager. He played in 354 games for Liverpool, scoring 34 goals.

Jones, mentioned as a recipient of the Military Medal in the war, played in a variety of positions.

Centre-forward, inside-left, right-back and half-back, he was ever dependable. He was a full England international as a centre-half. Bill played in 278 games, scoring 17 goals.

Centre-half Laurie Hughes also

'Taylor was another **splendid** Liverpool servant who would serve the club as player, captain and manager. A **classy wing-half,** he won three England caps'

played for England. He was strong in the air and relaxed in his style for a defender, making 326 appearances. Laurie's career started in 1945-46, he won a Championship medal in 1947 and was still playing going into the 1957-58 season.

Of course, we must mention the irrepressible **Billy Liddell** who is a prominent Forties and Fifties Hall of Fame candidate. The man was and is still idolised by Liverpool fans as a winger of pace and power and a centre-forward who scored blockbusting goals.

Below: Laurie Hughes went on to play for England

How the panel called it:

It was noted that goal heroes Balmer and Stubbins were the two post-war heroes of the fans. Balmer set a record for three consecutive hat-tricks and scored 61 goals in 138 post-war games. Stubbins scored more, 66 in 116. The panel noted that full-back Ray Lambert played a lot of games in this decade (148), but it wasn't enough to wipe out the hero status of the two nominees.

Only 40 games separated these stars, which was not deemed to be a significant number to alter the panel's view.

One big issue confronted the panel - Bob Paisley. Bob's 133 games in the decade was comparable with all the other stars, and he was also a member of the Championship-winning side. He played in 278 career games, but more significantly Liverpool FC was his life (1945-1983, longer still including his spell as a director). The panel felt that it was crucial to salute Bob in his own right in the Hall of Fame, along with others like Bill Shankly and that if this principle was observed, they were happy to stick with Balmer/Stubbins for the Forties.

I would also point out (possibly for further discussion) that of the candidates discussed, Phil Taylor was the only Liverpool player to play for England in this spell (winning three caps in 1947) amongst the candidates discussed. Laurie Hughes' caps were secured in the 1950 World Cup. Taylor served Liverpool as a quality player from 1935 to 1954 before becoming coach and then manager prior to Bill Shankly (24 years service), but the panel remained behind Stubbins and Balmer.

Scoring hero with true star **quality**

No.11: ALBERT STUBBINS

Albert Stubbins was one of the most popular players ever to wear the famous Red and a championship winner in 1946-47.

Chief executive Rick Parry said: "Albert was a great player and the panel recognised just how much our fans idolised and respected him during his time on Merseyside. Because of his standing, it was one of the easier decisions. It was a unanimous choice for the panel.

"Even if you were not fortunate enough to see him play, his name still stood out as a true Liverpool legend."

Stubbins was guaranteed hero status amongst Liverpudlians from the moment he snubbed Merseyside rivals Everton to sign in at Anfield.

At the time he was one of the most sought-after players in the game and was already a superstar in the eyes of his fellow Geordies, having scored 237 goals in 199 matches for Newcastle United.

Albert was English football's top scorer during wartime football and many of the country's leading sides were desperately keen to sign him. Liverpool's George Kay had powerful ambitions for the Reds going into the 1946-47 season, encouraged by an opening-day win at Sheffield United. A disappointing defeat followed at home to Middlesbrough before a truly remarkable game unfolded at Anfield against Chelsea.

On September 7, 1946 Liverpool beat Chelsea 7-4 with doubles from Willie Fagan, Bill Jones and Billy Liddell, supported by a lone-goal effort from Jack Balmer. The 49,995 crowd certainly got value for money that day with an 11-goal thriller.

With eight goals scored in the opening three games, you would think that manager Kay would not see a problem in that area. But a shock 5-0 reversal at Manchester United inspired an instant decision to go for Stubbins after Newcastle finally indicated he was available for transfer.

The player himself had made it clear that he was determined to secure a move and advance his career further, but completing a transfer was the last thing on Albert's mind when he visited a Newcastle cinema, completely unaware that two Merseyside giants were en-route to the North East to try and sign him.

In the excellent book Three Sides Of The Mersey, Stubbins recalls what happened next.

He said: "A notice came up on the screen: 'Would Albert Stubbins please report to St. James' Park.' This was about six o'clock and I went up there to meet Mr George Kay, representing Liverpool, and Mr Theo Kelly representing Everton.

"Stan Seymour, the Newcastle director said: 'Which representative would you like to see first?' I said: 'Let's flip a coin. Heads Liverpool. Tails Everton.' It came down heads - Liverpool.

"Bill McConnell, the Liverpool chairman, and George Kay and myself discussed matters and I was impressed with them both, and with the possibilities of Liverpool, so I said I would go to Anfield. I met Mr Kelly, who was very gracious about it. I told him I had decided on Liverpool, and he wished me all the best, which I thought was very sporting."

It was a real coup and while £12,500 was a substantial fee in those days, it would be money >

'Because of **his standing,** it was one of the **easier decisions** to include Albert'

– Rick Parry, Panel member

> well spent. Liverpool would put the United result behind them to win 3-1 at Bolton and Stubbins scored on his debut in between strikes by Berry Nieuwenhuys and Jack Balmer.

Indeed, with Billy Liddell supplying much of the ammunition from the wings, the Stubbins/Balmer partnership would be prolific. Stubbins figured in 36 league games and scored 24 goals as the Reds powered to the first post-war title. Balmer matched the goal tally in 39 games.

Albert's first season also coincided with a famous run in the FA Cup with victories over Walsall, Grimsby Town, Derby County and Birmingham before the Reds finally lost in a semi-final replay against Burnley at Maine Road. It was against Birmingham at Anfield that Stubbins would score a goal that many people still rate as the finest ever scored at Anfield.

It was not just the spectacular nature of the goal that impressed the fans that day, but also the bravery of the player. Stubbins launched himself at a cross to score with a remarkable diving header on an ice-bound pitch. It was part of a magnificent hat-trick in a 4-1 win and 51,911 Liverpudlians stood as one on the final whistle to salute a wonderful player.

The Liverpool FC Illustrated History shows an equally spectacular Stubbins diving header from 1947 and credits it as this legendary effort against Birmingham, but the muddy pitch is the clue.

Stubbins' classic strike, as the text in the book indicates, was scored during one of Britain's worst-ever winters. The Liverpool Daily Post correspondent described it as 'the best goal ever seen at Anfield.'

It is worth repeating the goal description: 'Liddell operated with a free-kick from about 18 yards. The ball is lashed by intense driving force across the goal area.

'Two players trying to contact it find it too fast. The crowd are yelling their "Ohs", feeling the ball will pass out of play when Stubbins, out of position, flinging his body forward, connects with the rocket ball, and, at a distance of no more than a foot or two from the ground, the ball is positively rammed into the net.'

It should be emphasised that Stubbins was not just a goalscoring machine, but also a player with outstanding ball skills and the ability to lead and control the forward line. Albert was also an absolute gentleman off the pitch and a real sportsman on it. No wonder he became such a great favourite with the Liverpool crowd, thousands of whom travelled to Molineux on the final day of the 1946-47 campaign to roar the players on as their title quest

'It should be emphasised that Stubbins was not just a **goalscoring machine,** but also a player with outstanding ball skills and the **ability to lead** and control the forward line. Albert was also an absolute **gentleman'**

reached its climax.

Wolves were the top flight's leading scorers with 97 goals and it was not going to be an easy game. Equally, even a victory would not necessarily secure the Reds the title because Stoke were only two points behind with a superior goal difference and a game to come at Sheffield United.

All Liverpool could do was win and they obliged with a tremendous 2-1 victory in which goalkeeper Cyril Sidlow was truly outstanding against his former club. Balmer put the Reds ahead and then Stubbins scored a gem that had the Liverpool Echo reporter purring with delight. He wrote: 'It was a picture goal that should be drawn and framed and hung in the dressing room. Stubbins covered the half-field in record time with the ball at his toe.'

Among those Wolves players who were left trailing as the Geordie star sprinted through was the legendary Stan Cullis, who was making his final appearance in his side's famous gold colours. Albert later recalled: "I think there was a tear or two in his eyes because he had lost a last chance of winning league title medal. Then, of course, it was great for Liverpool. We sang all the way home in the bus."

The Reds would then play Everton in the Liverpool Senior Cup final and it was during this match that the news came through that Stoke had lost at Sheffield. Anfield was packed for the final with the fans on parade in expectation of good news. Nevertheless, it would be a tense afternoon.

ALBERT STUBBINS

Born 13.07.1919 at Wallsend.

Career: Whitley & Monkseaton F.C. 1935.
Amateur.
Newcastle United. March 1936.
Amateur, 1937 professional.
24 appearances 4 goals + 1 F.A.C 1937-38 & 1938-39. Division 2.
W.W.II 6 seasons 187 appearances 231 goals for Newcastle Utd.
Sunderland - guest, 1942-43 3 appearances 1 goal.

Signed for Liverpool on 12.09.1946. Fee £12,500.
Club honours: First Division Championship winner 1946-47.
FA Cup finalist: 1949-50.
League: 159 appearances, 75 goals.
FA Cup: 19 appearances, 8 goals.
Liverpool Senior Cup winner: 1946-47, 1947-48 and 1951-52.
Representative honours: Only England recognition came in a Victory International against Wales at West Bromwich on October 20, 1945. Wales won 1-0. Albert scored 5 goals in a Football League v Irish League game.

Ashington: September 1953 to 1954.
LFC scout 1954 to 1960.
USA national coach 1960 -
New York coach.
Later sports journalist in the North East.
Died 28.12.2002.

Liverpool appearances :

	League		FAC	
	App	Gls	App	Gls
1946-47	36	24	6	4
1947-48	40	24	2	2
1948-49	15	6	3	1
1949-50	28*	10	7	1
1950-51	23	6	1	0
1951-52	12*	5	0	0
1952-53	5	0	0	0
Totals	**159**	**75**	**19**	**8**

Overall: 178 appearances 83 goals

Besides appearances in the Lancashire Cup and Liverpool Senior Cup he also played at least 12 friendly games notably in the 1948 tour of U.S.A and Canada when he scored 17 goals in 8 appearances.

Notes: 2 appearances differ to those in statistical book "Liverpool, A Complete Record:
*29.03.1950. Liverpool Daily Post reported Stubbins had a knee injury, Cyril Done coming in as replacement.
* 5.04.1952 Stubbins missing, Jackson coming in at 7 and J.T. Smith moved to centre forward.
NB: 1948-49 season - missed first 13 games due to refusal to sign a new contract.

The Football Echo recalled what happened next: 'All interest in the match went west five minutes before the finish when Mr George Richards, the Liverpool director, announced over the loud-speaker system that Sheffield United had beaten Stoke, and that Liverpool were therefore league champions after an interval of 24 years.'

The report added: 'The roar which greeted this announcement made the Hampden Park roar sound almost like a childish whisper. The crowd threw their arms in the air, many lost their hats and did not bother to look for them after they had tossed them up in a burst of joyful celebration.'

The referee soon blew his whistle and the fans swarmed on to carry Stubbins, Liddell and the rest from the pitch shoulder high. The irony was that Everton were the last champions before the war. Now Liverpool, on the day they met the Blues in the Liverpool Senior Cup, were the first post-war title heroes.

The following season, 1947-48, Stubbins was Liverpool's top scorer in the league with 24 goals from 40 games.

This included all four in the hammering of Huddersfield Town.

Albert had become a little bit unsettled because his wife had expressed a wish to return to Tyneside, but Liverpool were reluctant to release such a star talent.

He would remain on Merseyside for a further four seasons and while injuries dogged him at times, he finished with 83 goals in 178 appearances. The slim, red-haired centre-forward eventually returned to his native North East in 1953.

He retired in 1954 and became a Liverpool scout. He also took on the challenge as USA national coach in 1960, having spent some time in the States as a youngster before returning to Newcastle where he joined his home-town club in 1937

In his later years, Albert would write about the game he graced as a freelance journalist. He would never be forgotten here on Merseyside where he was always welcome. He also treasured his Anfield memories.

Albert's goalscoring feats, his qualities as a sportsman and a gentleman will never be forgotten.

Albert Stubbins looks on as a Payne shot is saved by the Arsenal keeper in the 1950 FA Cup final at Wembley

The day the Fab Four chose fab no. 9 Albert to be a Sergeant Pepper cover star!

Albert Stubbins achieved icon status twice in his life, first and foremost as a centre-forward who was idolised by the Anfield Kop and then as an unexpected image in a sea of legendary faces on the Beatles' famous Sergeant Pepper album.

Millions of people down the years have scanned that most famous of covers and instantly picked out the likes of Marlene Dietrich, Laurel and Hardy, Bob Dylan and Marlon Brando.

Few recognised the prominent smiling face tucked in behind Dietricht and Betty Davis as that of Stubbins, not an icon of the world of movies and entertainment, but a legendary football figure in Liverpool and Newcastle and a man whose name intrigued John Lennon.

Neil Aspinall, who worked closely with the Beatles says: "I remember being in the studio when we were making the album and everyone was asking: 'Who do you want to be in the band?'

"All these crazy suggestions were coming out. John was talking about Albert Stubbins. No one knew who he was. John said he was a Liverpool centre-forward."

Liverpool FC Museum Curator Stephen Done throws further light on why Albert was chosen by Lennon. He told LFC Magazine: "Ironically, representations were being made to Sir Paul to see if he would come and meet Albert after all these years to finally end the mystery as to how our great player ended up on that famous cover. I was told that Lennon and McCartney just thought that Albert Stubbins was a wonderful name for a sporting hero, so down to earth! It had a lovely ring about it. It was always my ambition to see if we could get Sir Paul to meet Albert. I know it meant a lot to him that he was on that Beatles cover."

Liverpool Fooball Club's official Hall of Fame panel smiled at the connection between John, Paul, George, Ringo - and Albert!

Cult striker and hat-trick **expert**

No. 12: **JACK BALMER**

There are certain football achievements that stick in the hearts and minds of fans forever. Sometimes it's a spectacular or visionary goal - scored at a crucial time. Other times it's linked with a trophy-winning moment.

Liverpudlians can reel off a catalogue of sensational memories - like St John's jack-knife winning header against Leeds in the 1965 FA Cup final, Tommy Smith's soaring European Cup final header against Borussia Moenchengladbach in 1977, Kenny Dalglish's delicate chip that beat Bruges at Wembley a year later, Alan Kennedy's unexpected but sensational European Cup goal against Real Madrid in 1981 or even Steven Gerrard's late equalising goal in the 2006 FA Cup final.

For years, the feat that stood head and shoulders above the rest and brought a smile to the face of every Liverpudlian who remembered it was achieved by a scheming inside-forward whose goals helped to light up Anfield after the Second World War.

Jack Balmer was the man who became famous for scoring hat-tricks in three consecutive league matches. And the fact that they came during Liverpool's eventful Championship-winning campaign of 1946-47 gave Balmer folklore status.

Indeed, Jack was the first player in the Football League to achieve such a goalscoring feat and the Hall of Fame panel took little persuading to elevate him into the club's official Hall of Fame for the Forties alongside his partner in goals Albert Stubbins.

Jack was from a famous football family. Two of his uncles had played full-back for Everton before World War One and it was no surprise when young Balmer chose the Blues to start his career as an amateur. However, Liverpool continued to monitor his potential and he soon crossed the park to serve the Reds for more than 12 years, his first-team career beginning in 1935-36.

Of course, like many of his team-mates, Jack's football ambitions had to go on hold for over five years because of the Second World War. Billy Liddell had been too young to enroll when the war started, being just 17. However, he would later qualify as an RAF navigator and come home safe following service in Europe and Canada.

Eddie Spicer survived after being wounded and he was decorated for bravery. Jim Harley was mentioned in despatches and defender Bill Jones brought great pride to city and club when he was awarded the Military Medal for helping rescue wounded comrades while under fire. Bob Paisley came through the desert campaign in North Africa.

Sadly, club captain Tom Cooper was killed in a motorcycle accident while on despatch duty. For his part, Jack Balmer had been at Dunkirk and witnessed that remarkable episode in British military history.

With the war over, he began the challenge of re-launching his career although it was something of a formality. During the war years Jack had won unofficial international honours for England and was clearly highly rated, not just on Merseyside but also throughout the country.

In the four years up to the war he had figured in >

'Jack Balmer scored **goals** for **fun.** Players with a **natural** eye for goal are like **gold dust**'

– Ian Callaghan, Panel member

> 130 games and demonstrated his scoring prowess with 39 goals.

The 1946-47 season, the first after hostilities had ended, proved to be momentous for Balmer and Liverpool. The League Championship had come to Merseyside in 1939, the last year before the war, won by Everton. It would stay in our city as the Reds powered to the first post-war league title in 1947.

Balmer's impact was phenomenal. He would play in 39 of the 42 league games and score 24 goals, fittingly a tally that was equalled by his partner Albert Stubbins who stands alongside him in Liverpool's official Hall of Fame for the Forties.

This striking combination had everything. Jack was both a schemer and a finisher from the inside-right position. He had good skill and a tremendous shot.

Stubbins was more of a natural centre-forward, brave and good in the air as well as having a powerful shot. They linked well, not least because they had the attacking support of the great Billy Liddell whose power and pace also helped to make the Reds such an unstoppable force during that Championship year.

The team had quality in all areas. In defence Phil Taylor and Lawrie Hughes had real ability. Bill Jones had some injuries that year but played his part in the back line. Bob Paisley was a brave and determined wing-half who played in 33 games.

But it was the goal input of the two main front men that regularly raised the Kop roof.

Balmer's great claim to fame - his three successive hat-tricks - came at home to Portsmouth (3), away at Derby (4) and at home to Arsenal (3). The other remarkable thing about it was that Jack had found the back of the net 10 times without another Liverpool player scoring in between.

The Championship season is still talked about by senior Liverpudlians, not least because of the final game at Molineux where the Reds faced Wolves. It seemed that half the population of Merseyside made the trip with them. Liverpool had to win to have a chance of clinching the trophy and faced a home side who were the top flight's leading scorers at that time with 97 goals.

The title was also still within the grasp of the Wolves. However, Balmer gave the Reds the perfect start.

Stubbins grabbed a second after racing half the length of the field. The home side pulled one back, but Liverpool had the points in the bag.

Ironically, they had a tantalising wait to find out if they were to become champions because Stoke had re-arranged their final game for June 14 and were two points behind with a better goal average. As it turned out, Balmer, Stubbins, Liddell and the rest had done enough and when Stoke went down to Sheffield United, the Red half of Merseyside exploded in delight.

Balmer had been vice-captain that season and he then became skipper in his own right for the following two seasons.

Jack's Anfield career ended in 1951 after 312 games and 111 goals. He had his Championship medal. He had his remarkable hat-trick record. He also had the thanks of all the fans who watched him score all of those crucial goals in a red shirt. He fully deserves his inclusion in the official Liverpool Hall of Fame.

JOHN (JACK) BALMER

Born 6.02.1916, Liverpool
Career: Everton. 1933. Amateur. Collegiate Old Boys. Representative game (amateur) - Northern Counties Championship: Replay - Liverpool County v Lancashire, 16.12.1933. Won 4-1 - Balmer 2 (1 pen)
Signed for Liverpool: May 1935 Amateur. Professional 23.08.1935.
Position: Inside forward.
Club captain: 1947-48, 1948-49, 1949-50. Vice captain 1946-47.
First Division Championship winner: 1946-47.
League: 291 appearances, 99 goals.
FA Cup: 21 appearances, 12 goals.
L.F.C. WWII 101 appearances, 53 goals.
Lancashire Senior Cup winner: 1945-46, 1946-47 13 + appearances 10 goals.
Liverpool Senior Cup winner: 1935-36 (shared), 1936-37, 1945-46, 1946-47, 1947-48. 11 appearances, 7 goals.
Friendly games: 18 appearances 12 goals plus 1946 USA tour 9 games 19 goals, 1948 USA tour 11 games 16 goals.
Renowned for his feat of 3 hat-tricks (10 goals) in 3 consecutive games.
Brighton & Hove Albion WWII guest
15,03,1941 - 31.05.1941 8 appearances 9 goals.
20.09.1941 - 11.10.1941 6 appearances 7 goals.
Newcastle United WWII guest. 1941-1942 6 appearances 1 goal.
Retired from playing May 1952. Club trainer May 1952 to 1955.
Later in business in Liverpool.
Died 25.12.1984 in Liverpool.

Liverpool appearances and goals:

	League		FAC	
	App	Gls	App	Gls
1935-36	17	3	0	0
1936-37	33	8	1	0
1937-38	30	13	1	0
1938-39	42	10	3	4
1939-40	3*	1	0	0
1945-46	0	0	2*	1
1946-47	39	24	6	4
1947-48	40	15	1	0
1948-49	42	14	4	2
1949-50	9	1	0	0
1950-51	34**	10	1	1
1951-52	2	0	2	0
Total	**291**	**99**	**21**	**12**

Overall: 312 games, 111 goals

LFC WWII appearances:

1939-40	8	5
1940-41	2	0
1941-42	12	6
1942-43	16	4
1943-44	26	22
1944-45	3	0
1945-46	34	16
Total	**101**	**53**

* Normal league competition abandoned after 3 games and the F.A.Cup competition resumed in 1945/46 before normal league football in 1946-47.
** Difference to other sources - Balmer (along with Sidlow) reported absent with 'flu, 7.10.1950. L.Echo.

LFC Hall of Fame

'TRYING TO STOP LIDDELL WAS LIKE TRYING TO STOP A FIRE ENGINE'

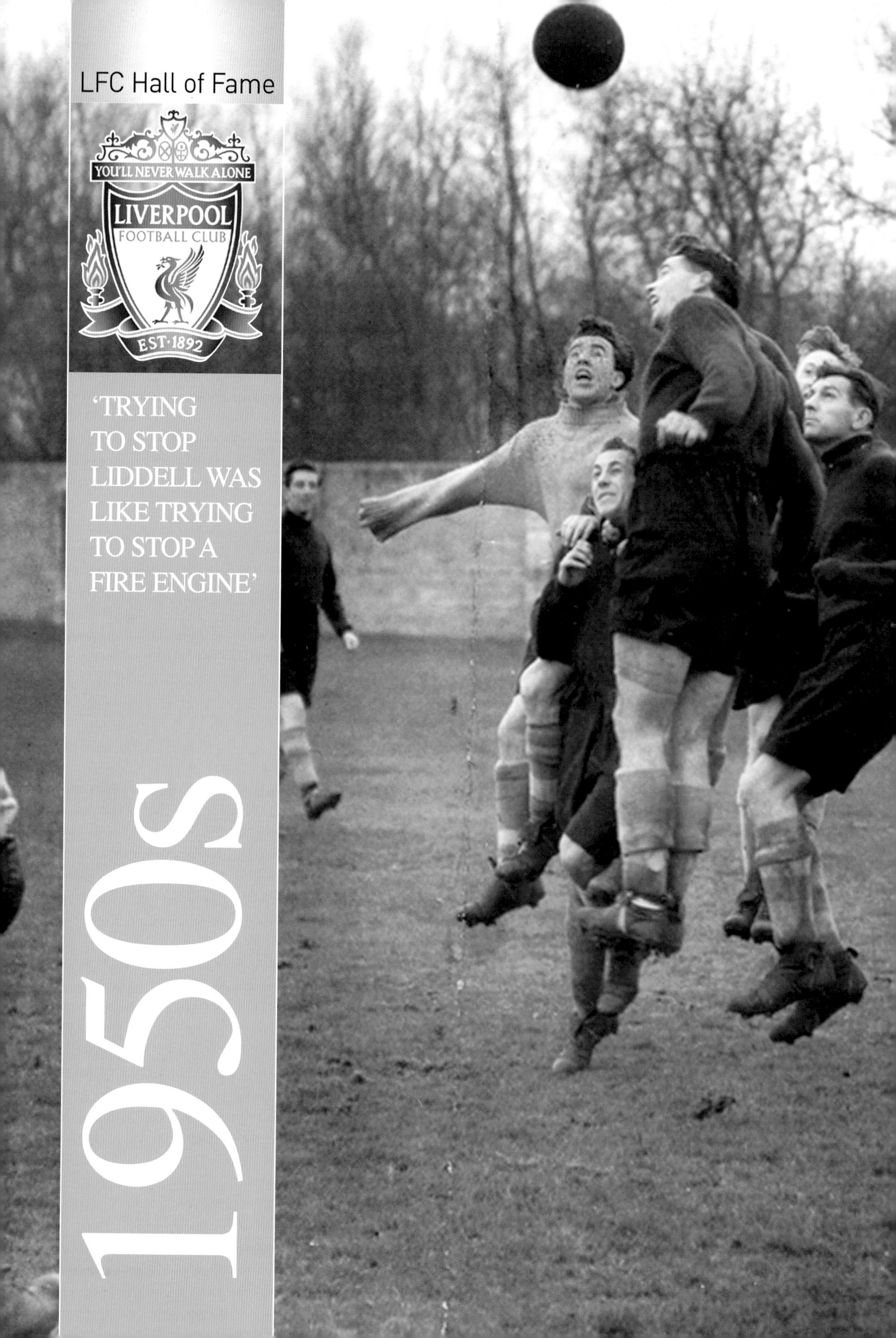

1950s

1950
J.MERCER
A. STUBBINS
R.LAMBERT

Rollercoaster ride

One man dominated the Anfield scene during an up and down decade, although a new messiah would begin a football revolution as the 1950s drew to a close

The Liverpool squad in the close season of 1951

The 1950s were a rollercoaster ride for Liverpool fans. The decade began with a Wembley FA Cup final appearance against rivals Arsenal, an occasion that has become more famous for the dropping of semi-final hero **Bob Paisley** than the result which went against the Reds.

In 1953-54, Liverpool found themselves relegated from the top flight after nearly 50 years in Division One. The fact that Everton came up at their expense added to the frustration.

Twice before, the Reds had made a swift return after a relegation campaign, but this time the fans would have to steel themselves to an uncomfortably long stay in Division Two and it would take the arrival of an inspirational Scottish manager to spark the revival as the Sixties dawned.

In some respects, the Fifties were forgettable for Liverpudlians, but as soon as you say it you begin to think of heroes and games that are part of folklore. After all this was the age of "Liddellpool." This, in itself, is enough to make this era very special.

Billy Liddell, or "King Billy" to give him his correct title, came to Merseyside from Dunfermline Athletic, where he played for Fifeshire junior club Lochgelly Violet. The Second World War interrupted Liddell's early football ambitions. He became a navigator in the RAF, but by 1946-47 his soccer dreams were beginning to take shape and he won a championship medal with Liverpool in his first peace-time season.

A speedy and durable winger with an explosive shot, Liddell was equally at home at centre-forward as on the flanks. In full flow he was almost unstoppable and the Liverpool fans adored him. Between his first season and his last (1960-61), Billy made 537 explosive appearances and scored 229 goals. Along the way he won 28 Scotland caps, but a true measure of his greatness was the fact that he was one of only two players in that era to be selected twice for specially-named Great Britain sides for games against the Rest of the World (1947 and 1955). The fact that Liddell was selected as a Second

Division player in 1955 highlights the fact that his brilliance transcended the perceived gulf between the divisions.

Billy Liddell was not just a great player, but also a modest, intelligent and likeable individual who the fans could relate to in every way.

The good news/bad news contrasts of the Fifties meant that the rollercoaster was always going full pelt, on an upwards curve one minute and plummeting downwards the next. In that first season down in 1954-55 **John Evans** became only the second Liverpool player to score five in a league match, at home to Bristol Rovers. All the goals came in open play.

Against this, the Reds crashed 9-1 at Birmingham, their heaviest ever defeat, and also lost 6-1 at Rotherham. In all, they conceded 96 goals that season, but we also scored 92, their highest total for half a century.

The side finished 11th when at one stage it had looked as if it might be relegated again, to the old Third Division! The turning point was a solid 4-0 FA Cup win at Everton, the club's first away success of that season and the inspiration to finally turn around an otherwise disastrous campaign.

'Billy Liddell was not just a **great player,** but also a modest, **intelligent** and likeable individual who the fans could **relate to**'

Liddell was not the only character to stamp his mark on the Fifties. Speedy winger **Alan A'Court** was skilful enough to be selected for England as a Second Division player, making his debut against Northern Ireland at Wembley in 1957.

He went on to make three appearances in the 1958 World Cup in Sweden against Austria, Brazil and USSR.

Laurie Hughes, a man who commanded the centre of the field, was another around in the Fifties who earned England recognition, although his three caps came in the ill-fated 1950 World Cup finals in Brazil when he was a member of the team embarrassingly beaten by the United States, then a non-entity in the world >

Hall of Fame

1950s

SCROLL OF FAME

1950-1959: Men who made a first team appearance, players in gold shortlisted for Hall of Fame

A'COURT Alan
ANDERSON Eric
ARNELL Alan
ASHCROFT Charlie
BALMER Jack
BANKS Alan
BARON Kevin
BIMPSON Louis
BLORE Reg
BRIERLEY Ken
BURKINSHAW Keith
BYRNE Gerry
CADDEN Joseph
CAMPBELL Bobby
CAMPBELL Don
CARLIN Willie
CHILDS Albert
CHRISTIE Frank
CROSSLEY Russell
DICKSON Joe
DONE Cyril
EVANS John
FAGAN Willie
GERHARDI Hugh
HAIGH Jack
HARROWER Jimmy
HEYDON Jack
HICKSON Dave
HUGHES Laurie
HUNT Roger
JACKSON Brian
JONES Alan
JONES Bill
JONES Harold
JONES Mervyn
LAMBERT Ray
LEISHMAN Tommy
LIDDELL Billy
LOCK Frank
MALONEY Joe
McNAMARA Tony
McNULTY Tom
MELIA Jimmy
MINSHULL Ray
MOLYNEUX John
MORAN Ronnie
MORRIS Fred
MORRISSEY Johnny
MURDOCH Bobby
NICHOLSON John
PAISLEY Bob
PARR Steve
PAYNE Jimmy
PERRY Fred
PRICE John
ROWLEY Antonio
ROWLEY Arthur
RUDHAM Doug
SAUNDERS Roy
SHEPHERD Bill
SHIELDS Samuel
SIDLOW Cyril
SLATER Bert
SMITH Jack
SMYTH Sammy
SOUTH Alex
SPICER Eddie
STUBBINS Albert
TAYLOR Phil
TOMLEY Fred
TWENTYMAN Geoff
UNDERWOOD Dave
WATKINSON William
WHEELER Johnny
WHITE Dick
WHITWORTH George
WILKINSON Barry
WILLIAMS Bryan
WOAN Don
YOUNGER Tommy

Wembley hopefuls: The teams walk out ahead of the 1950 FA Cup final

of football. Hughes had won a championship medal with the Reds in 1946-47 and was the man who replaced Paisley in the 1950 FA Cup final, returning after a broken toe. He was virtually an ever-present in 1956-57, but managed just one appearance the following year when his long Anfield career ended after 326 appearances and just one goal.

Bill Jones' bravery won him the Military Medal during World War Two and he was one of Liverpool's finest utility players. He had occupied five different positions in the championship year of 1947 and was still going strong in the early Fifties, always dependable. He qualified as a Hall of Fame candidate for the Forties and Fifties and was a real all-round sportsman.

Another Forties/Fifties man was **Ray Lambert**, who signed for the Reds as an amateur before his 14th birthday. A defender who played centre-half and full-back during his career, Lambert was a Welsh international who was always cool under pressure.

Jimmy Melia was an England Schoolboy and Youth international who would eventually be one of those who would help inspire the club's return to the top flight in 1961-62 when he was ever-present. He was full of running and had an excellent football brain. Jimmy would eventually become a manager and take Brighton & Hove Albion to the 1983 FA Cup final, ironically masterminding a defeat against Liverpool along the way.

Ronnie Moran joined the club as a 17-year-old in 1952. He would serve the Reds for a lifetime as player, coach and acting manager. A solid left-back with a tremendous shot, Ronnie made his debut in November 1952 and by 1955 he had become an automatic choice. He was a penalty expert whose playing career carried on into the Sixties when he played his part in the promotion push as well as winning a championship medal in 1963-64. Ronnie remains one of Liverpool's greatest servants.

Bob Paisley, mentioned already, deserves a wider accolade. Born in Hetton-le-Hole in the North East, he won an FA Amateur Cup winners' medal with the famous Bishop Auckland in 1939 after which he joined Liverpool. The War interrupted his career, but he won a Championship medal in 1947. Again, his career bridged the Forties and Fifties. Bob was a tremendous tackler with an unquenchable spirit and he became an outstanding wing-half with a powerful throw-in.

He scored the first goal in the 1950 FA Cup semi-final victory over Everton and while his omission from the final was controversial, his professionalism carried him through and he never questioned the decision,

Hall of Fame candidate Louis Bimpson challenges a Northampton defender on a snowy day at Anfield in January, 1958

something he would use in the future when, as a manager, he was forced to make difficult selection decisions. He retired as a player in 1954 after 278 appearances and would go on to become trainer, coach, assistant to the great Bill Shankly and later the most successful English manager of all time in his own right.

Albert Stubbins, elected to the Hall of Fame for the Forties, was still going strong at the start of the Fifties.

Phil Taylor was a quality wing-half who made 345 appearances for the Reds. He captained the side at Wembley in 1950, by which time he had already won a championship medal with Liverpool as well as appearing for England. He played for the last time in the fateful 1954 relegation campaign, but became manager in 1956 when he succeeded Don Welsh.

He gave everything to try and get the club back up, but this honour would ultimately go to a certain Mr Shankly who brought the Fifties rollercoaster existence to a halt.

The Fifties would not just see the emergence of the legendary Shankly, but also top-class young stars like **Ian Callaghan** and **Roger Hunt**, who would later become household names for Liddellpool … sorry, LIVERPOOL!

Above: Future club manager Bob Paisley was a spirited wing-half

How the panel called it:

No debate about Liddell. It was Billy and one other. Defender Laurie Hughes was a Championship winner in 1947 and entered the decade with five years service already behind him. He won three England caps at the start of the decade. Putting Liddell to one side, the panel noted that Hughes was one of three players with over 200 games in this decade and over 300 career games for the Reds. The others were Alan A'Court and Ronnie Moran. A'Court won five England caps in this spell, notably in the 1958 World Cup in Sweden.

Again, putting the unmatchable Liddell to one side, A'Court also finished with the most career appearances amongst the candidates in this decade (382), followed by Moran (379). Ronnie would go on to win a Championship medal in the Sixties, but the panel opted to give the skilful A'Court the Fifties vote over Hughes and Moran.

Explosive talent and **Kop talisman**

No. 13: **BILLY LIDDELL**

Millions of words have been written about Billy Liddell. He wasn't just a footballer. He was a Merseyside icon, loved and respected by fans everywhere.

Of course, Reds fans re-named the club in honour of their super hero. In Billy's days, it was definitely LIDDELLPOOL.

And so when the Hall of Fame panel sat for the first time and asked itself if there were any certainties within the eventual prestigious list of 22, two stars for each decade, the name Billy Liddell was the first on everybody's lips. No debate was needed and Rick Parry, Phil Thompson, Alan Hansen, Ian Callaghan and Brian Hall rubber-stamped his inclusion without a second thought. Ask any fan to name the greatest Anfield player of all time and the name Billy Liddell will always roll off the tongue as a prime candidate.

Yes, goalkeeper Elisha Scott was an immortal, but Liddell would go on and beat the Irishman's record number of appearances. Yes, Kenny Dalglish was a visionary forward who had magic in his boots. Billy was just a phenomenon.

Billy Liddell was one of the greatest players in the British game - good enough to be one of only two players (the other was the legendary Stanley Matthews) to play for Great Britain in both games against specially selected Rest of Europe opposition in 1947 and 1956. A measure of his talent was that he was selected on the second occasion as a Division Two player with Liverpool.

Liddell was an explosive talent, equally happy storming down both flanks or leaving defenders in his wake in a more central attacking role. Former *Liverpool Echo* sports editor Ian Hargraves, a man who was a great personal friend of the Scottish international and who saw him play many times, summed up this special talent perfectly when he said: "Speed and strength were Billy's greatest assets, combined with a lethal shot with either foot. He frequently appeared to go straight through opponents rather than round them."

Liddell was born on January 10, 1922. He was first capped by Scotland as a schoolboy in 1936 and signed as an amateur for Liverpool in July, 1938 and turned professional in April, 1939.

Billy served in the RAF between 1942 and 1946, and played for the Scots in a wartime international for the first time in April, 1942.

His first full international (not counting the 1945-46 'Victory' games) came against Wales in October, 1946.

In 1947 came that Great Britain honour against the Rest of Europe, to be repeated in 1956. Billy would captain Liverpool for three years in the mid-Fifties and beat Elisha Scott's record of 430 league appearances for Liverpool in November, 1957.

The record-breaking continued when he broke Ted Sagar's Merseyside record of 465 games for Everton on March 27, 1958. Billy was made a Justice of the Peace in October 1958 and would serve the city magnificently in this respected role.

Billy made his first team debut for Liverpool in a wartime regional match against Crewe Alexandra at Anfield on New Year's Day, 1940, and scored in two and a half minutes ina 7-1 victory. >

1950s: BILLY LIDDELL
'Billy was picked because he was a legend in the hard times. He was a hero'
– Phil Thompson, Panel member

In 1946-47 Liverpool won the first post-war Championship with Liddell inspirational. He played in 34 league games and six FA Cup ties that season. All of his games were at outside-left in this campaign except one, at inside-left.

Another memorable season unfolded in 1949-50 when the Reds reached the FA Cup final, sadly a losing experience against Arsenal. The Gunners put robust defender Alec Forbes on the Scot and one very heavy tackle meant that Liverpool's most important weapon was not as effective as it might have been.

Liverpool were not defeated until their 20th game in that season. Liddell missed only one match and finished as leading scorer for the first time, claiming 17 as a winger!

Incredibly, during the following summer Liddell was approached by an agent of a South American club and asked to go to Bogota, Columbia, where several English players had journeyed to try and make their fortune. Billy was offered £2,000 to sign on, a King's Ransom in those days, but he turned the offer down to stay at Anfield where he again finished top scorer.

Liddell was involved in one of the most controversial moments ever to unfold at Anfield on February 22, 1956, as a replayed FA Cup tie against Manchester City reached its climax. Ian Hargraves recalls: "It was an extraordinary incident. City had grabbed the lead and held out despite all of Liverpool's frantic late efforts to equalise. Suddenly Liddell managed to break clear and to a tumultuous roar of applause thundered a mighty shot past City's famous German goalkeeper Bert Trautmann.

"As the excitement began to die down, it was noticed that the players were shaking hands and leaving the pitch instead of preparing for extra time. It gradually dawned on the huge crowd that the referee had blown for time half a second before the ball had entered the net.

"It caused tremendous controversy and argument, but this was silenced the following day when *Liverpool Echo* photographer Neville Willasey developed a film from the game which showed the referee with the whistle in his mouth while the ball was in mid-air." Not that Liddell himself disputed the victory. He was a gentleman whose modesty and calm nature made him stand out even more amongst his peers. When Bill finally hung up his boots, the *Echo* produced a 16-page broadsheet special edition,

'He was a man who **moved fast** and resolutely, taking the ball with head or feet in a **breathtaking** way. His shooting was as fierce and accurate as has **been known**'

Hall of Fame 1950s

Billy Liddell in an aerial duel against Southend in January, 1958

which was packed cover-to-cover with salutes from the world of football. Former Liverpool captain Matt Busby, by now manager of Manchester United, said: "I have known the great Billy Liddell throughout his entire career, first as a boy at Anfield and again on the occasion of his entry into first class football while still very young.

"I well remember his hat-trick against the great Frank Swift (later killed in the Munich Air Disaster) in one of his very early matches in the first team. I feel I was responsible, to some extent, for Billy having his first chance in the Scottish international team as I recommended him to the Scottish FA at that time.

"My managerial experiences watching the tilt of two great players in opposition, Billy Liddell and our own Johnny Carey, was, I felt, a highlight of the game. He has not only been one of the greats as a footballer, but off the field has always been a big >

WILLIAM BEVERIDGE LIDDELL

Born 10.01.1922 at Townhill, Dunfermline, Scotland
Died 3.07.2001, Liverpool.
Clubs: Kingseat Juveniles, 1936. Blairhill Colliery trial, 1937. Hearts of Beath trial, 1937. Lochgelly Violet, 1937. Partick Thistle trial ,1938. **Liverpool FC amateur July 1938. Signed professional 17.04.1939 to May 1961. Club vice captain:** 1953/54, 1954/55; **captain** 1955/56; 1956/57; 1957/58.

Liverpool appearances:

	League		FAC	
	App	Gls	App	Gls
1945-46	0	0	2	1
1946-47	34	7	6	1
1947-48	37	10	2	1
1948-49	38	8	4	1
1949-50	41	17	7	2
1950-51	35	15	1	0
1951-52	40	19	3	0
1952-53	39	13	1	0
1953-54	36	7	1	0
1954-55	40	30	4	1
1955-56	39	27	5	5
1956-57	41	21	1	0
1957-58	35	22	5	1
1958-59	19	14	0	0
1959-60	17	5	0	0
1960-61	1	0	0	0
Total	**492**	**215**	**42**	**13**

Overall totals: 534 apps, 228 goals

War competitions

	App	Gls
1939-40	16	9
1940-41	37	12
1941-42	35	22
1942-43	15	5
1943-44	6	4
1944-45	15	13
1945-46	26	18

International appearances: 28, 6 goals:
1946 v Wales; N. Ireland.
1947 v N. Ireland; Wales.
1948 v England.
1949 v Wales.
1950 v England; Portugal; France; Wales; N. Ireland; Austria.
1951 v England; N. Ireland; Wales.
1952 v England; USA; Denmark; Sweden; Wales; N. Ireland.
1953 v England; Wales.
1955 v Portugal; Yugoslavia; Austria; Hungary; N. Ireland. Also Aug. 1946 England v Scotland Bolton Disaster Fund.

War Internationals: 8 apps, 5 goals:
1942 v England (h); v England (a);
1943 v England;
1945 v England (a); Wales;
1946 v N. Ireland; England; Switzerland.

Great Britain: 2 appearances 1947; 1955

Liddell on the spot against Huddersfield at Anfield in 1960

asset to our game. His retirement will be a great loss to football."

Joe Mercer described him as "surely the greatest player ever to wear the famous red of Liverpool."

We leave the last tribute to famous local football journalist Leslie Edwards, whose father Ernest, when sports editor of the Liverpool Echo, was the man who gave the 'Kop' its name earlier in the century.

Paying one last tribute to Billy, Leslie said: "Deeds, rather than words, spoke for him. I never knew him utter a foul word. He always played hard and fairly and only rarely got ruffled.

"He was feared as much at grounds other than Anfield. I don't suppose there is a place on the football map where his name stands for anything save hard shooting, sportsmanship and all-round competence, whether he figured on the wing or in the centre.

"They say he was never a ball player of the Mannion, Carter, Matthews or Finney breed. That may be so, but he was better. He was a man who moved fast and resolutely, taking the ball with head or feet in a breathtaking way. His shooting was as fierce and accurate as has ever been known.

"He had a remarkable physique and when he went down the right wing, the task of the back facing him must have seemed like trying to stop a fire engine."

That was the legend of Billy Liddell.

'**Deeds,** rather than words, spoke for him. I never knew him utter a **foul word.** He always played **hard and fairly** and only rarely got **ruffled**'

22 SEP 1960

16 THE LIVERPOOL ECHO AN

A night to remember for all Liverpool and Liddell

By MICHAEL CHARTERS

1 - MAY 1961

PETER PRICE REPORTS The Stage of Sport

Players chair Billy Liddell on his final exit from Anfield

The days the Kop showed how much they loved Anfield hero Billy

The archives of the Liverpool Daily Post and Echo provide fascinating reading, showing without doubt what a hero Billy Liddell was to the people of Liverpool.

The Kop's favourite was awarded a testimonial in September, 1960, during his final season wearing the famous shirt.

Describing an emotional night, the Liverpool Echo's Michael Charters wrote: "On a wet, uncomfortable evening, 38,789 people poured into the ground to pay their tribute to the idol of Anfield in the way they know best - cheering, cheering all the way.

"It was a wonderful thing to be one of that crowd and feel the surge of affection, respect and regard flowing out form them to Liddell as he led the teams on to the pitch and then again when he ran off through a lane of players down the tunnel.

"These were moments of drama, of emotion, of pride such as one rarely experiences in football.

"This was the occasion when all Liverpool supporters who could be at Anfield were there to say to Liddell: 'Thank you for all the joy and thrills and entertainment you have given us for so many years'."

Liddell played for an 'All-Stars' side which featured Stanley Matthews and Tom Finney. Even though they ended up losing to a Liverpool team - thanks in part to a Dave Hickson hat-trick - this was a night for Liddell to savour.

"By his sportsmanship, great ability and ideal demeanour on and off the field, he has made himself the model footballer," added Charters.

"The Anfield fans showed him last night that there'll never be another like him in their eyes."

A few months later, it was time to say farewell for good as Liddell bowed out as a Liverpool player.

Even though his final appearance was in a reserve team game, the fans again turned out in their numbers to chant their idol's name. His colleagues also ensured there would be no low key ending to an amazing Anfield career by carrying him shoulder high from the pitch.

"A crowd awaited his return to his car and after a session of signing autographs, his admirers took up the chant: "For he's a jolly good fellow!'"

It would be some years before such hero worship was seen again around the fields of Anfield Road.

Speed **merchant's** **express** delivery

No. 14: **ALAN A'COURT**

One in a long line of incredible Liverpool wingers, Alan A'Court may have been less famous than Billy Liddell, Peter Thompson, Steve Heighway and John Barnes, but he was just as much a hero to the thousands who watched him regularly from the Kop.

"They used to put their hands out to catch me when I went flying in among them after crossing at top speed," he recalls. "That was a big help, because opposing wingers were left to crash into the stanchions."

A'Court becomes the second player from the Fifties to be elected to the official Liverpool Hall of Fame, standing proudly alongside the legendary Liddell, which is something that fills him with pride.

Alan's greatest asset was probably his speed, which enabled him to get to the corner flag and send over a cross while the opposing defence was still retreating. His footwork was also quite nimble, but especially during his early days at Anfield the emphasis was all on direct play, with everyone charging downfield once possession had been gained.

In this respect he was probably fortunate to play in front of two excellent full-backs in Ronnie Moran - the only player other than Alan to turn out for Liverpool before relegation and again after promotion back to the First Division - and Wembley hero Gerry Byrne.

Alan's other big asset was his cheerful, bubbly personality that made him popular with everyone. He was just the man to cheer up the other players after a poor first half or the horrific kind of train journey that was all too common in those days.

His crossing of the ball, mainly with his famous left foot, was first class, which explains why the mighty Liddell scored so many headed goals, and he had quite a useful shot himself, though he would be the first to admit that he was not really a marksman. Tactically, he was also well aware, but it must be remembered that back in the Fifties football was a straightforward game featuring any number of individual contests and hardly any of the intricate tactical moves so common today.

In this context, it is interesting to note that, unlike his boss Bill Shankly, he was an early supporter of the FA's coaching courses at Lilleshall, and went on to enjoy an extremely successful coaching career after he stopped playing.

Periods at Norwich and Crewe were followed by a lengthy spell as Tony Waddington's chief coach at Stoke, a period when the Potteries outfit enjoyed more success than they have ever done, before or since, claiming their only major trophy in the League Cup and even competing reasonably effectively in Europe.

Born in Rainhill and educated at Prescot Grammar School - which was rather unusual for a pro footballer at that time - Alan turned down the chance to sign for Bolton Wanderers and instead agreed to join a Liverpool club then managed by Don Welsh in 1952.

A schoolboy star who represented his country against the famous Amateur Cup side Pegasus, he made rapid progress through the ranks before >

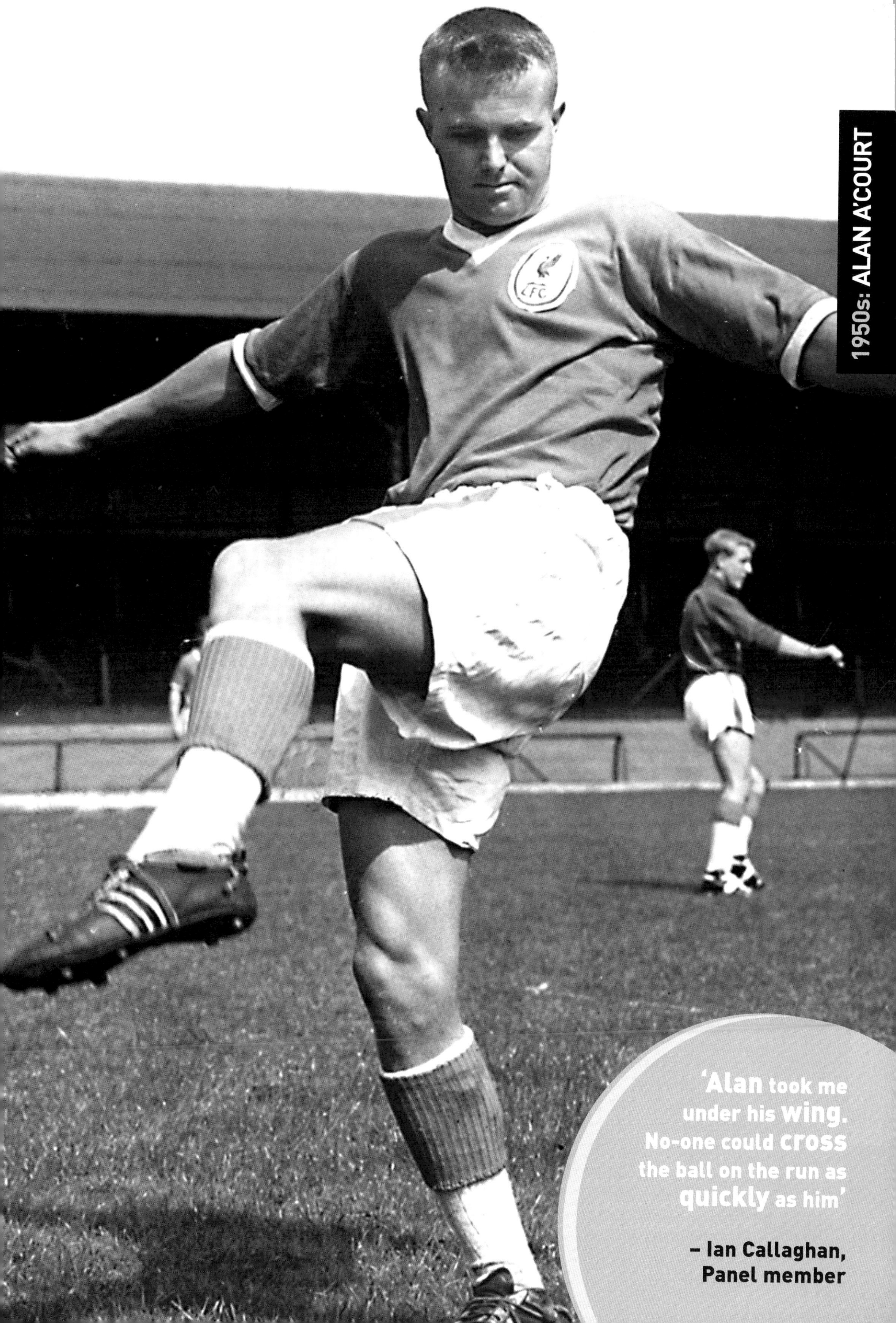

'Alan took me under his wing. No-one could cross the ball on the run as quickly as him'

– Ian Callaghan, Panel member

> making his first team debut at Middlesbrough the following February. Remarkably, he avoided National Service through failing his medical, though he has never suffered from health problems.

Surprisingly for a comparatively frail person who relied heavily on speed, he ended up playing in his favourite position on the wing after the great Billy Liddell switched to centre-forward.

That switch soon became permanent, and so successful that Liddell scored countless outstanding goals thanks to the service from A'Court. Unfortunately, the quality of these two players was not matched elsewhere, and the youthful A'Court found himself relegated at the end of his second season.

There followed eight seasons of disappointment, as managers Don Welsh and Phil Taylor strove with great determination but very little luck to take the Reds back to their rightful station, and it is a tribute to A'Court's skill that he still managed to attract plenty of attention.

One early highlight was provided by a share in a 4-0 cup victory over old rivals Everton in front of 72,014 who, having leapfrogged above Liverpool, started as hot favourites. Another was a starring role in the 7-0 rout of then fashionable Fulham, a side

'Alan's **greatest asset** was his speed, which enabled him to get to the corner flag and send over **a cross** while the opposing defence was still **retreating**'

boasting the likes of Jimmy Hill and Johnny Haynes, who would become a great England captain.

In the end, however, it was Alan's performances away from Merseyside that attracted most attention. After appearing for the new England U23 team, he he won his first England cap against Northern Ireland in 1957 when the legendary Tom Finney had to drop out with an injury. He was then picked for England's 1958 World Cup squad in Gothenburg, Sweden, and ended up playing in three of their four matches against the Soviet Union , Brazil and Austria, but unfortunately the darkest of clouds hung over both the event and the team.

Six months previously England had been among

the favourites, but then came the Munich air disaster to deprive England of three key Manchester United players, while Nat Lofthouse, Jimmy Greaves, Brian Clough and Bobby Charlton were left at home. England were knocked out by the Russians.

Further disappointment was to follow. Alan's style of play never fitted in with that of Haynes, who now became an automatic England selection, and he had to be content with just one more cap, while the Liverpool side continued to splutter.

Fortunately the latter stage of Alan's career was given a massive boost by the arrival of Bill Shankly, who took over from Phil Taylor as manager. "We knew very little about him when he arrived," Alan recalls, "but he soon woke us up. He walked into the room where we were waiting, stared at us for a minute or two, then said grimly: 'Some of you boys have been here for too long.'"

What followed is well known and well loved history, and A'Court eventually found himself part of a brilliant promotion team featuring a forward line of Ian Callaghan, Roger Hunt, Ian St John and Jimmy Melia as well as himself.

Liverpool were promoted with 62 points, eight more than their nearest rivals Leyton Orient, and A'Court had the satisfaction of scoring twice when the teams met in a vital encounter just before the season's end.

Sadly, he managed only one season in the First Division - Liverpool's first for a long time.

Then the first injury of a 12-year Liverpool career, which saw him play 381 first team games and score 63 goals, withdrew him to the sidelines.

Despite going on tour with the club the following summer, he found himself replaced by close season signing Peter Thompson, who had attracted Bill Shankly's attention by scoring a goal for Preston against them in the cup.

Neither Thompson nor Ian Callaghan missed a match the following season, and so Alan had to watch in frustration as his friends romped to their first Championship since the war.

Next autumn he crossed the Mersey for two seasons with Tranmere Rovers, after Shankly had brought him back for an emotional farewell in the European Cup at Anfield against Reykjavik (Liverpool's first excursion in Europe).

ALAN A'COURT

Born 30.09.34, Rainhill.

Career:
Prescot Grammar School, Prescot Celtic, Prescot Cables. Amateur.

Signed for Liverpool in 1952.
Position: Left-wing.
Second Division Championship winner: 1961-62.
5 caps for England: v Northern Ireland (1957), Brazil, Austria, Soviet Union, Wales (1958).

Liverpool appearances and goals:

	League		FA Cup		Lge Cup		Europe	
	App	Gls	App	Gls	Apps	Gls	App	Gls
1952-53	12	2	0	0	0	0	0	0
1953-54	16	3	0	0	0	0	0	0
1954-55	30	2	3	1	0	0	0	0
1955-56	40	6	5	0	0	0	0	0
1956-57	38	10	1	0	0	0	0	0
1957-58	39	6	5	0	0	0	0	0
1958-59	39	7	1	0	0	0	0	0
1959-60	42	8	2	0	0	0	0	0
1960-61	33	7	2	0	2	0	0	0
1961-62	42	8	5	1	0	0	0	0
1962-63	23	2	0	0	0	0	0	0
1964-65	0	0	0	0	0	0	1	0
Totals	**354**	**61**	**24**	**2**	**2**	**0**	**1**	**0**

Overall 381 appearances, 63 goals

Signed for Tranmere Rovers in October 1964.

Took coaching and assistant managerial positions at Chesterfield, Crewe and Stoke.

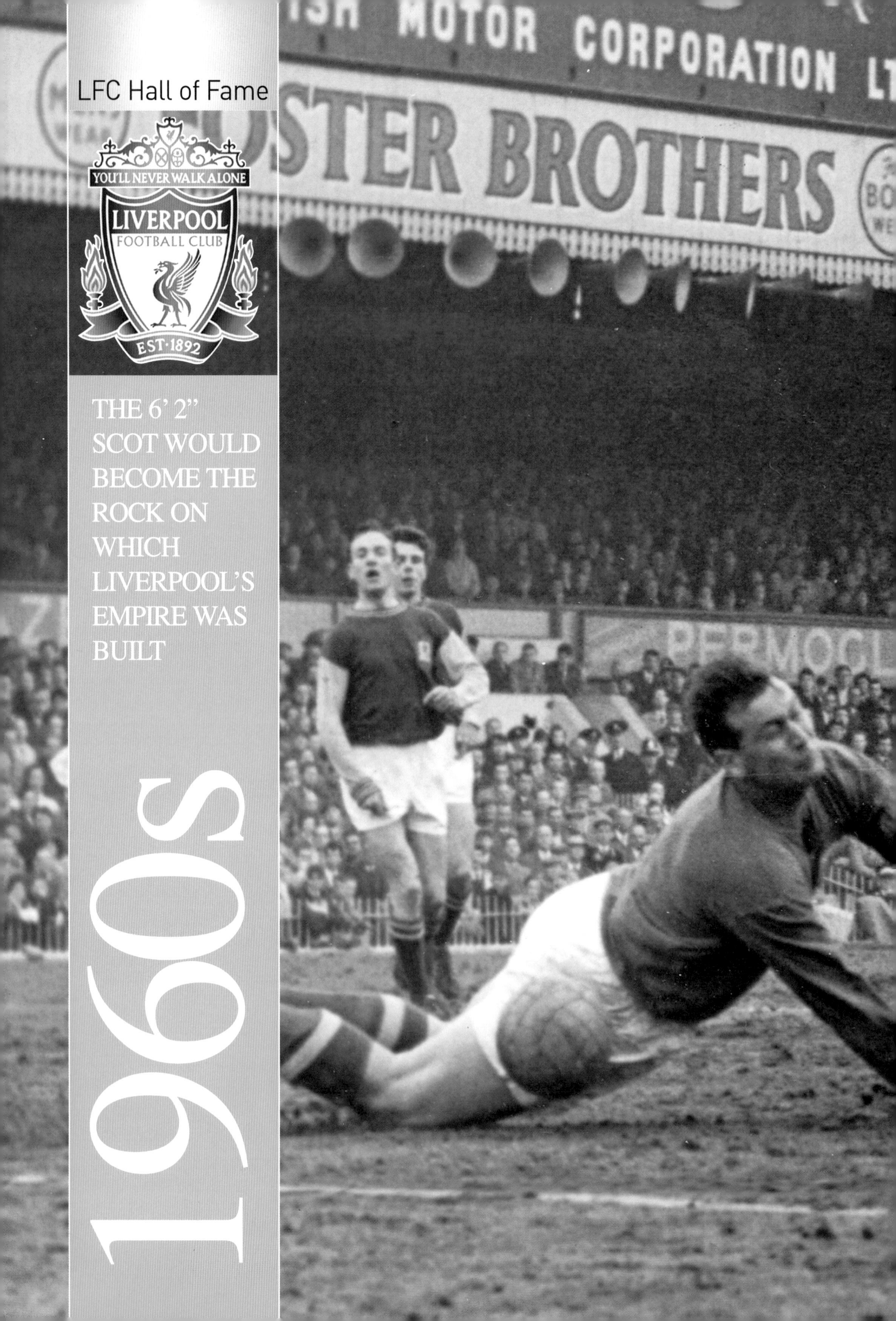

THE 6' 2" SCOT WOULD BECOME THE ROCK ON WHICH LIVERPOOL'S EMPIRE WAS BUILT

1960s

WOLSELEY
MORRIS COMMERCIAL
Riley
SAVE
by using
BIRMINGHAM
MUNICIPAL
AUSTIN

The Shankly family

Bill Shankly dragged the club out of the Second Division and back into the big time, creating his first great team which won leagues and the FA Cup

When you reflect on the 'Swinging Sixties' you instinctively think of Liverpool, music, fashion, *The Beatles* - and football!

Liverpool Football Club came alive in this decade after an unhappy spell in the doldrums. It was the age of the "Colossus", the "Saint", the "Flying Pig", the "Anfield Iron" and "Sir" Roger...

If you are a young fan and haven't got a clue what we are talking about, look up the mighty deeds of super heroes like **Ron Yeats, Ian St John, Tommy Lawrence, Tommy Smith** and **Roger Hunt.**

Melwood photo call: The Liverpool squad, pictured in 1965

These are just some of the giants who danced brilliantly to the football tune hummed by the man who was arguably the greatest manager of all-time - Bill Shankly.

From the moment the great Scot arrived on Merseyside, he was the undisputed "King of the Kop" and a man of the people. Shankly's down-to-earth policies captured the imagination of players and fans alike. He wanted the very best for Liverpool FC - and he achieved all of his dreams.

He once said: "The socialism I believe in is not really politics. It is a way of living. It is humanity. I believe the only way to live and be truly successful is by collective effort, with everyone working for each other, everyone helping each other, and everyone having a share of the rewards. It is the way I see football and the way I see life."

Seemingly everything at the modern Liverpool leads back to the foundation stones that were put in place by Shankly.

The 1960s started with a Second Division title triumph (1961-62) as the Reds powered back to the big time, scoring 99 goals and finishing eight points ahead of their nearest rivals Leyton Orient.

Shankly decided on day one that he needed a giant at the back, a rock on which he would build the new Liverpool. He signed **Ron Yeats** from Dundee United for £30,000 in July, 1961. When the press came to see the new man, Shankly declared: "Walk around him. He's a Colossus!"

Dick White remained captain at the start of the season before Yeats took the mantle at the end of December, never looking back.

He would link up with another inspirational Scot, **Ian St John,** who had been signed from Motherwell for £35,000, a record for Liverpool at that time. This pair provided strength and determination down the middle.

Nothing got past big Ron's telescopic left foot. Up front the diminutive St John, standing just over 5ft 7inches tall, was an explosive and fearless figure. He had already won seven Scottish caps by the time he arrived at Anfield and would win another 14 with the Reds.

Ian's final career statistics with Liverpool showed 425 games and 118 goals, a tremendous return for a man who could not have made a better start in a red jersey. He scored a Liverpool Senior Cup hat-trick on his debut against Everton.

'Nothing got past big Ron's **telescopic** left foot. Up front the diminutive St John, standing just over **5 ft 7 inches** tall was a **fearless** figure'

Four players were ever-present in the Second Division championship-winning side - **Gerry Byrne, Gordon Milne, Jimmy Melia** and **Alan A'Court.** Yeats, Hunt and **Tommy Leishman** missed >

Taking time out: 1960s stars (left to right) Ian Callaghan, Roger Hunt, Tommy Lawrence

Hall of Fame

1960s

SCROLL OF FAME

1960-1969: Men who made a first team appearance, players in gold shortlisted for Hall of Fame

A'COURT Alan
ARNELL Alan
ARROWSMITH Alf
BANKS Alan
BOERSMA Phil
BYRNE Gerry
CALLAGHAN Ian
CAMPBELL Bobby
CHISNALL Phil
CLEMENCE Ray
EVANS Alun
FERNS Phil
FURNELL Jim
GRAHAM Bobby
HALL Brian
HARROWER Jimmy
HATELEY Tony
HICKSON Dave
HIGNETT Alan
HUGHES Emlyn
HUNT Roger
JONES Alan
LAWLER Chris
LAWRENCE Tommy
LEISHMAN Tommy
LEWIS Kevin
LIDDELL Billy
LINDSAY Alec
LIVERMORE Doug
LLOYD Larry
LOWRY Tom
MELIA Jimmy
MILNE Gordon
MOLYNEUX John
MOLYNEUX William
MORAN Ronnie
MORRISSEY Johnny
OGSTON John
PEPLOW Steve
ROSS Ian
SEALEY John
SLATER Bert
SMITH Tommy
STEVENSON Willie
ST JOHN Ian
STRONG Geoff
THOMPSON Peter
THOMSON Bobby
WALL Peter
WALLACE Gordon
WHEELER Johnnie
WHITE Dick
WILSON Dave
YEATS Ron

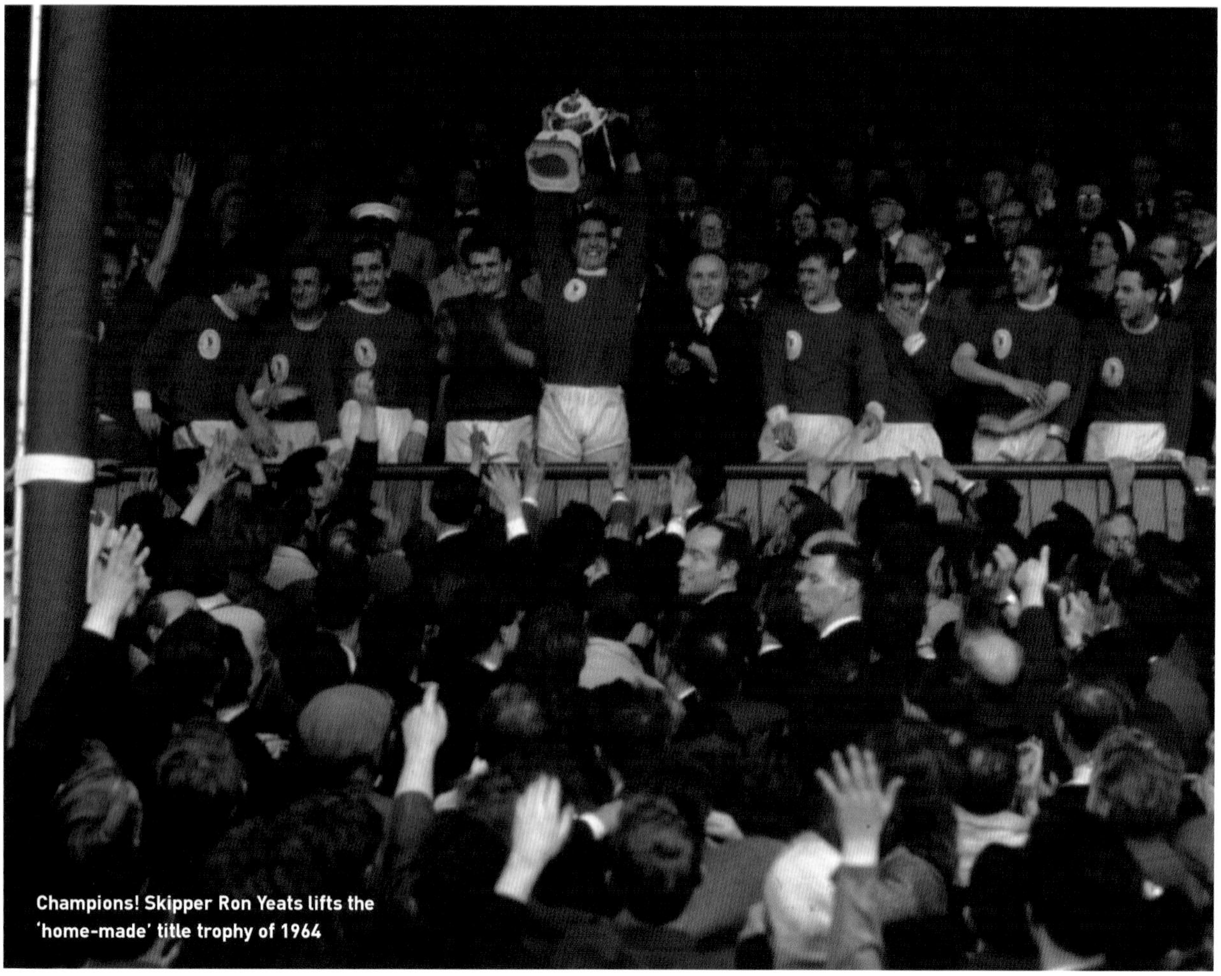

Champions! Skipper Ron Yeats lifts the 'home-made' title trophy of 1964

just one game, **Roger Hunt** one and St John two. This was the kind of consistency Shankly was looking for, although he was determined that the club would not stand still and immediately began to look to the future.

Byrne was a local full-back with a crunching tackle. He would become part of Anfield folklore when the Reds won the FA Cup for the first time in 1965. The defender sustained a broken collar bone against Leeds, one of the toughest sides in the country at that time, but he showed remarkable courage to play on in an era when substitutes were not allowed.

He even played into extra time and was the provider of the cross from which Ian St John scored the winning goal!

Liverpool had followed the promotion campaign of 1962 with a year of consolidation in the top flight, finishing eighth. Striker Hunt was by now one of the most feared attackers in the land and he would plunder 31 goals as the Reds won the championship in 1964.

Roger had joined the Reds in 1959 and was a goal machine from the start.

He rarely missed a scoring opportunity and even scored for England on his debut, against Austria. He would go on to win 34 caps, but his real claim to international fame came in 1966 as a member of the only England side to win the World Cup. By the time he left the club for Bolton Wanderers, he had scored an astonishing 285 goals in 484 Reds appearances, a club scoring record.

This 1960s side was jam-packed with heroes, not least two famous wingers. On the right, **Ian Callaghan's** industry made him a marathon man in every game. Cally's career would bridge the 1960s and the 1970s (by which time he had tucked into midfield). He would complete an astonishing 857 games

for the Reds scoring 68 goals - and he was only booked once!

Peter Thompson was a flying left winger who would torment defenders time and again. Another England player, his finest game possibly came in 1963-64 when he ran the Arsenal defence dizzy and scored twice in a 5-0 win as the title beckoned.

Of course, Liverpool had steel as well as skill and **Tommy Smith** was the man all rivals feared for his fearsome tackling.

Like Callaghan and **Chris Lawler,** Tommy's career would bridge the 1960s and 1970s. A local lad who could play football as well as dig in, no one showed more commitment than the "Anfield Iron" who was red through and through.

As the 1960s unfolded, Shankly would secure another powerhouse defender, a young man who would eventually go on to captain club and country - **Emlyn Hughes.**

'Ian Callaghan's career would **bridge** the Sixties and Seventies. He would complete an astonishing **857 games** for the Reds, scoring **68 goals**'

Nicknamed "Crazy Horse" by the fans because of the way he would surge forward, Hughes was a tackler and a good player.

His greatest moments possibly came in the 1970s when he held aloft the European Cup, but he still had a major impact on the late 1960s. This was the team that Shankly built and would then rebuild.

Above: The Liverpool squad line up ahead of an away trip in 1969; note Bill Shankly 'next off' on the coach.

How the panel called it:

The panel found itself with 11 players on its original 1960s list of candidates, highlighting this golden era when Bill Shankly's boys walked tall on the football fields of England and Europe. These were Byrne, Callaghan, Hunt, Lawler, Lawrence, Milne, Smith, Stevenson, St. John, Thompson and Yeats. This was a mix of defensive power, courage, skill and world class attackers.

It was in the goalscoring stakes that the panel looked for its first inductee in this decade in the shape of "Sir" Roger Hunt who was a World Cup winner with England in 1966.

The debate then followed for the second inductee with a simple question asked. Who would Shanks have picked? He idolised all of his players, but had total respect for his great captain Ron Yeats, the rock on which the new Liverpool was built.

Goal machine who kept game **simple**

No. 16: **ROGER HUNT**

The 1960s was a remarkable era, not just in the context of Merseyside football history, but also on a national scale.

Liverpool Football Club won its first FA Cup in the middle of this incredible decade, having powered back into the top flight and screamed out its intent to become the future powerbrokers of English football under the inspirational Bill Shankly.

England won its first and only World Cup in 1966 as Alf Ramsey's wingless wonders stamped their mark on the global game.

The playing link from an Anfield point of view was a gentleman footballer who emerged from the tiny village of Culcheth, nestling just off the East Lancashire Road which links the great soccer strongholds of Merseyside and Manchester. Roger Hunt was assured of his place in English football folklore on that day at Wembley when Ramsey's men showed power, passion and skill to overshadow West Germany and lift the hearts of a nation.

When the Liverpool FC Hall of Fame panel of judges sat down to consider and debate the claims of a host of 1960s super heroes, Roger's achievements, both for club and country, were impossible to ignore.

Legendary skipper Ron Yeats, Shankly's Colossus, secured the first of the two places available in this most momentous of decades. That Hunt will stand alongside him demonstrates the remarkable quality of the men who were the rock on which the modern Liverpool Football Club was built.

In Hall of Fame terms we are now in really exciting territory. Yes, the panel studied and gave due diligence to the early years and the pioneers who won those first championships, suffered relegation years and bounced back time and again with the kind of pride and passion that would become the hallmark of a great club. But this early journey had been taken in a football time machine. The panel relied on unquestionable statistical facts. They studied the folklore passed down from grandfather to son to grandson. The heroes they considered from this bygone age wore the famous red, but as their famous feats were pieced together, it was inevitably in terms of black and white images encapsulated in old photographs and rare flashes of historic newsreel footage.

But now it was the ‘Swinging Sixties’ and the black and white was replaced by a dazzling splash of colour, predominantly red.

In London, this was the age of trendy Carnaby Street. In Liverpool it was the age of Mathew Street, the Beatles, increasingly long hair, outrageous fashions and footballers who would become as famous as any Hollywood movie star. Enter the George Best phenomenon on one side of Manchester and the Rodney Marsh antidote on the other.

Here on Merseyside, we had skill on both sides of Stanley Park. But it was a different type of star quality. It can be explained this way. Many clubs of the day, not least the London giants, had a breed of what Bill Shankly might have called the ‘Fancy Dans’ of football. The Reds had their skill

>

'Roger Hunt has always been one of my **heroes** and our only World Cup **winner'**

– Phil Thompson, Panel member

merchants, Peter Thompson being the most obvious example. But it was skill harnessed to the discipline of a Roman army. Shanks was beginning to preach the doctrine of pass and move. His most telling phrase in the dressing room was 'support your mates.' It was one for all and all for one.

Shankly wanted solidity right down the middle and got it with a new goalkeeper, Tommy Lawrence, a towering centre-half in Ron Yeats and a mobile, fast-raiding centre-forward in Ian St John. The roots were sunk into the Anfield turf and now the branches began to spread out from a solid trunk.

The emerging talent that was Roger Hunt, playing for Stockton Heath (later Warrington Town) was courted by Portsmouth and then snatched by Second Division Bury. It was all part of the apprenticeship. Hunt's typical level-headed logic told him that it made sense to learn his trade low down and work his way up to the top.

It would be tough. Incredibly, the man who would eventually help to make English football history, found his career held up at Gigg Lane where he had become a reserve to the reserves. He returned to the Mid-Cheshire League and Stockton Heath - just to get a game! Roger had always scored goals and he got more than his fair share at this level.

A spell in the army followed with less than glamorous postings to Oswestry and then Rhyl, followed by the bleak Salisbury Plain, one of the most isolated places in England. No roaring crowds here, just roaring sergeants who instilled the kind of discipline into young Roger that a certain Mr Shankly would have approved off.

He would play for the army team and one or two scouts began to take notice, but when an offer came, it was not from an Arsenal, Manchester United or Liverpool. Devizes Town tempted him into further non-League action and he helped them win the Wiltshire Cup while continuing with his army duties.

Former Liverpool defender Bill Jones saw him in action and he immediately alerted Anfield manager of the day Phil Taylor. The young, unassuming striker soon signed on the dotted line and what a sound decision that was for all concerned.

He would come under the wing of reserve coach Joe Fagan, who told him what was required to take the step from second string to senior side. 'Graft, graft and more graft' was what Joe demanded from the new boy.

The character of the man was such that he was prepared to give everything to impress the man who had, by now, become his boss - Bill Shankly.

As Liverpool took off under Shankly, so the city took off as Beatlemania swept the country and then the world. Quite simply, for a few short, spectacular mind-blowing years, Liverpool seemed like the centre of the universe.

Hunt's style of play was swashbuckling - all cut and thrust. Roger was not an orthodox centre-forward, but someone who would lie deep and then explode into forward space to send a stunning shot into the roof of the net. He wasn't tricky like a Peter Thompson, but then nobody was. He had a body-swerve, but there was nothing fussy or over-elaborate about Roger's game.

He got the ball and put it in the back of the net. Well, they say football is a simple game.

Liverpool won the championship in 1963-64 and the explosive Hunt hammered home 31 league goals. In 1965 came that first Liverpool FA Cup final victory when the Reds beat Leeds United at Wembley after extra time. Roger scored Liverpool's opener, paving the way for St John's eventual match winner with that now legendary jack-knife header.

Speaking in the book 'Three Sides of the Mersey', Roger recalled: "My ambition was always to win an FA Cup winners' medal. In 1963 we got to the semi-final and were very unlucky to go out. In 1964 we got to play Swansea at home in the sixth round. They were lying near the bottom of the old Second Division and we were near the top of the First.

"We lost that one 2-1. You get to think, 'How many chances do you get to go to Wembley? Some people never go.' >

ROGER HUNT MBE

Born 20.07./1938, Golbourne, Lancashire.

Career: Croft Youth club, Bury, Stockton Heath.
Signed for Liverpool on 29.07.1959.
Position: Inside right.
Second Division championship winner: 1961-62.
First Division championship winner: 1963-64, 1965-66.
FA Cup winner: 1964-65.
World Cup: Winner 1966.
European Cup Winners Cup: Finalist 1965-66.
Charity Shield: 1964, 1965 (both shared); 1966 winner (as captain).
Liverpool Senior Cup winner: 1961-62. Scored 1 in 2-1 win.
34 caps for England, 18 goals, (record for England for Liverpool player before Michael Owen).
1962 v Austria (scored 1 on debut); 1963 v East Germany (1);
1964 v Scotland, U.S.A (4). Portugal (1), Wales;
1965 v Spain (1).
1966 v Poland, W. Germany, Finland (1), Norway, Poland (1), Scotland (2), Uruguay, Mexico (1), France (2), Argentina, Portugal, W.Germany (Final). Northern Ireland (1), Wales, Czechoslovakia.
1967 v Spain (1), Austria, Wales , Northern Ireland, USSR.
1968 v Spain, Spain (a), Sweden (1), Yugoslavia, USSR, Romania.
1969 v Romania.
Representative games:
Football League v Scottish League, 2 goals in 2-3 defeat.
24.05.1963. FA centenary/ FL 75th anniversary at Highbury. Hunt for FL scored 1 in 3-3 draw.
2.10.1963 FL v League of Ireland, Dalymont Park, Dublin, lost 1-2.
18.03.64 FL v Scottish League, Roker Park Drew 2-2.
1.05.1964 England v Young England. Scored 1 goal in 3-0 win.
9.05.1964 FL v Italian League, San Siro Stadium, Milan. Lost 0-1.
28.10.1964 FL v Irish League, The Oval, Belfast. Won 4-0.
20,03.1968 FL v Scottish League, Ayresome Park. 1 goal in 2-0 win.
Friendly games: 1960 Friendship Cup v Nantes. Scored 1 in 2-0 win (a), 1 in 5-1 win (h).
1961 Tour of Czechoslovakia 4 games 1 goal.
1961 Floodlit Cup v Everton, scored 2 in 2-2 draw.
Signed for Bolton Wanderers on 10.12.1969 for £32,000.
1969-70 to 1971-72 77 (7) appearances, 25 goals.
Awarded MBE in 2000 New Year's honours list.

Liverpool appearances and goals:

	League		FAC		Lge C		EC		ECWC		Fairs C	
	App	Gls	App	Gls	App	Gls	App	Gls	App	Gls	App	Gls
1959-60	36	21	2	2	0	0	0	0	0	0	0	0
1960-61	32	15	1	1	3	3	0	0	0	0	0	0
1961-62	41	41	5	1	0	0	0	0	0	0	0	0
1962-63	42	24	6	2	0	0	0	0	0	0	0	0
1963-64	41	31	5	2	0	0	0	0	0	0	0	0
1964-65	40	25	8	5	0	0	9	7	0	0	0	0
1965-66	37	30*	1	1	0	0	0	0	7	2	0	0
1966-67	39	14	3	1	0	0	5	3	0	0	0	0
1967-68	40	25	9	2	2	0	0	0	0	0	6	3
1968-69	38	13	4	1	3	2	0	0	0	0	2	1
1969-70	15(3)	6	0	0	2	0	0	0	0	0	(2)	1
Total	**401(3)**	**245**	**44**	**18**	**10**	**5**	**14**	**10**	**7**	**2**	**8(2)**	**5**

Overall: 487 (5) appearances, goals 285.
Charity Shield: 3 games, 1 goal.
* Some sources credit an o.g. 12.03.1966.

"The following season we actually got through to the semi-final. We beat Chelsea 2-0 at Villa Park and it was one of the greatest days of my career."

His colleague Tommy Smith picks out Hunt as a 'great player' but he would soon become a 'world class' player and and all because of a famous day in 1966 when he ran out under the Twin Towers alongside Gordon Banks, George Cohen, Ray Wilson, Nobby Stiles, Jack Charlton, Bobby Moore, Alan Ball, Bobby Charlton, Geoff Hurst and Martin Peters. Of course, the afternoon would not be short on controversy. Indeed, that controversy still rages in German football circles. Was Geoff Hurst's famous goal truly over the line? Every photograph shows Roger nearest to the incident as the ball thudded down off the underside of the crossbar.

He recalls: "Geoff swivelled and hit a strong, clean shot which hammered against the bar and bounced down. I was running in, sniffing for rebounds, and was about six yards out when the ball hit the ground. I saw it cross the line and I turned instantly to celebrate the goal. I believed at the time it was over the line and I believe it now."

'There was nothing **fussy** or **over-elaborate** about Roger's game. He got the ball and put it in the back of the net. Well, they say football is a **simple game**'

Modern computer graphics suggest otherwise, but who cares? Hurst would stride forward and get another. Roger, like the whole England team, never stopped running in pursuit of the Jules Rimet Trophy. Liverpool FC's pride in his achievement will never fade. Equally, the feats of 'Sir Roger' in a red shirt demand that he is included in the Hall of Fame.

Because of the sheer quality of his peers, the great debate might continue, but who would deny Hunt and Yeats the honour of being the icons of the 1960s?

They were heroes amongst heroes.

It truly was a special era.

'We canvassed fans and the names of Roger Hunt and Ron Yeats came out on top'

Heroes of the Sixties: Roger Hunt and (below) Ron Yeats carried the hopes of the fans

Red All Over The Land's JOHN PEARMAN on the Hall of Fame candidates that stood out in the golden era of the Sixties for his fanzine's readers

When I first met with Liverpool's chief executive Rick Parry a few years ago I suggested to him that the club should have a Hall of Fame. At the time I can remember that he was impressed by the idea and he went through a few suggestions as to how such a thing could be implemented.

Although Hall of Fame was never forgotten, other things became more pressing.

However, I'm delighted that the idea is now underway. It's great that everybody can participate in the debate, whether they be fanzine readers, a supporters' club or just a couple of fans sitting down in a pub suggesting that old so-and-so should be thought about for the Hall of Fame!

A few years ago Red All Over The Land fanzine canvassed subscribers to nominate an Anfield hero from the Sixties who they thought should be considered for the Hall of Fame. The names of Roger Hunt and Ron Yeats came out on top.

Roger first came into the side in the very late Fifties at a time when Liverpudlians were facing up to the fact that Billy Liddell wouldn't be able to carry the burden of their hopes for too much longer. In Roger, they saw a man they could turn to once King Billy had abdicated his Anfield throne.

While you can't forget the records that Roger Hunt broke and set you shouldn't forget either the way he worked for the club during those heady days of the Sixties. Most of the great goalscorers of the time wouldn't have listed work-rate as one their greatest attributes, but Roger could.

I don't think that Hunt ever got the national recognition that was due to him. Although he was a goalscoring genius he was not flamboyant like a Jimmy Greaves or a Denis Law.

But his record is there for all to see and the history books on this occasion don't lie!

Ron Yeats was probably your typical centre-half of the Sixties era. 'Rowdy' was the sort who preferred not to take too many prisoners.

Over the park at Goodison they had one of their finest defenders of any era in Brian Labone and it was great to be able to argue the toss with any Blue about which giant was actually the best.

Back in the mid-Sixties if you were the centre-half on Merseyside then you had the right to claim to be the best defender anywhere and I always argued that Rowdy Yeats was not only bigger than Brian Labone, but he was better as well.

So as far as the Red All Over The Land recommendations are concerned for the Sixties section of the Hall of Fame, as they say in court, we rest our case!

It has to be Yeats and Hunt.

'Captain **Fantastic**' in a team **of stars**

No. 15: **RON YEATS**

Ron Yeats was a man-mountain of a centre-half who Bill Shankly knew would stand like an impenetrable barrier in the heart of the Liverpool defence - the rock on which a modern football empire would be built.

Signed by the Reds from Dundee United in 1961, the story about the new centre-half's introduction to the press is now part of Anfield folklore. "Take a walk around him, gentlemen," was Shankly's invitation to those gathered around. "He's a Colossus."

The description could not have been more apt and the 6 feet 2 inches tall Scot would become the cornerstone of Liverpool's great revival in the 1960s, supported by some of the finest players to have ever worn the famous red.

Just to run through the squad that won the championship in 1964 is a journey through a million and one Anfield memories. Lawrence, Byrne, Moran, Milne, Yeats, Stevenson, Callaghan, Hunt, St John, Thompson, Melia and Arrowsmith. Each and every one of them played the Shankly way with a camaraderie that raised the spirits of every supporter fortunate enough to have watched them.

By the time the FA Cup was won for the first time in sensational fashion the following year, one or two new names were beginning to support this all-star cast, not least emerging young local heroes like Smith and Lawler.

The leader of the gang was Ron Yeats. It's a remarkable statistic, but in the 454 games he played for Liverpool, he was skipper in almost every one. That highlights his strength of character and influence. And so when Liverpool's official Hall of Fame panel considered the options for the 1960s - arguably the most colourful era in the history of the club - the support for this 'Captain Fantastic' was powerful and unequivocal.

It's certain that if Bill Shankly himself had been around today and inevitably on the panel, he would have given his personal sanction to the man who never let Liverpool down in any situation, and was truly a leader of men.

Yeats gave a lifetime's service to Liverpool FC, as a player and later as a chief scout. He retains a fierce passion for the Reds and was thrilled when told of his Hall of Fame honour.

He said: "It's special because we had so many good players in that era. I think we had 14 internationals in our squad at one time."

Giants like Ron Yeats are few and far between. He had this long telescopic left leg that would flick out like the tongue of a deadly snake. The tackle that followed would have all the venom of the strike of a cobra. Because of his giant frame, you could always see the big man coming, but you couldn't get out of the way.

Because the left foot was so dominant, Bill Shankly decided that he would give Ronnie a right foot in the shape of Tommy Smith. The 'Anfield Iron' provided the perfect insight into this strategy in his book 'My Anfield Secrets'.

He said: "Shanks told me that I would be Ron's right leg. It suited me. You were always happy to have him with you rather than against you. He was a very inspirational captain and few centre-forwards,

>

'I appreciate **great** centre-backs. Ron Yeats was called the **Colossus** and that's what he was'

– Phil Thompson, Panel member

> if any, got the better of him.

"Ronnie's attitude was simple. Get stuck in! He could intimidate opponents with his sheer size, let alone his outstanding ability. He was one of those who would say to a team-mate: 'Send him down the line and I'll kick him over the stand!'

"We got off to an interesting start. Liverpool used to have this famous pre-season game, the Reds versus Whites. The management would pick two teams from the first team and reserves and thousands of fans would turn up to gain an early insight into the way the season might evolve for particular individuals.

"I was just 16 and found myself on the bench. At half-time the boss said: 'Get your boots on. You're going on at centre-forward for the Whites'. I was thrilled and then suddenly realised that my marker would be none other than Shankly's Colossus. More than that, Yeats was fired up for the occasion, determined to impress the fans and the manager at the start of what would become a famous Liverpool career.

"As I stepped out at Anfield, I realised that Ronnie was not going to adopt any half measures just because he was marking a young lad and he got stuck in to me. My team, the Whites, were 2-0 down to a couple of Roger Hunt goals. Then we forced a corner and Johnny Morrissey whipped it in. I met it perfectly with my head and the ball flew into the net.

"I looked at my giant marker and said: 'Pick that out, you Scottish ****!'

"It was my Scouse edge coming out, even as a 16-year-old. He gave me a look that could kill and, as I said, I was glad that I was soon alongside him and not against him. His strength was his aerial power

'I tried to be **a leader** on the pitch, doing the job as well as I could. My view was that if I gave **100 per cent** in every situation, then others **would follow**'

and that telescopic left leg that would shoot out and steal the ball from attackers, just when they thought they were past him. He stood up for himself and his team-mates and I learned a lot from the big man. With crunching tackler Gerry Byrne also in the last line of that 1960s defence - and my old pal Chris Lawler - we were the rearguard that took no prisoners. Anfield was becoming a fortress under Bill Shankly and Ron Yeats was an inspirational figure in what would become a remarkable success story."

Ron looks back with happy memories. He said: "I have always had a great relationship with the Merseyside people. I couldn't believe it on my first day down here. I arrived by train and there were up to a hundred at the station to greet me. I had never experienced anything like it before and I knew straight away that the passion would be special.

"I took to Bill Shankly straight away. When he was grilling me in Edinburgh before I signed, I said to myself: 'I like this man.'

"I had not worked with good managers before

that. I had three different bosses in a short space of time at Dundee United. I didn't know any of them that well because I was only part-time. To meet someone who was so inspirational and clearly knew what he was talking about had a real impact on me. I suppose being Scottish was a bonus!"

Shankly, of course, had also signed mobile and fiercely competitive striker Ian St John from Motherwell. The manager knew that he would get nothing less than total commitment from this tartan duo.

Yeats picked up on the theme. He said: "I had been captain of Dundee United at 19 and Shanks told me that I would now skipper Liverpool. I tried to be a leader on the pitch, doing the job as well as I could. My view was that if I gave 100 per cent in every situation, then others would follow.

"I never had to shout. My style was to buck up my team-mates, not pull them down. Anybody can make a mistake. But our thinking was that if something went wrong, your mate would be there to cover for you. We looked out for each other. We were always together.

"Shanks played his part in that. He was a remarkable character."

Looking back, Ronnie's proudest moment was undoubtedly the day he became the first Liverpool captain to hoist aloft the FA Cup after victory over Leeds United in 1965. He said: "It was an unbelievable occasion. It was not the best cup final neutrals will have ever seen, but to our supporters and the players it was an afternoon we will never forget. Looking back, we were very lucky to play in front of this remarkable crowd, so humorous and full of passion.

"Just think about the standing Kop. We had 25,000 people roaring us on from behind that one goal!

"What a sight that was. When you stepped out of the tunnel, the hairs stood up on the back of your neck. I always thought that we could win every game. If we were 1-0 down, I felt we could score two, or three. We felt invincible."

Ian Callaghan, Ron's team-mate and Hall of Fame panel member, says: "Ronnie was a real leader and a great influence on us. He fully deserves this honour."

RON YEATS

Born 15.11.1937, Aberdeen.

Career: Aberdeen Lads' Club, Scottish schoolboy international, Dundee United (116 appearances. 1 goal).
Signed for Liverpool on 22.07.1961. Fee £30,000.
Position: Centre-half.
Club captain from December 1961 to 1970.
Second Division championship winner: 1961-62.
First Division championship winner: 1963-64, 1965-66
FA Cup winner: 1964-65 (first Liverpool captain to win cup).
European Cup Winners' Cup: Finalist 1965-66.
Charity Shield winner: 1966-67; shared 1964-65 & 1965-66.
Liverpool Senior Cup: Winner 1961-62.
Testimonial game Liverpool v Glasgow Celtic, 13.05.1974.
Friendly games - 1964 tour U.S.A. & Canada - 2 appearances
1967 European tour - 5 games
Also 20 testimonial and other games.
League: 1 & 2 - 358 appearances 13 goals.
FA Cup: 50 appearances.
League Cup: 7 appearances
European games: 36 appearances, 2 goals.
Charity Shield: 3 appearances, 1 goal.
Two caps for Scotland: 3.10.1964 v Wales at Cardiff, lost 2-3. 7.12.1965 v Italy at Naples, lost 0-3.
Signed for Tranmere Rovers on December 30th 1971 as player/assistant manager); player/manager 1972-1975.
110 appearances, 6 goals.
Stalybridge Celtic 1975 as player.
Barrow - player/manager 1976.
Liverpool chief scout from 1986-87 until retirement November 2002.

Liverpool appearances and goals:

	League		**FA C**		**Lge C**		**EC**		**ECWC**		**UEFA**		**Ch Sh**	
	App	Gls	App	Gls	App	Gls	App	Gls	App	Gls	App	Gls	App	Gls
1961-62	41	0	5	0	0	0	0	0	0	0	0	0	0	0
1962-63	38	0	6	0	0	0	0	0	0	0	0	0	0	0
1963-64	36	1	5	0	0	0	0	0	0	0	0	0	0	0
1964-65	35	0	8	0	0	0	9	1	0	0	0	0	1	0
1965-66	42	2	1	0	0	0	0	0	9	0	0	0	1	1
1966-67	40	2	4	0	0	0	5	0	0	0	0	0	1	0
1967-68	38	2	9	0	2	0	0	0	0	0	6	1	0	0
1968-69	39	2	4	0	3	0	0	0	0	0	2	0	0	0
1969-70	37	3	6	0	2	0	0	0	0	0	3	0	0	0
1970-71	12	1	2	0	0	0	0	0	0	0	2	0	0	0
Total	**358**	**13**	**50**	**0**	**7**	**0**	**14**	**1**	**9**	**0**	**13**	**1**	**3**	**1**

Overall: 454 appearances, 16 goals

SPORT
15/6/61
LIVERPOOL MAKE FIRM OFFER FOR YEATS
In Region Of £20,000
NOW FAVOURITES
By MICHAEL CHARTERS
Liverpool have made an offer of about £20,000 for Dundee United centre-half Ron Yeats, who is on the transfer list at his own request because he wants to

LFC Hall of Fame

FROM 'MIGHTY MOUSE' TO A NEW KING OF THE KOP

1970s

MOBI
RWICH UNION

Masters of Europe

A decade in which Liverpool became two-time European champions as Shankly and then Paisley oversaw a memorable period littered with honours

The sensational 1970s had Liverpudlians purring with satisfaction as the Reds claimed an array of honours that put the club in a league of its own.

It was a decade in which Liverpool collected a European trophy for the first time - the UEFA Cup in 1973. That victory over Borussia Moenchengladbach, with Tommy Smith as captain, was an appetiser for the main course which would come in 1977 against the same opposition in the Olympic Stadium in Rome.

This time the European Cup would be the prize and while Emlyn Hughes had by now replaced Smith as captain, it was the Anfield Iron's soaring header that would capture many of the headlines. A year later the trophy was successfully defended, this time at Wembley against FC Bruges courtesy of a **Kenny Dalglish** classic.

The Reds would finish the decade with five league championships (including 1979/80), two European Cups, two UEFA Cups, the FA Cup and the European Super Cup.

Bill Shankly had been determined to get his side back amongst the trophies as the 1970s dawned. The club had not won the league title since 1966 and Shanks knew he had to start to rebuild a new team. It meant that legendary 1960s heroes like Ron Yeats, Ian St John, Tommy Lawrence and Peter Thompson would have to step aside. It was difficult for Shankly, as mentally tough as he was, because of the respect he had for these heroes.

But having made the decision, he set about the challenge with a fire and a passion that would soon equip the squad with the strength in depth to march forward.

Some of the signings were masterstrokes, including the capture of **Ray Clemence** and **Kevin Keegan** from Scunthorpe United, **Steve Heighway** from local non-league side Skelmersdale United, **Larry Lloyd** from Bristol Rovers and **Alec Lindsay** from Bury. People looking in from the outside could have been forgiven for wondering if the great Shankly had lost his way by looking down the divisions to rebuild his great team.

Far from it. He had already demonstrated the importance of

swooping for the game's brightest young stars by grabbing **Emlyn Hughes** from Blackpool in 1967. By the time the 1970s dawned, Hughes was a fixture in Shankly's evolving new team. Men like Keegan, Clemence, Heighway, Lloyd and Lindsay would certainly not look out of place alongside established stars like Smith, Ian Callaghan and Chris Lawler. Far from it. They would become Kop heroes in their own right.

The 1970s revolution was about to begin. **John Toshack** arrived from Cardiff City to lead the attack and a young man by the name of **Phil** >

'Paisley would steady the ship as the Reds finished **second again** in 1975. What we didn't know was that Bob would go on to become the **most successful** manager in the game'

Mighty Emlyn: With European Cup no. 2 at Wembley in 1978

Hall of Fame

1970s

SCROLL OF FAME

1970-1979: Men who made a first team appearance, players in gold shortlisted for Hall of Fame

ARNOLD Steve
BOERSMA Phil
BROWNBILL Derek
CALLAGHAN Ian
CASE Jimmy
CLEMENCE Ray
COHEN Avi
CORMACK Peter
DALGLISH Kenny
EVANS Alun
EVANS Roy
FAGAN Kit
FAIRCLOUGH David
GRAHAM Bobby
HALL Brian
HANSEN Alan
HEIGHWAY Steve
HUGHES Emlyn
IRWIN Colin
JOHNSON David
JONES Joey
KEEGAN Kevin
KENNEDY Alan
KENNEDY Ray
KETTLE Brian
KEWLEY Kevin
LANE Frank
LAWLER Chris
LAWRENCE Tommy
LEE Sammy
LINDSAY Alec
LIVERMORE Doug
LLOYD Larry
McDERMOTT Terry
McLAUGHLIN John
NEAL Phil
OGRIZOVIC Steve
ROSS Ian
RYLANDS Dave
SMITH Tommy
SOUNESS Graeme
ST JOHN Ian
STORTON Trevor
STRONG Geoff
THOMPSON Max
THOMPSON Peter
THOMPSON Phil
TOSHACK John
WADDLE Alan
WALL Peter
WHITHAM Jack
YEATS Ron

> **Thompson** showed that local talent would also not be overlooked.

Liverpool would finish fifth in 1970 and 1971, third in 1972 and then finally regain the title in 1973 when they also won that first European crown, the UEFA Cup. The following year, 1974, they were Division One runners-up, but would grab the FA Cup at the expense of Newcastle United - some consolation for losing out at Wembley three years earlier to the Double-winning Arsenal. The real sensation of 1974 was the announcement that the legendary Shankly was to quit.

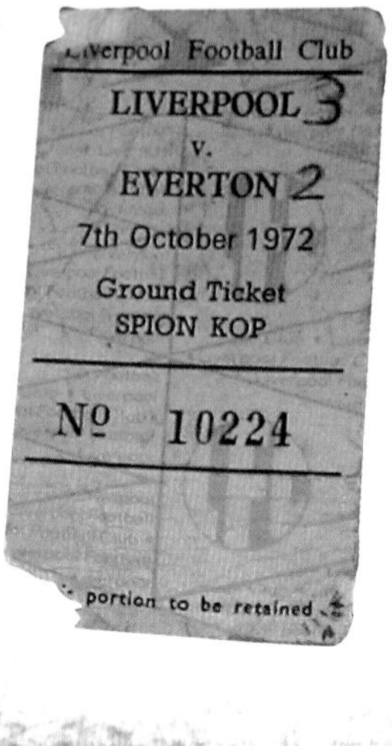

But Bob Paisley would steady the ship as the Reds finished second again in 1975. What we didn't know then was that Bob would go on to become one of the most successful managers in the game. When we think of the 1970s, we instinctively think of the incomparable Paisley who would win his first title in 1976, combining it with a famous UEFA Cup triumph over FC Bruges. The title would be retained in 1977 and sit alongside the European Cup in the trophy room.

The Reds had to settle for the league runners-up berth in 1978, but this was completely overshadowed by a second European Cup success for Bob and his boys. Again, Bruges were his victims.

As the 1970s drew to a close, the

Liverpool Football Club
LIVERPOOL 3
v.
EVERTON 2
7th October 1972
Ground Ticket
SPION KOP
Nº 10224
portion to be retained

league championship trophy was in familiar residence at Anfield.

The revolution started by Shankly had been completed in style by Paisley. Along the way a string of super heroes had captivated the imagination of the fans.

It all pointed to a powerful list of individuals who would be considered for places in the Liverpool Hall of Fame in this decade. This was possibly one of the hardest eras for the panel to call, but it once again highlighted the supreme quality of candidates across the board.

'The **revolution** started by Shankly had been **completed** in style by Paisley and along the way a series of **super heroes** had captured the fans' **imagination'**

Seventies hero: Kevin Keegan - 'Mighty Mouse' - celebrates his vital equalising goal in the title clinching 3-1 win at Wolves in 1976

How the panel called it:

This was one of the most difficult decades for the panel to call with so many successes and so many great players involved as Liverpool won two European Cups. The shortlist was Callaghan, Clemence, Heighway, Hughes, Keegan, R. Kennedy, Neal, Smith, Phil Thompson and Toshack. Seven of these had 300-plus games under their belt in the decade, many more across their wider careers. Hughes, Clemence and Keegan all gained significant England caps in this decade.

Seven players won two European Cups in the decade (Clemence, Heighway, Hughes, Ray Kennedy, Neal, Case and McDermott). Smith was desperately unlucky, missing the second final after a freak accident at home cost him a second final appearance. It was noted that Kevin Keegan was a European Footballer of the Year, but that accolade came with Hamburg.

Ian Callaghan and Phil Thompson, as panel members, could not vote in this decade - both being on the shortlist. There was tremendous admiration shown for Keegan and Hughes by the remaining panelists, but after extensive discussions they were unanimous on their first decision. They named world class keeper Clemence in the Hall of Fame.

At the second vote, Callaghan - ultimately with more career matches than any other rival and one of the most respected players in the game - gained the second Hall of Fame place.

It was one of those eras with a wealth of talent, but the panel had its clear remit to name just two.

Few would question the stature of Messrs Clemence and Callaghan.

Saving **grace** and consistent **class**

No. 17: **RAY CLEMENCE**

Strikers and visionary midfielders often claim the limelight when the plaudits are handed out, highlighting the achievements of any great team.

But football managers, without exception, will point to the crucial need for a goalkeeper of the highest class.

Without one you can kiss goodbye to any dreams you might have of picking up the silverware that makes you stand out in the annals of football history.

Liverpool Football Club have been blessed with contrasting, but nevertheless outstanding custodians down the years.

It is not just coincidence that the club's famous old telegraphic address was 'Goalkeeper' - based on the legend of men like Elisha Scott.

The roll of honour on this particular front is a long one.

In the Hall of Fame investigations we have already highlighted the remarkable talents of men like Matt McQueen who, in the 1890s, was as adept at playing between the posts as he was playing up front.

This type of versatility, of course, should not be confused with that of a Bruce Grobbelaar who also found himself playing outside his own area at times, but while wearing the No. 1 shirt!

Grobbelaar was a different breed again, ready to go where previous keepers had feared to tread. There have been others who have been top class, like England's Sam Hardy and Scotland's Tommy Younger.

But the ultimate tribute to the latest star to Ray Clemence of Liverpool and England is that he was good enough to be compared to arguably the greatest of them all - Elisha Scott.

In many respects, the Seventies and the one that followed were the most difficult for the panel to call.

The shortlist was outstanding. Ian Callaghan, Clemence, Emlyn Hughes, Kevin Keegan and Tommy Smith were all in the mix, along with other illustrious candidates like Phil Thompson, Phil Neal, Steve Heighway, Ray Kennedy and John Toshack.

Four of those mentioned had 300-plus games in the decade: Clemence 410 league games, Hughes 360, Heighway 322 and Callaghan 304. Smith, Thompson, Keegan and Neal all had over 200 decade league games and Ray Kennedy was just short on 199.

However, the remarkably consistent Clem, who would have doubled his England tally but for world class competition from Peter Shilton with whom he shared the international No. 1 jersey, finally received the first 1970s vote from the judges.

The Skegness-born keeper made 48 league appearances for Scunthorpe before being snatched by Bill Shankly, who paid the Third Division side a bargain £18,000 for his services.

Ray would understudy Tommy Lawrence for two seasons and then force his way in during the 1969-70 campaign.

By the following season he was the automatic choice and in the following 11 years missed only seven league games in total. >

'No-one **dominated the box** as well as Clem. He made things look **easy**'

– Ian Callaghan, Panel member

His international career started in earnest in 1970-71 and he would soon win four U23 caps, making his full debut in 1972. His 61 full caps is a remarkable achievement in itself, bearing in mind the fierce competition from Peter Shilton.

Clem missed just one game in 1970-71 as the Reds equalled their own record of only conceding 24 goals in a 42-match league season.

Perhaps the most amazing campaign of all was in 1978-79 when Liverpool conceded just 16 goals with Ray ever-present. It was only one goal more than Preston had conceded in 1888-89 from a 22-match campaign in the Football League's inaugural season.

Clemence was fundamental to the success achieved in the 1970s which included five championships, one FA Cup, two UEFA Cups, three Charity Shields, one European Super Cup and, of course, two European Cups. Clemence also played in the 1980-81 European Cup final.

He looks back on his Anfield career with real pride. Speaking in 'This Is Anfield - An Official Modern History of Liverpool', he says: "People say to me,'what was your greatest save?' I always say that you can see the lads in the park make fantastic saves equal to anything you might see in a World Cup final. But it is the importance of the save. How does it influence the game?

"For me, that penalty save at Anfield - in the first leg of the old Fairs Cup final against Borussia Moenchengladbach - was one of the most important saves made in my career.

"We were winning 3-0 and there were only 15 to 20 minutes to go. Steve Heighway brought down a German player. Heynckes took the penalty and I managed to save it.

"At the time it didn't seem important as we were winning 3-0. But when we went out to West Germany two weeks later, within 20 minutes we were 2-0 down, and Borussia were absolutely running the show. We held on somehow to only lose 2-0 and won the cup 3-2 on aggregate.

"You look back and you think: 'If I'd let the penalty in then they would have won on the away goals.' So that, for me, was one of the most important saves I ever made for the club."

Ian Callaghan, Clem's team-mate and one of the panel who have voted him into the Hall of Fame, said: "Ray was one of the best goalkeepers I have ever seen. He is in England's top three alongside Gordon Banks and Peter Shilton.

"Ray is certainly the best Liverpool keeper I have ever seen. He was very forceful. He used to build himself up before every game. No one dominated the box as well as Clem. He made things look easy because he was so good. That is the sign of a great keeper. Possibly Shilton looked more spectacular, but Clem was always in control. Of course, he was playing behind a tremendous defence and starring for a team that dominated games for long periods.

"He managed to keep his concentration through every phase of the game and made many match-winning saves in the last five minutes.

"This focus is crucial if a goalkeeper is to be truly world class, which Ray was. I would have hated to have been understudy to someone like Ray.

"The other keepers never got a look-in for years. He was one of those people who was really enthusiastic in training.

"He always wanted people to take shots at him. He defied you to try and put the ball in the net."

It was a stunner when Clemence joined Spurs in August 1981 for £300,000 while still at the peak of his career. He would win another FA Cup winners medal at White Hart Lane, but he could have gone on to achieve much more if he had stayed.

As a keeper he was totally dominant in his area. No one got in his way when he came to collect the ball, not even his own team-mates.

If they did, the Clemence knees would thud into their back with the words screaming out over their heads: 'My ball!'

'Ray was truly **world class.** I would have hated to have been **understudy** to someone like Ray. The other keepers never got a look-in **for years'**

RAYMOND NEAL CLEMENCE MBE

Born 5.08.1948, Skegness, Lincolnshire.

Career: Skegness Schools, Skegness Youth Club, Notts County amateur, Scunthorpe United. Professional 1965.
Appearances 1965/66 to 1966/67 League 48; FA Cup 2; Total 50.
Signed for Liverpool on 12.06.1967. Fee £18,000.
Position: Goalkeeper.
Division One championship (5): 1973, 1976, 1977, 1979, 1980.
FA Cup winner: 1974; finalist 1971, 1977.
League Cup winner: 1981; finalist 1978.
European Cup winner (3): 1977, 1978, 1981.
UEFA Cup winner (2): 1973, 1976.
61 International caps for England; (56 with Liverpool).
England under 23 internationals.

Representative games:
Football League v Scottish League 15.03.1972 won 3-2.
Football League v Scottish League 29.03.1974 won 5-0.
Testimonial game 14.05.1980v Anderlecht; lost 6-8 (Clemence 1 goal).
59 Friendly and Testimonial games including:
Mathias Testimonial at Tranmere 21.04.1976 lost 5-6
(Clemence 3 goals - 2 pens).

Signed for Tottenham Hotspur on 15.08.1981 for £300.000.
Appearances 1981/82 to 1987/88:
League 240; FA Cup 25; League Cup 38; UEFA Cup 15; E.C.W. Cup 12; Total 330.
FA Cup winner 1982; finalist 1987.
League Cup finalist 1982.
Reserve team coach June 1989 to May 1992.
Barnet manager January 1993 to August 1996.
England goalkeeper coach.
Southampton goalkeeper coach
Career total appearances - 1045 games.
Received a MBE in the summer of 1987.

Liverpool appearances:

	League	FAC	Lge C	EC	ECWC	UEFA	Ch Sh	Super C
1968-69	0	0	1	0	0	0	0	0
1969-70	14	1	0	0	0	2	0	0
1970-71	41	7	3	0	0	10	0	0
1971-72*	42	3	3	0	4	0	1	0
1972-73	41	4	7	0	0	12	0	0
1973-74*	42	9	6	4	0	0	0	0
1974-75*	42	2	4	0	4	0	1	0
1975-76*	42	2	3	0	0	12	0	0
1976-77*	42	8	2	9	0	0	1	0
1977-78	40	1	9	7	0	0	1	2
1978-79	42	7	1	2	0	0	1	1
1979-80	41	8	7	2	0	0	1	0
1980-81	41	2	9	9	0	0	1	0
Total:	**470**	**54**	**55**	**33**	**8**	**36**	**6**	**3**

*Denotes ever-present in all competitions.
Overall total: 665 games.
Goalkeeping statistics for 665 games:
Goals against 488; per game 0.73; clean sheets 323;
% clean sheets 48.6%.

Super **Cally** the **marathon** man

No. 18: IAN CALLAGHAN

If ever a player reflected the spirit, honesty, endeavour and skill of the true professional, it was Ian Callaghan.

He started as a traditional right-winger. He finished as a midfield marathon man. Here was a player every manager in British football would have loved to have signed. Cally was football's 'Mr Consistent' in an astonishing 857 games for Liverpool Football Club.

When chief executive Rick Parry began to formulate the panel charged with the almost impossible task of naming just two players from every decade for the club's first official Hall of Fame, Ian's name immediately came to mind. Here was a man respected by every fan in the country, let alone Liverpool's red army. Here was a respected figure who was beyond reproach and who would bring a wealth of experience and sound judgement to the panel.

Cally therefore took his place alongside Mr Parry, Alan Hansen, Phil Thompson and Brian Hall as the comprehensive selection procedure began to name the players for Hall of Fame. Of course, when it came to the resurgent 1960s and 1970s, Ian was quick to sing the praises and highlight the achievements of his famous team-mates from that era.

The other panel members were quick to point out that Cally was a leading candidate in his own right. To demonstrate fair play, he sat out the subsequent debate that dealt with the claims of a host of household names.

However, at the end of it all, the panel members were steadfast in their final nominations for the 1970s, the era in which Ian figured in a host of famous trophy successes and one in which he became the first Liverpool player to surpass 800 games. Having revealed that great goalkeeper Ray Clemence would go into the Hall of Fame for the 1970s, it was quickly confirmed that Ian Callaghan would join him, and there is not a single Liverpudlian - fan, player or director - who would begrudge Cally his place among the true Anfield greats.

From the day he made his home debut against Bristol Rovers in April 1960, Ian had the respect of supporters and colleagues alike. Indeed, the young winger received a standing ovation that day from team-mates, opponents, the crowd and even the referee.

It would not be the last time he brought an appreciative Anfield audience to its feet.

In many respects, Cally had two Liverpool careers - the 1960s and 1970s. He could have earned his place in Hall of Fame in either decade.

In the first instance, he was a traditional winger who mirrored the pace and penetrative ability of Peter Thompson on the flank. But while Peter's game on the left was all about twisting and turning and often going back to beat the same man twice just for good measure, Ian's game on the right was much more straightforward. He fitted in perfectly with Bill Shankly's master plan for the new Liverpool.

There was nothing fancy about Callaghan. Yes, he was as skilful as they come, but he was a real team player who would complement the bag of tricks that was team-mate Thompson. >

'Ian Callaghan played over 850 games and epitomised everything that's good about Liverpool'

– Phil Thompson, Panel member

'He was never a **prolific goalscorer** himself, but that did not make him any less effective. It was the **cover play,** the accurate pass, the telling cross and the work-rate that made him **stand out'**

By the time the 1970s dawned, Ian had become a dynamo in midfield and his consistency was such that he would actually win another England cap at the age of 35! This highlighted the esteem in which he was held all over the country.

In the 1960s, the likes of Ian St John and Roger Hunt would benefit from the direct style and support play of Callaghan. He was never a prolific goalscorer himself, but that did not make him any less effective. It was the cover play, the accurate pass, the telling cross and the work-rate that made him stand out on any stage.

Then, at the start of the 1970s, Cally was forced to have a cartilage operation that sidelined him for four months.

This enabled another right-winger, the emerging Brian Hall, to seize his chance and some wondered if Ian's Kop days were numbered. However, Bill Shankly continued to have total belief in Callaghan's ability and, just as significantly, his ability to adapt in midfield to a more modern approach.

Instead of playing as a natural winger, Ian became the definitive midfield marathon man, working from box to box and never giving anything less than 100 per cent. It's a tribute to his staying power that he would miss just four games in the next five seasons. His contribution to the game was recognised with an MBE and he was voted Footballer of the Year. This reflected his status as one of football's most respected stars.

Callaghan was truly the 'Peter Pan' of football. He never seemed to age. Indeed, his passion and work-rate seemed to increase with every passing season. The Liverpool hero received many accolades, but he always kept his feet on the ground. Ian remains a modest individual.

He set the standard for others to try and match. The roll of honour included five championships, two European Cups, two UEFA Cups, two FA Cups and one European Super Cup. This is not to mention his individual accolades.

In 1978, Cally had a summer loan spell in America with Fort Lauderdale. His team-mate and room-mate Tommy Smith also travelled Stateside that summer and when they returned, they accepted an audacious offer from John Toshack to join Swansea City. The duo proved to be the catalyst that set the Swans on a remarkable promotion drive that took them all the way to the top flight.

But Cally - and Smithy - would never be remembered for the Welsh connection. These great friends would forever be local lads who helped bring pride and success to Liverpool FC.

Reflecting on his elevation to the Hall of Fame, Ian said: "It fills me with tremendous pride. It's an honour that I will treasure. But I accept it in the name of all of the great players who turned out for Liverpool in the 1960s and 1970s. Like Smithy, they are all legends in their own right.

"I gave my best for the Reds. I had the honour of being at a club early on that still had the great Billy Liddell in its midst. I was fortunate to be part of the Bill Shankly and Bob Paisley success stories. I will be forever grateful to both men who were contrasting but wonderful characters.

"I also have to mention Joe Fagan, who was another inspirational figure behind the scenes. The Anfield Boot Room, which included Ronnie Moran, became world famous. They were as much a part of the success as the players.

"I'm just so proud to have played my part in the building of the modern Liverpool."

IAN ROBERT CALLAGHAN MBE

Born 10.04.1942, Toxteth, Liverpool.

Career: Turned professional for Liverpool on 28.03.1960.
Position: Outside right, later midfield.
First Division championship winner (5): 1963-64; 1965-66; 1972-73; 1975-76; 1976-77.
Second Division championship winner (1): 1961-62.
FA Cup winner (2): 1964-65; 1973-74. Finalist (2) - 1970-71; 1976-77.
League Cup finalist: 1977-78.
World Cup: Winners medal as member of the squad.
European Cup winner (2): 1976-77; 1977-78.
UEFA Cup winner: 1972-73; 1975-76.
European Cup Winners Cup: Finalist 1965-66.
European Super Cup winner: 1976-77.
European Team of the Year: Medal 1976.
Charity Shield winner (6): 1964, 1965 (both shared); 1966, 1974; 1976; 1977.
Liverpool Senior Cup winner: 1961-62. Finalist 1960-61.
4 caps for England (member of the 1966 World Cup winning squad).
1966 v Finland (Man of the Match Award), France.
1977 v Switzerland, Luxembourg.

Representative games:
Football League v League of Ireland, 2.10.1963. Lost 1-2.
Football League v Scottish League, 15.03.1967. Won 3-0
England v Young England 13.05.1966. Drew 1-1.
Football Writers Player of the Year 1974.
Awarded a MBE in 1975.
Testimonial game 19.09.1977 v Shankly's Lancashire XI.
Fort Lauderdale, U.S.A. Loan May 1978 to July 1978. 19 games
Swansea City 14.09.1978. Free transfer. 91 games; 1 goal.
Cork City 1981 3 games.
Soudifjord 1981.
Crewe Alexandra 29.10.1981 to March 1982. 15 league, 2 F.A.Cup games.
Total 17.

Liverpool appearances and goals:

	Lge		FAC		Lg C		EC		ECWC		UEFA		Ch Sh	
	App	Gls	App	Gls	App	Gls	App	Gls	App	Gls	App	Gls	App	Gls
1959-60	4	0	0	0	0	0	0	0	0	0	0	0	0	0
1960-61	3	0	0	0	2	0	0	0	0	0	0	0	0	0
1961-62	23	1	5	0	0	0	0	0	0	0	0	0	0	0
1962-63	37	2	6	0	0	0	0	0	0	0	0	0	0	0
1963-64*	42	8	5	0	0	0	0	0	0	0	0	0	0	0
1964-65	37	6	8	1	0	0	9	1	0	0	0	0	1	0
1965-66*	42	5	1	0	0	0	0	0	9	0	0	0	1	0
1966-67	40	3	4	0	0	0	5	1	0	0	0	0	1	0
1967-68	41	3	9	0	2	1	0	0	0	0	6	3	0	0
1968-69*	42	8	4	1	3	1	0	0	0	0	2	0	0	0
1969-70	41	3	6	0	2	0	0	0	0	0	4	2	0	0
1970-71	23	0	5	0	1	0	0	0	0	0	5	0	0	0
1971-72	41	2	3	0	3	0	0	0	4	0	0	0	1	0
1972-73*	42	3	4	0	8	1	0	0	0	0	12	0	0	0
1973-74*	42	0	9	0	6	3	4	0	0	0	0	0	0	0
1974-75	41	1	2	0	3	0	0	0	4	1	0	0	1	0
1975-76	40	3	2	0	3	0	0	0	0	0	12	1	0	0
1976-77	33	1	5	0	2	1	7	0	0	0	0	0	1	0
1977-78	26	0	1	0	7	0	5	1	0	0	0	0	1	0
Total	**640**	**49**	**79**	**2**	**42**	**7**	**30**	**3**	**17**	**1**	**41**	**6**	**7**	**0**

Plus one appearance in the European Super Cup
Overall: 857 games, 68 goals
* Denotes ever-present in all competitions.

LFC Hall of Fame

THERE'S TRULY ONLY ONE . . . KENNY DALGLISH

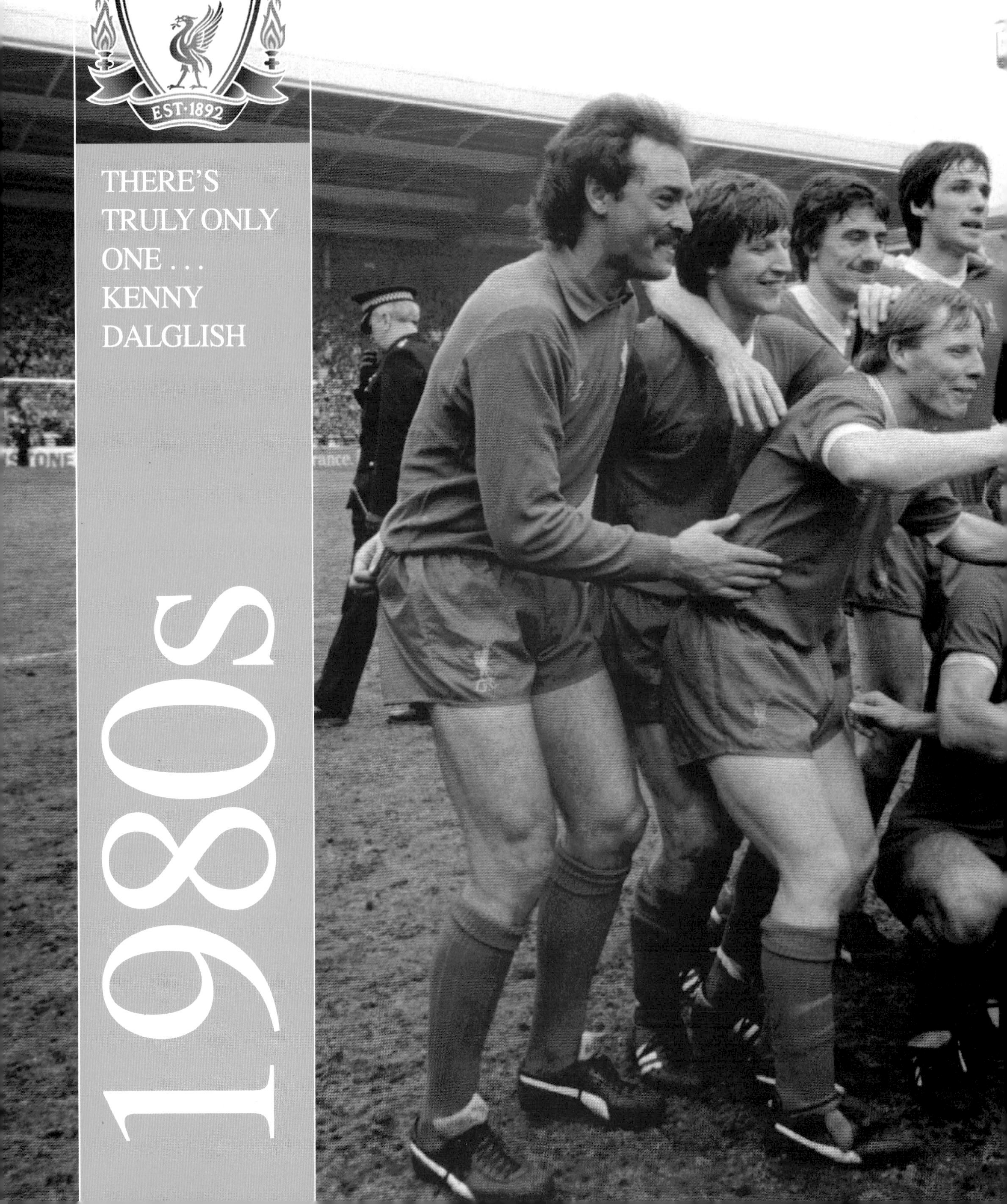

Heroes to heartache

A decade of success and silverware at home and abroad would be overshadowed by off-field tragedies and so the club needed its respected leaders

The 1980s could easily be described as the most eventful decade in the history of Liverpool Football Club. On the one hand it was a tremendously successful period in terms of honours won, an age packed full of famous victories inspired by a host of playing legends.

Against this, the club found itself desperately trying to come to terms with two tragedies, the Heysel Stadium Disaster of 1985 and the Hillsborough Disaster of 1989.

Great Scots: Alan Hansen and Kenny Dalglish celebrate League Cup success in 1981 after both had scored in the final replay against West Ham at Villa Park

In many respects, it was fortunate that the Reds were led during this period by men of honour and vast experience. The club cannot and will not hide from the events in Brussels that cost so many Juventus lives after a wall collapsed during fighting between rival supporters prior to an ill-fated European Cup final.

Before the decade was out, the Reds had to cope with the terrible events of Sheffield that took 96 loyal fans and brought so much pain.

In looking back at the 1980s, we remember all of those who lost their lives. They will never be forgotten.

The irony is that it was a golden football period during which the club had three legendary managers - Bob Paisley, Joe Fagan and Kenny Dalglish.

The great Paisley, the most successful English boss of all time, won his third European Cup at the start of the decade (1980-81). By the time he retired in 1983, Bob had served the Reds for 43 years as player, trainer, coach, assistant-manager and manager. During his time in the Anfield hot-seat he won six championships, three consecutive League Cups, three European Cups and one UEFA Cup.

Paisley had achieved the impossible by following so successfully in the footsteps of the legendary Bill Shankly. Now Fagan had to replace an immortal and he established his own special place in the history of Liverpool Football Club when he guided the Reds to three major trophies in his first season - the championship, the League Cup and the European Cup. Sadly, Joe would retire in 1985, devastated by the events of Heysel.

The Brussels experience cast a shadow over the world of football, but not on the man who retired with honour and dignity after serving Liverpool so magnificently for over 30 years.

Kenny Dalglish would become the club's first-ever player-manager in 1985. He was already an Anfield super hero at that time and proved he had a sharp and inventive football brain off the pitch as well as on it when he guided Liverpool to an historic league and FA Cup Double in his first sensational managerial campaign, 1985-86.

He would also guide the club to two further titles in 1988 and 1990 and win his second FA Cup in 1989.

Dalglish was a powerful Hall of Fame candidate for the 1980s as well as the 1970s. His playing career bridged two eventful decades. Liverpool paid Celtic £440,000 for the Scot in time for the 1977-78 campaign and while he was replacing another super hero, Kevin Keegan, Dalglish arrived with a proven pedigree. He had scored over 100 league goals at Parkhead in 204 appearances, and Liverpudlians immediately took the visionary attacker to their hearts.

Dalglish could make goals and take goals of the highest quality. He had this knack of shielding the ball from defenders in the tightest situations and he seemed to have a sixth sense when it came to finding

'**Dalglish** was one of those who was a **powerful** Hall of Fame candidate for the **1980s** as well as the 1970s. Liverpudlians took the **visionary** attacker to their hearts'

his team-mates with pinpoint passes or finding the target with a shot out of nothing.

Dalglish had some outstanding playing allies, not least **Ian Rush,** who made his debut on December 13, 1980. The young Welshman was the master striker who benefited from the world class support of men like Dalglish, **Graeme Souness** and, early on, **Terry McDermott.** Later, midfielders like **Ronnie Whelan,** >

Hall of Fame

1980s

SCROLL OF FAME

1980-1989: Men who made a first team appearance, players in gold considered for Hall of Fame

ABLETT Gary
ALDRIDGE John
BARNES John
BEARDSLEY Peter
BEGLIN Jim
BURROWS David
CASE Jimmy
CLEMENCE Ray
COHEN Avi
DALGLISH Kenny
DURNIN John
FAIRCLOUGH David
GAYLE Howard
GILLESPIE Gary
GROBBELAAR Bruce
HANSEN Alan
HEIGHWAY Steve
HODGSON David
HOOPER Mike
HOUGHTON Ray
HYSEN Glenn
IRVINE Alan
IRWIN Colin
JOHNSON David
JOHNSTON Craig
KENNEDY Alan
KENNEDY Ray
LAWRENSON Mark
LEE Sammy
MACDONALD Kevin
MARSH Mike
McDERMOTT Terry
McMAHON Steve
MOLBY Jan
MONEY Richard
MOONEY Brian
NEAL Phil
NICOL Steve
OGRIZOVIC Steve
ROBINSON Michael
RUSH Ian
RUSSELL Colin
SEAGRAVES Mark
SHEEDY Kevin
SOUNESS Graeme
SPACKMAN Nigel
STAUNTON Steve
TANNER Nick
THOMPSON Phil
VENISON Barry
WALSH Paul
WARK John
WATSON Alex
WHELAN Ronnie

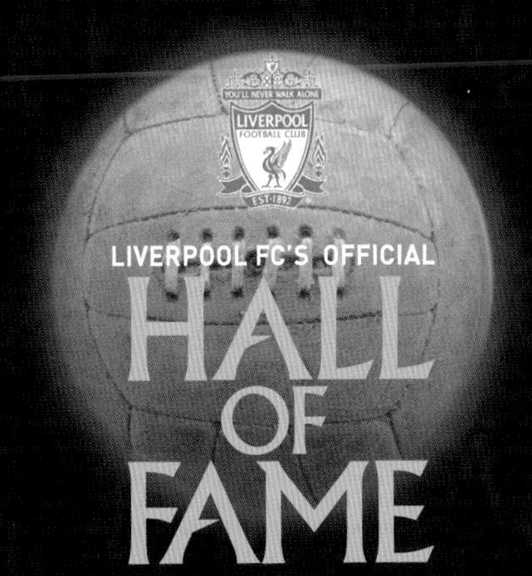

> **Steve McMahon** and **Jan Molby** would also give Rush no end of ammunition to help him rifle shots into the back of opposing nets.

Liverpool won the title in 1980 with the great Ray Clemence still in goal. The England star made 41 appearances in 1980-81, but the Reds had to settle for fifth place. The following season, 1981-82, a young and supremely confident **Bruce Grobbelaar** was between the posts as the club powered to another championship success, its 13th. Grobbelaar was a showman who would stand on his hands to impress the fans. Not surprisingly, he was dubbed the Clown Prince of football.

This cavalier approach meant he would occasionally lose concentration, but he was tremendously agile and his ability to act like an extra defender, constantly racing out to the edge and beyond of his own box to deal with through balls, proved highly effective.

Silver lining: The 1986 FA Cup winners at Wembley and the 1984 European Cup winners in Rome

Liverpool had an outstanding backline at the start of this decade which included **Phil Thompson.** Kirkby-born Thompson was red through and through and he was a born leader who was extremely proud when he captained the side. An authoritative central defender with good passing ability, Thommo was international class and won 42 England caps.

Alan Hansen was the most creative defender of his day, always ready to take the ball from his keeper and start attacks from the back. Another leader who would captain the club, he would later form a tremendous central pairing with **Mark Lawrenson,** whose timing in the tackle was second to none at his peak.

This 1980s side had players with remarkable consistency, none more so than right-back **Phil Neal** who missed only one league game in 10 seasons between 1975-76 and 1984-85. Not surprisingly, he would become Liverpool's most decorated player and win 50 caps for England. The bonus, if one was needed, was that he was a lethal penalty taker.

In the other full-back berth, Geordie **Alan Kennedy** was brave and tough tackling. He scored the goal that won the 1981 European Cup final against Real Madrid and his penalty won the shoot-out at the end of the drawn 1984 European Cup final against AS Roma.

Liverpool were blessed with great midfielders throughout the 1980s. **Graeme Souness** was world class, a man no-one messed with when it came to a 50-50 tackle.

Equally he was a tremendous footballer who scored some fantastic goals.

Sammy Lee was England class; enthusiastic, full of running and a fierce tackler.

Ronnie Whelan was an Irishman with an eye for a goal from the midfield area. Later in the decade, he would form an outstanding partnership with **Steve McMahon** whose strength, shooting power and tackling ability made him a formidable opponent.

Steve Nicol was one of Liverpool's most versatile and consistent performers who made his mark in defence and midfield. **Jan Molby** came from Ajax, a midfield heavyweight in stature, but a real skill merchant.

How the panel called it:

Support for Kenny Dalglish was unanimous. Ian Rush received a similar level of backing but the debate seemed to push him into contention for the 1990s. It was acknowledged that Alan Hansen, who was ineligible to vote in this section, played in an outstanding 508 games in the 1980s. Bruce Grobbelaar notched up 435 games and the quality and consistency of Phil Neal and Ronnie Whelan was also noted.

At a second vote, the panel opted to elect Hansen alongside Dalglish - two great and deserving Scots - with Rush now a powerful 1990s candidate.

Double act: John Aldridge and Ian Rush kept the goals flowing during the 1980s - here they celebrate a strike against West Ham in May, 1989

King Kenny – **the greatest** of all?

No.19: KENNY DALGLISH

There is a famous chant in football. 'THERE'S ONLY ONE . . . ' You add the name of your super hero and you have instant adulation.

However, it's a chant that has become over-used. You will hear it sung in the lower reaches of the Football League about players whose 'legendary status' would certainly not hold up in a football court of law.

It's a chant that should be used sparingly because it actually refers to individuals who are unique.

When Liverpool Football Club began its search for the legends who would stand proudly in the first ever official Hall of Fame, the panel was looking for individuals who were not just giants of the game, but who had something about them that fans would recognise immediately as being the hallmark of true greatness.

It's fair to say that three names immediately jumped out from the powerful list of candidates that panellists Rick Parry, Ian Callaghan, Phil Thompson, Alan Hansen and Brian Hall studied. This trio did not automatically select themselves for the Hall of Fame, but their status was such that the panel did not need much persuading.

This trio was . . . Elisha Scott, Billy Liddell - and Kenny Dalglish.

Dalglish was inducted for the 1980s, a decade of almost non-stop success for the Reds, following on from the equally sensational 1970s.

To gain one of the two places in either of these eras demanded very special talents. With so many star candidates, you had to be extra special. No one would question Dalglish's right to be up there on that pedestal. He was a visionary footballer who stands alongside the cream of Britain's greatest footballers.

Manchester United fans would talk about Bobby Charlton, Denis Law and George Best. Tottenham and Chelsea fans would reflect on the remarkable goalscoring ability of Jimmy Greaves. Newcastle United would nominate Alan Shearer.

For their part, Liverpudlians naturally refer to immortals like Scott and Liddell, World Cup-winning hero Roger Hunt - and the unique Kenny Dalglish. Fittingly, each of these stars is now installed in the official Liverpool Hall of Fame. It highlights the sheer quality of this very special 'club' within a club.

Author Ivan Ponting, writing in the excellent book 'Liverpool, Player by Player', described Kenny in these terms:

'His exploits for Celtic alone would fill a book, but it was the sublime gifts he displayed for Liverpool that lifted him onto the highest plain. Kenny was one of those rare performers who brought true beauty to sport, his football at once exhilarating and aesthetic. Some of his goals were acts of artistic creation and those who saw him at his peak were privileged indeed.'

As a football journalist, I was fortunate enough to cover Liverpool home and away during the reign of Dalglish. It was easy to write about the 'Prince of Parkhead' who became the King of Anfield. In the >

'Kenny Dalglish had skill and vision that raised him to another level'

– Phil Thompson, Panel member

'When Kenny gained possession, it was almost **impossible** for defenders to get a foot in. He would **seize control** and hold his marker at bay by bending forward to **protect the ball**'

> same way that Ivan Ponting was inspired to wax lyrical about this very special performer, I found myself amongst an army of colleagues in press boxes all over the country who constantly ran short of superlatives to describe his unique style of play.

I have already used the word visionary. Kenny seemed to have eyes in the back of his head. He had this in-built personal radar that presented his razor-sharp football brain with an instant mental picture of the shape of the action going on around him. He would swivel and sweep a pinpoint pass to a team-mate in one movement. It also enabled him to penetrate opposing defences with the most telling of through balls; slide-rule football that more often than not ended up with partner Ian Rush striding forward to apply the lethal finish.

When Kenny gained possession, it was almost impossible for defenders to get a foot in. He would seize control and hold his marker at bay by bending forward to protect the ball.

Here was the all-round player - a man who would work like a Trojan, tackle back and cover and then produce an exquisite moment of attacking play, resulting in a magical assist for a team-mate or a devastating finish of his own.

His goals all came with a distinctive trademark of sheer class. He scored many, but the one that leaps out in many people's minds was plundered under the Twin Towers of Wembley in 1978 as Liverpool retained the European Cup with a famous victory over Bruges. The Graeme Souness delivery was matched by the speed of thought of the master finisher who reacted superbly to dink his shot over the advancing keeper.

Even before the ball hit the back of the net, Kenny was en route towards the fans at that end, that famous smile declaring to those supporters that football is a game to be celebrated.

Many people believed that Kevin Keegan was simply irreplaceable when he left for West Germany and Hamburg in the summer of 1977 after an equally dramatic European Cup success.

Bob Paisley's masterclass in manipulating the home transfer market produced the swoop for a player who was hardly a secret weapon, having won countless honours north of the border with Celtic for whom he scored 167 goals in 321 appearances. The only surprise was that no one else had been able to persuade the Scots to part with their most treasured possession.

A British record £440,000 fee did the trick. More significantly, Kenny was ready for a new challenge

and Anfield offered the perfect stage.

In his autobiography, Kenny recalls the move south. He says: "I had captained Celtic, won every trophy in Scotland, but nothing in Europe. It was time to move on to a club capable of giving me the European success I craved. I didn't want to go abroad so Liverpool fitted the bill perfectly.

"They were the champions of Europe with the family atmosphere I needed to make me feel comfortable. I wanted to be at a club where I could celebrate trophies with a tour of the city in an open-top bus, looking down to see all the happy faces sharing our success.

"I knew a lot about Anfield, about its history, its success, its friendliness. Having been on a trial there at 15, I already had a bit of an insight. I was only an unknown kid then, but Liverpool's first team players were friendly. They took time out to talk to me."

Kenny went on to reflect on the men who pointed Liverpool towards glory and inspired respect from all and sundry - the famous Boot Room team. Of course, the wily Bob Paisley signed him, but he knew all about the impact of Bill Shankly and what the great Scot had achieved as he built his Liverpool empire.

Kenny said: "Everyone who went to Liverpool could relate to Shanks. He had everybody pulling in the same direction, on and off the pitch. People quickly felt an affinity for Liverpool because Shanks was totally enthusiastic. He set up a great football tradition of making people understand the principles that Liverpool Football Club stood for, almost moulding them to the Liverpool way.

"This approach was inherited by Bob Paisley, because Bob was part and parcel of the way Shanks worked. The tradition was passed on to Reuben Bennett, Ronnie Moran, Roy Evans and Joe Fagan. It enshrined the Boot Room where the staff met to discuss anything that would make Liverpool more successful. >

And could he play: Dalglish was on the mark twice in a 4-1 friendly win against Bangor City in the snow in January, 1979. Opposite page: In action against Bayern Munich at Anfield in a European Cup game from April, 1981

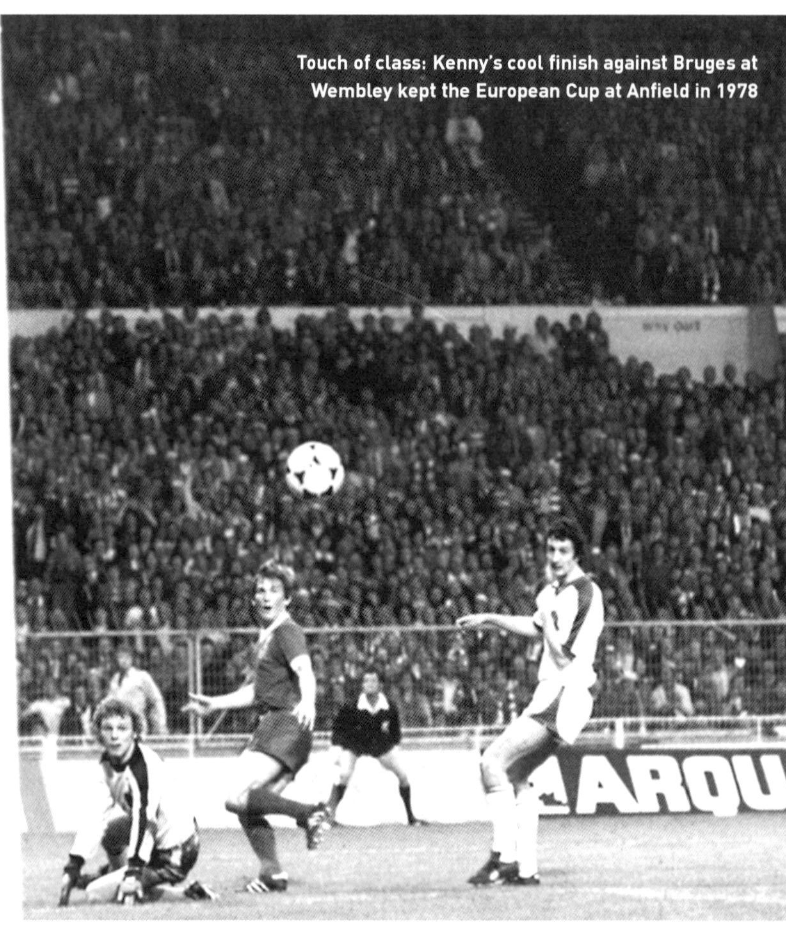

Touch of class: Kenny's cool finish against Bruges at Wembley kept the European Cup at Anfield in 1978

"So I knew where I wanted to go. It had to be Liverpool."

Ray Clemence gives a perfect comparison between Keegan and Dalglish in the Liverpool history book 'This Is Anfield'. He says: "Kevin was exceptional, Kenny was different. Kenny was the complete player because he could score goals, he could create goals, he could hold the ball for you until you could get up and support him.

"Kenny could do that and he wasn't afraid to defend. If we were under real pressure he would get back, try to win tackles and work hard to close people down. Shanks and Bob both said that good defending starts at the front. Kenny would do that for us."

Phil Neal had actually played against Kenny when Scotland played England at Wembley soon after the 1977 Rome European Cup final. The Reds full-back didn't realise that the magician he was trying to mark would soon become his team-mate.

'Kevin was **exceptional,** Kenny was different. Kenny was the **complete player** because he could score goals, he could **create goals,** he could hold the ball for you until you could support him'

Phil told 'This Is Anfield' author Andrew Thompson: "I came up against this Dalglish bloke. I couldn't get the ball off him. He would always have the ball where the defender couldn't get it. In the end, I got so frustrated that I kicked him off his feet and, from the free-kick, Gordon McQueen scored. Little did I know that a few weeks later Kenny would be my team-mate and how happy I would be to have him in my side."

Dalglish became a permanent fixture, David Johnson recalling: "The only person in our side who ever knew that he was definitely playing was Kenny. The boss had this habit of naming about 16 players and it wasn't until the next day when you went out and saw your boots were actually underneath the shirt that you realised you were actually playing."

No surprises in Jonno's statement. Kenny did pick himself, but only because he was such a special match winner, good enough to win two Footballer of the Year awards, in 1979 and 1983.

Of course, he would become player-manager of Liverpool in 1985 after the Heysel Stadium Disaster took its toll on one of the most honest and down-to-earth men in the world of football, Joe Fagan. When Joe resigned after the tragedy of Brussels, the Liverpool board took what some possibly believed was a gamble, promoting from within the dressing room.

Inside the club, Peter Robinson and the rest knew that it was no gamble at all. They knew Kenny could stand above the players' banter and was tough enough to make the most difficult of decisions, even if it affected individuals who might still look on him as one of the lads.

By 1990, Kenny's managerial achievements were beginning to match his remarkable success story as a player. Of course, in 1985-86 he had become the first Liverpool boss to achieve the famous league and FA Cup Double. That he secured it as player-manager adds to the prestige.

By 1987-88 we were assessing Dalglish the manager rather than the player as Liverpool stormed to their 17th league championship. Another Double was denied the Reds when Wimbledon pulled off one of the greatest FA Cup final upsets of all time.

In 1988-89 a tragedy would unfold that would swamp the entire city, indeed the entire nation. The Liverpool v Nottingham Forest FA Cup semi-final was abandoned after six minutes with 96 fans either dead or dying following crushing at Hillsborough's Leppings Lane End. >

KENNETH MATHIESON DALGLISH MBE

Born: 4.03.51; Dalmarnack, Glasgow.
Career: Glasgow United, Possilpark YMCA, Drumchapel Amateurs YC (junior), Glasgow Celtic (with loan spell at Cumbernauld United)
Celtic record: 321 appearances, 167 goals.
Scottish League winner (4) 1971-72, 1972-73, 1973-74, 1976-77.
Scottish FA Cup winner (4) 1971-72, 1973-74, 1974-75, 1976-77.
Scottish League Cup winner 1974-75.
Signed for Liverpool on 10.08.77. Fee £440,000.
Championship winner (6): 1978-79, 1979-80, 1981-82, 1982-83, 1983-84, 1985-86. As player-manager: 1987-88, 1989-90.
FA Cup winner: 1985-86, 1988-89.
League Cup winner (4): 1980-81, 1981-82, 1982-83, 1983-84.
European Cup winner (3): 1977-78, 1980-81, 1983-84.
European Super Cup winner: 1977-78.
Charity Shield winner (5): 1979-80, 1980-81, 1982-83. Shared 1977-78, 1986-87.
Football Writers' Association "Footballer of the Year": 1978-79, 1982-83.
Record 102 caps for Scotland with 30 goals (equals Scottish record).
Manager of the Year 1986, 1988, 1990.
Awarded an MBE in 1985 New Year's Honours List.

Further managerial career: Blackburn Rovers manager 12.08.91 to 1995, then Director of Football to 22.08.96, Promotion to Premier League 1991/92; Premier Champions 1994/95, Glasgow Rangers scout, November 1996, Newcastle United manager 14.01.97 to 27.08.98. Glasgow Celtic Director of Football 10.06.99; caretaker manager 10.02.2000 to June 2000.

Liverpool appearances and goals:

	League		FAC		Lge C		EC		Ch Sh	
	App	Gls	App	Gls	App	Gls	App	Gls	App	Gls
1977-78*	42	20	1	1	9	6	7	3	1	0
1978-79*	42	21	7	4	1	0	2	0	0	0
1979-80*	42	16	8	2	7	4	2	0	1	1
1980-81	34	8	2	2	8	7	9	1	1	0
1981-82*	42	13	3	2	10	5	6	2	0	0
1982-83	42	18	3	1	7	0	5	1	1	0
1983-84	33	7	0	0	8	2	9	3	1	0
1984-85	36	6	7	0	1	0	7	0	1	0
1985-86	21	3	6	1	2	1	0	0	0	0
1986-87	18	6	0	0	5	2	0	0	1	0
1987-88	2	0	0	0	0	0	0	0	0	0
1988-89	0	0	0	0	1	0	0	0	0	0
1989-90	1	0	0	0	0	0	0	0	0	0

Totals (goals in brackets): League 355 (118); FA Cup 37 (13); League Cup 59 (27); EC 47 (10); Charity Shield 7 (1).

Total: Appearances 505, Goals 169

Also World Club Championship 2; European Super Cup 4, 1 goal; Mercantile Credit Centenary Trophy 1; Screen Sport Super Cup 3, 2 goals; Dubai Super Cup 1.

Overall: 516 apps, 172 goals.

Note: Dalglish's autobiography gives 2 FA Cup appearances in 1981-82, but reports clearly indicate 3.

* Denotes ever-present in all competitions.

Bowing out: Kenny on his testimonial night (left) and (right) getting a soaking in a dressing room title celebration!

> Kenny Dalglish felt the pain during that time as much as any fan. It was to be admired the manner in which he worked tirelessly with his wife Marina to give support to the families of the bereaved. Of course, his players, countless former stars and an army of Merseysiders pulled together at that time. However, Kenny was the figurehead and the genuine compassion he and his family showed and the manner in which he led the club at that time earned him the respect of the whole city.

Kenny says: "I will never forget 15 April, 1989. I cannot even think of the name Hillsborough, cannot even say the word without so many distressing memories flooding back. I find it very difficult to write about Hillsborough, where terrible mistakes by the authorities, both police and football, ended with 96 of our supporters dead.

"The memory will remain with me for the rest of my life. I was offered the manager's job at Sheffield Wednesday after I left Liverpool, but I could not take it because of what had happened at Hillsborough.

"I don't know how many funerals I went to. Marina and I went to four in one day. We got a police escort between them. All the funerals were harrowing. All those families mourning the loss of their loved ones. Most of the church services finished with the singing of You'll Never Walk Alone. I couldn't sing through any of the songs or hymns. I was too choked up.

"I did what I had to do after Hillsborough, certainly not through any delusions of grandeur. Marina's mum and dad said to me: 'You've got to go to the funerals, be there to help and support.'

"We just had to go out and help people. If I had to face the consequences of stress at a later date, then so be it. All that mattered was to support the people of Liverpool because they had always supported me."

Of course, life had to go on although many people involved at that time realised that Bill Shankly's famous saying about football being more important than life or death would have to be reappraised.

The following year, Dalglish would lead Liverpool to their 18th league championship and it was during this campaign that he would wear the famous red for the last time, on May 1, 1990 when he came on as a 72nd minute substitute for Jan Molby in the 1-0 home win over Derby County. The season would end with Kenny named Manager of the Year for the third time.

We could not have envisaged at that time that his Anfield days were numbered. In February 1991, with Liverpool top of the league and caught up in an FA Cup fifth-round marathon against Everton, the manager stunned the football world by announcing that he was quitting football. The news

broke after a sensational 4-4 draw at Goodison Park.

By his own admission, Kenny felt unwell and under severe strain at that time. His body had become covered in big blotches and he still doesn't know if the rash resulted from general strain. As the fans drifted away from Goodison Park on the night of that famous draw, Kenny knew he had to take a break from football. In fact, he had made up his mind before the game.

Again, talking in his autobiography, he says: "Resigning was a decision made primarily in my best interests, but I was also thinking of Liverpool. A manager who cannot make decisions has to go. I left the club I loved out of necessity, not choice."

This, of course, is all history. The story needs to be told because it is part of Liverpool folklore. But in announcing Kenny's inclusion in the official Liverpool Hall of Fame, it's all about Dalglish the player. And what a superstar he was.

They once said Martin Peters of West Ham was years ahead of his time as he helped England win the World Cup.

If that was the case, Kenny Dalglish was decades ahead. Here was the complete footballer. If you saw him play, you were privileged. If you never, you will have been told about his skill, his great goals and his ability to bring any football crowd to its feet with one moment of magic.

To return to the chant that started this salute.

THERE'S ONLY ONE KENNY DALGLISH.

Winning smile: Kenny Dalglish celebrates after scoring his first against Stoke City in March 1983 – a game that also saw him reach a 300-goal milestone

The **ultimate ball playing** defender

No. 20: **ALAN HANSEN**

There was a time when defending was about one thing and one thing only: THE TACKLE.

Truly great defenders were those who put their foot in or who could rise above towering centre-forwards and dominate them in the air.

Defenders who dallied on the ball or who had aspirations to be constructive in possession were a liability. Managers focused their rearguard on a safety-first mentality with a simple maxim drilled into them. 'If in doubt, put it out, preferably beyond Row Z.'

I'm not suggesting there had never been defenders in the British game capable of playing with elegance, vision and control. As early as the 1960s, teams in Europe were building their tactics around a libero, or sweeper.

As more English teams ventured into Europe, we grasped the importance of building from the back with that new-style central defender working behind the back line one minute, and then stepping in front the next to spring an attack. Liverpool, more than most, were exposed to this type of play as their great European adventure began to unfold under Bill Shankly and Bob Paisley.

Whether either legendary boss ever considered the possibility of making an audacious swoop into the world of Italian or Spanish football for a defensive playmaker is unlikely.

After all, why shop in Madrid or Milan when you can find genius at . . . Partick Thistle!

Enter Alan Hansen, bought (or was it stolen) by Paisley for the princely sum of £100,000 in May 1977. Bob, like Bill before him, had made some canny moves in the transfer market, but this would prove his most astute. Supporters were revelling at that time in the acquisition of another Scot from the heart of Glasgow - the supremely talented Kenny Dalglish. One brought skill and vision to the attack. The other brought the same qualities to the defence.

Young Hansen might have inspired a look of panic on the faces of one or two team-mates early on as his instincts to play his way out of trouble rather than find 'Row Z' raised a few eyebrows. But his ability to read the game and dominate with intelligence rather than brute force made him stand out as the most effective defender in the British game throughout the 1980s. Liverpool had vision at the front in the shape of Dalglish and vision at the back where Hansen was as constructive as he was destructive.

The sight of him majestically striding out with the ball at his feet, the springboard for another Liverpool attack, was fundamental to the pass-and-move game that made Liverpool the greatest team in Europe. It is fitting that Hansen would join his great friend and fellow Scot Dalglish in the official Liverpool FC Hall of Fame for the 1980s. Both men, along with Phil Neal, set a British record by winning an astonishing eight championship medals.

Hansen said: "To be in there amongst the 22 players who have initially been elected is probably the biggest honour I have ever had. I came to Anfield in 1977 with the club riding high thanks to

'Alan Hansen had a confidence bringing the **ball** out that made him **stand out** as a **class** player'

– Ian Callaghan, Panel member

'If I'd gone to an **Italian side,** I'd still be playing now! People ask me if I would have liked to have played anywhere else. It's a **simple answer.** I would not have wanted to be anywhere but **Liverpool'**

> the achievements of Bill Shankly and Bob Paisley. I knew Liverpool had a great tradition of signing Scottish players and I was proud to be one of them.

"The club became my life. I was there for 14 tremendous years. Liverpool have had so many legendary players down the years. It's a pity we couldn't have five or six Halls of Fame because we've had such an array of talent wearing that red shirt."

When you ask Alan to talk about the players he starred with during that immensely successful period when trophies were arriving at Anfield thick and fast, he says: "I have to mention two in particular, both of them Scotsmen - Kenny Dalglish and Graeme Souness.

"Graeme is one of those who did not make it into the Hall of Fame, but what a great player he was. When you sat in the dressing room and saw those two opposite you, everything was possible. It didn't matter who we were playing. We always had a chance.

"I count myself fortunate to have played alongside so many great Liverpool players. The supporters recognised our passion for the club and our desire to win.

"To be fair, I played in three or four different Liverpool teams and while the first one was probably the best, every side had its qualities and kept driving forward to achieve success.

"When Bob left, Joe Fagan took over and won a treble. Then Kenny took over as player-manager and won the famous league and FA Cup Double in his first year. I remember we had this unbelievable finish. Our final game was at Chelsea where Liverpool teams have always struggled for a result down the years. We beat them and took the title. Just to play for Liverpool is a great honour. To be captain as well was fantastic for me."

So what about that special Hansen style of play? How did a boy in Scotland playing for Partick Thistle develop such a cultured game? Alan smiles and says: "I was always more of a Continental-style of player. Looking back, I was born to play in Italy rather than Scotland and England.

"If I'd gone to an Italian side, I'd still be playing now! People ask me if I would have liked to have played my football anywhere else. It's a simple answer. I would not have wanted to be anywhere but Liverpool.

"I've got a lot of medals to remind me of what we achieved, but it's more about the people I was involved with and the fans. You think about the games you played in, the dressing room banter, the supporters, the times we had winning things in Europe and the great camaraderie. Every day was special.

"We were expected to win every game and we were always up for the challenge. I could not have had better times. I have now worked at four World Cup finals for television, but you can never match that feeling of actually being in there amongst a successful set-up, winning cups and leagues and feeling the elation that comes with it."

ALAN DAVID HANSEN

Born 13.06.1955, Sauchie, Clackmannan, Stirlingshire.

Career: Sauchie Juniors, (Liverpool F.C. trial August 1971), Partick Thistle (1973-74 to 1976-77 making 108 appearances and scoring 7 goals, winning the Scottish League Division One championship in 1976)

Signed for Liverpool on 5.05.1977.
Fee: £100,000.
Position: central defender.
Club honours: Club captain 1985-86 to1987-88 and 1989-90.
First Division championship winner (8): 1978-79, 1979-80, 1981-82, 1982-83, 1983-84*, 1985-86**, 1987-88, 1989-90.
FA Cup winner (2): 1985-86**, 1988-89.
League/Milk Cups (4): 1980-81, 1981-82, 1982-83, 1983-84*.
European Cup winner (3): 1977-78, 1980-81, 1983-84*.
Charity Shield winner (5): 1979, 1980, 1982, 1989, and 1986 (jointly).
*Triple trophy winner. **League & F.A. Cup double winner.
Screen Sport Super Cup winner: 1986.

26 caps for Scotland 1979-1987. No goals.
Under 23 caps (3) 16.04.1975 v Sweden (Gothenburg) won 2-1; 16.12.1975 v Romania (Falkirk) won 4-0; 4.02.1976 (sub) v Wales (Wrexham) won 3-2.
1987-88 PFA Fair Play Team award (as team captain) presented by Gordon Taylor.
1999 AXA FA Cup Legend Award.
Retired through injury on 1.03.1991.

Liverpool Appearances, subs, goals.

	League		FAC		Lge C		EC		Ch. Sh.	
	App	Gls	App	Gls	App	Gls	App	Gls	App	Gls
1977-78	18	0	1	0	3	0	4	1	0	0
1978-79	34	1	6	1	0	0	0	0	0	0
1979-80	38	4	8	0	5	0	1	0	1	0
1980-81	36	1	0	0	8	1	9	1	1	0
1981-82	35	0	3	1	8	0	5	1	0	0
1982-83	34	0	3	0	8	0	6	0	1	0
1983-84	42*	1	2	0	13	0	9	0	1	0
1984-85	41	0	7	0	2	0	9	0	1	0
1985-86	41	0	8	0	7	0	0	0	0	0
1986-87	39	0	3	0	9	0	0	0	1	0
1987-88	39	1	7	0	3	0	0	0	0	0
1988-89	6	0	2	0	0	0	0	0	0	0
1989-90	31	0	8	0	2	0	0	0	1	0
Totals	**434**	**8**	**58**	**2**	**68**	**1**	**43**	**3**	**7**	**0**

Plus: European Super Cup 1978-79 2 appearances. 1984-85 1 appearance; Screen Sports Super Cup 1986-87 5 appearances; World Club Championship 1981-82 1 appearance, 1984-85 1 appearance.

Overall: 620 appearances 14 goals.

Also 82 tour, friendly and testimonial games, 2 goals.

'Incredibly I was trusted with the whole of Kenny's football career which was packed in my boot and delivered to Anfield'

Nobody followed the Liverpool Hall of Fame project more closely than Stephen Done, the curator of the Anfield Museum and Tour Centre.

Stephen is steeped in the history of the club on a daily basis. Not only is he a committed Liverpool fan, he is also the individual charged with the task of highlighting the achievements of the legends who have been inducted into the Hall of Fame.

It's not a job as far as Stephen is concerned. It's a passion and his dedication to the challenge comes across in every word as you speak to him about historic days and legendary Anfield characters.

It was fascinating to talk to Liverpool FC's Museum curator about some of the remarkable memorabilia that is now in the hands of the club and either on display or about to be displayed. In many respects he already has a 'Hall of Fame' of sorts – one that will now be strengthened and consolidated by the formation of the Official Liverpool Hall of Fame..

We all know about the famous radio show Desert Island Discs in which an individual selects his or her top 10 records of all time. We asked Stephen Done to talk to us in similar fashion about his 10 prized items in the Museum, and give a very personal assessment of Liverpool greats.

It was a bit like letting the Kop loose on a host of new songs and chants. Stephen is passionate about his club, to say the least.

He said: "Naturally, I was not on the panel, but that doesn't mean that I did not follow the Hall of Fame debate like every fan. Of course, I have my own personal favourites. In this job I have been fortunate enough to meet nearly all of the individuals who were my heroes when I was a kid and then a teenager.

"I was not lucky enough to watch the great Roger Hunt game after game, but I can recall seeing him in action on TV and, of course, I have viewed him as much as possible on every available bit of video footage we have at the Museum.

"Then I had the good fortune to meet him and he summed up for me what Liverpool FC is all about. Roger is completely down-to-earth and approachable, even though he is one of the legends who helped to win England the World Cup in 1966, not to mention his Anfield goalscoring achievements.

"For me, even the name has a special ring about it. ROGER HUNT. His biography was called 'Hunt For Goals.' It sounds perfect!

"To have Roger's World Cup semi-final shirt in the Museum is tremendous. I don't think Roger gets the national acclaim he deserves as a member of that great England side. But he certainly gets the acclaim from Liverpool fans for his achievements with us."

Like many fans, Stephen has a special affinity with the Eighties. He said: "We all had our own Hall of Fame thoughts for this era. If I had been given a vote it would have gone to Kenny Dalglish and Alan Hansen. I've had the pleasure to work with them both. >

Steeped in history: Stephen Done is proud of the collection at Anfield, while the World Cup semi-final shirt of Roger Hunt (left) is in the Museum

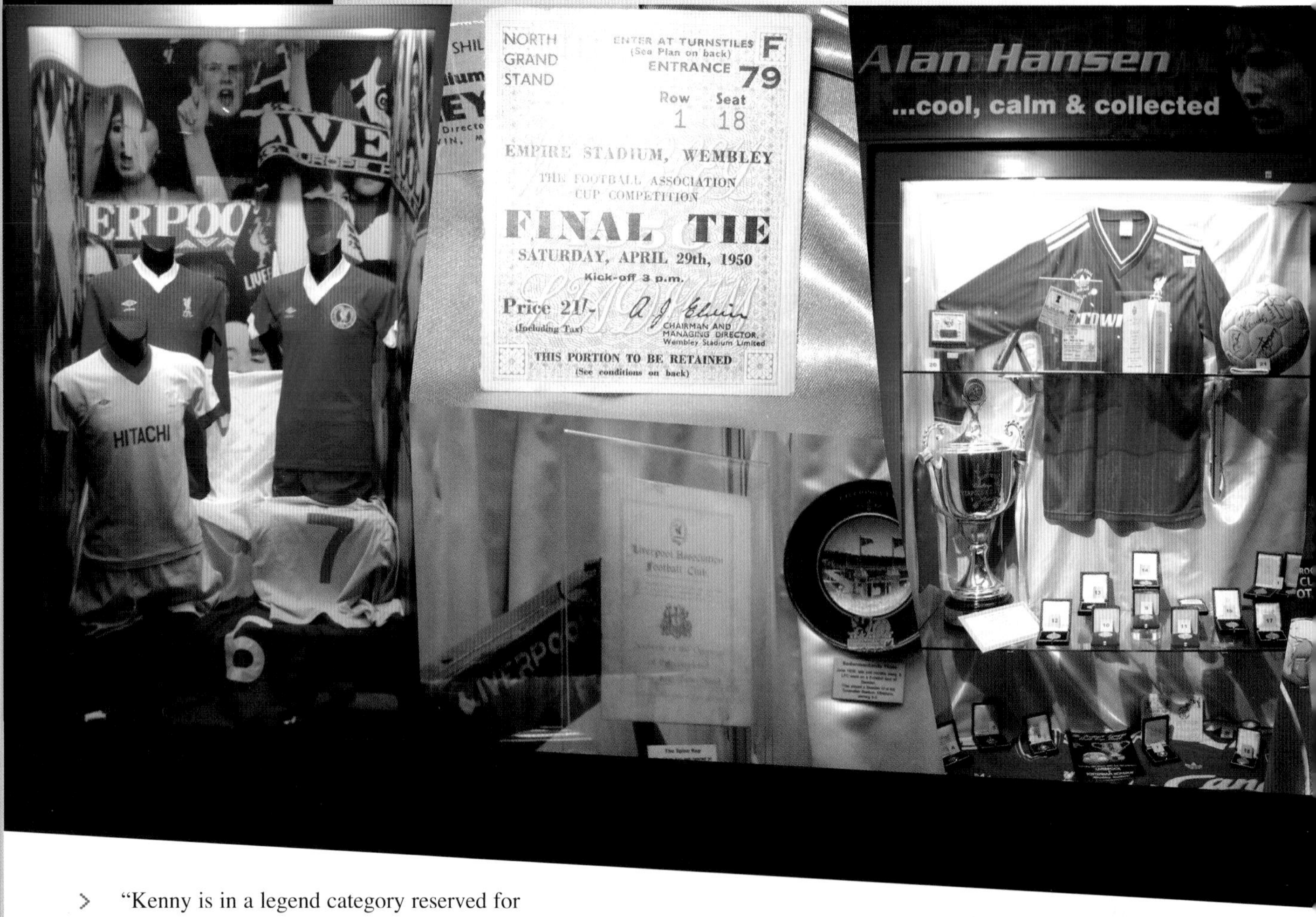

"Kenny is in a legend category reserved for people like Pele. Alan was also one of my favourite players of that era. Both of them have been real supporters of the Liverpool Museum and therefore the history of the club.

"Alan handed us all of his medals, awards and shirts for display. Working with him was a delight.

"I met Kenny when he was manager of Newcastle. I went up on a match day and I knew it would be difficult to get access to him. The Newcastle press officer arranged for me to speak to him just before kick-off and I asked him if he had anything we could display in the Museum. Two days later, back in Liverpool, I received a call from Kenny's wife Marina. She asked if I could pop round to their house.

"I was shocked when I arrived. Laid out on the kitchen table were all of Kenny's shirts, hat-trick balls and medals. We made an inventory of it all. I was able to search through thousands of matchday programmes he had collected during his career, many very rare.

"Incredibly, I was trusted with the whole of Kenny's football career which was packed in my boot and delivered straight to Anfield. What can you say? He wanted the fans to enjoy this material.

"I ended up with two cases bursting at the seams

with Dalglish and Hansen memorabilia. Neither batted an eyelid about lending their treasured possessions to Liverpool FC. It says everything about how they feel about the club."

We asked Stephen a very difficult question about the Museum and Tour Centre he continues to develop. If he could select one item from all the treasures collected, what would it be?

He said: "There are two ways of looking at it. What is the most valuable or what is the rarest item? Of course, nothing we have is for sale, but we have to put a price on things for insurance purposes. If Kenny Dalglish's shirt from the European Cup final

of 1978 was destroyed, no amount of money could buy it back.

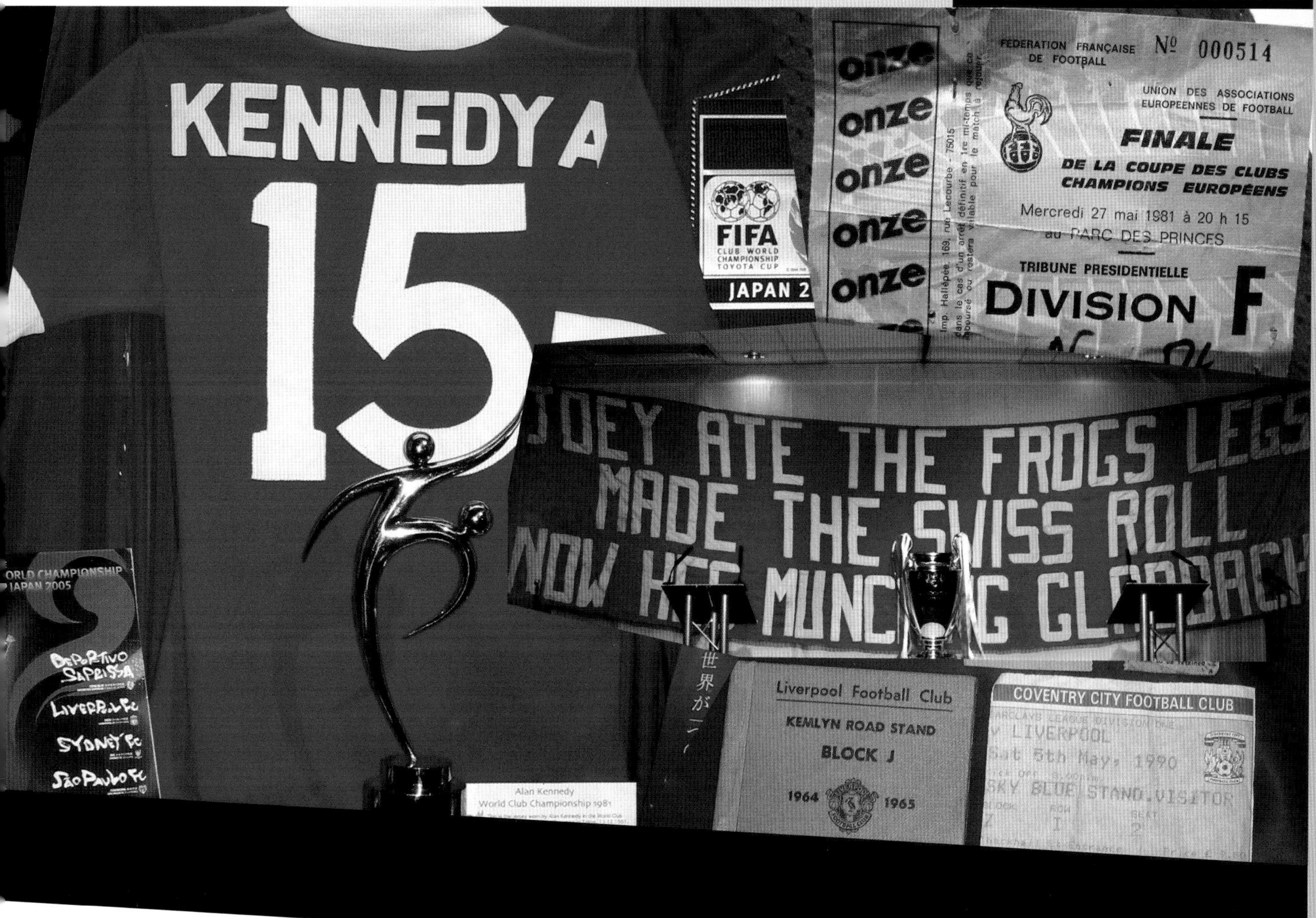

"If I had to pick one thing from the Museum, I would probably go for something on the emotional side.

"We've got one quite small item which is not dramatic to look at in the way a cup might be. It's a piece of paper from Companies Houses formally registering Liverpool as a football club.

"You have to look at it and think what it means. None of our history would have happened without that piece of paper."

Stephen's next favourite item?

"It has to be Kenny Dalglish's league and FA Cup final shirts from 1985-86 when we won an historic double. We've also got his tracksuit top. What a great season that was. I recall the moment at Chelsea in the final game when we won the league. Our player-manager scored the winner and the picture of him, fist in the air and flashing that beaming smile, is something I will never forget. The final followed, a victory over our great rivals Everton. Yes it was a very special year."

You might be surprised to hear that a shirt worn against Grimsby Town is one of Stephen's special Museum items. But if we told you that shirt was worn by Michael Owen on the day he scored his first hat-trick for the club, you will immediately understand the significance.

Stephen said: "Straight after that game I went down to the dressing room area and urged Ronnie Moran to get me the shirt. I said 'Please get it off Michael now. It will become very special one day.'

"I pointed it out to Michael when he visited. He forgot we had it and was delighted it was on display."

We've talked about small items. One of the biggest items will remind fans of famous European Cup nights and one in particular in 1977.

Stephen said: "You look at that Joey Jones banner which was put together by fans. Again, it's not a piece of silverware with an obvious price.

"But to us you simply cannot put a value on it. It smacks of passion, the flow of adrenalin that comes when you watch a big game.

"For me, it sums up Liverpool FC. The banner is something special and it captures the essence of the European Cup."

Treasure trove: A number of the artefacts at the Liverpool FC Museum, while the image of Kenny Dalglish (left) celebrating his winner against Chelsea in 1986 is a special one to curator Stephen Done

LFC Hall of Fame

FROM EVOLUTION TO RED REVOLUTION AND A NEW BREED OF KOP STARS

1990s

Reebok

Changing fortunes

The 1990s saw a massive turnover of players as changing circumstances brought silverware but saw the club fail to repeat the successes of the 1970s and 1980s

The 1990s will go down as a time of frustration for Liverpool when compared with the sensational achievements of the 1980s.

For some clubs a championship at the start of a decade, followed by FA Cup and Coca-Cola Cup triumphs, would mark a particular era down as eminently successful, but the Reds had previously set such high standards that these achievements could not hide the fact that the 1990s were challenging, to say the least.

But it was nevertheless a fascinating spell, an eventful time for the club and most certainly an emotional 10-year stretch.

Just look at the timeline:

1990: League champions.
1991: Dalglish resigns; Graeme Souness appointed manager.
1992: FA Cup winners.
1993: Robbie Fowler's debut.
1994: Significant FA Cup defeat by Bristol City; Souness leaves; Roy Evans appointed; Kop terraces demolished.
1995: Coca-Cola Cup winners.
1996: Wembley defeat by Manchester United in the FA Cup final; death of Bob Paisley.
1997: John Barnes leaves; Paisley Gates opened; Michael Owen's debut.
1998: Evans and Gerard Houllier become joint managers; Houllier later appointed sole manager; Phil Thompson appointed assistant; Shankly statue unveiled; Steven Gerrard's debut.
1999: Anfield Academy opens; Sami Hyypia signs.

There is certainly a whole range of issues to discuss and debate when looking back at a decade that is described in the official history of Liverpool FC as "Paradise Lost."

They say you should never look back, but it was hard for Liverpudlians to accept years without further title glory when the club had revelled in six championship successes in the 1980s (80, 82, 83, 84, 86 and 88). This had also been the age of further European Cup achievements, two FA Cup successes and a string of League Cup wins.

But there was no sign of the stresses that might follow when Kenny Dalglish's Reds claimed the first title of the new decade in 1990. It was a year in which **John Barnes** was at his majestic best and his Footballer of the Year mantle, inherited from team-mate **Steve Nicol,** was well deserved.

In the final game of that memorable campaign, a lone-goal win over Derby County, Dalglish brought the crowd to their feet when he came off the bench to make one final appearance in the red he had graced so magnificently over the previous 13 years. No one realised that day that King Kenny's reign would soon be over.

It was one of the most sensational events in the history of Liverpool and many fans found it incomprehensible. On February 22, 1991, with his team top of Division One and in the middle of an eventful series of FA Cup clashes with Everton, the manager announced he was quitting football. Dalglish had given everything to the Liverpool cause.

He had achieved everything he could as a player, becoming a living legend. He had proved himself as a thoughtful and successful manager. He had also been a rock for families and fans alike following the Hillsborough Disaster, an event that clearly took its toll on him as he and his wife attended one funeral after another with other Liverpool FC figures.

Now it was all over as Kenny succumbed to the pressures of the game he had graced. It would take a strong character to replace him and that man was Graeme Souness, a Liverpool playing great in his own right. As a manager, he had transformed Glasgow Rangers and he arrived back on Merseyside full of confidence.

Many believe Souness went too far, too quickly in trying to re-shape Liverpool in his own image. He changed tried-and-trusted training techniques and the players who had changed at Anfield every day and used the famous stadium as a base for everything from eating to treatment now only saw the ground on matchdays. **Mark Wright** and **Dean Saunders** were signed and youngsters like **Steve McManaman, Jamie Redknapp** and **Robbie Fowler** were introduced.

Against this, Souness broke one of the club's big rules by selling players who arguably still had a lot to offer, like **Peter Beardsley, Steve McMahon, Ray Houghton** and **Steve Staunton.** Souness embarked on revolution rather than evolution and the policy of steady progression and team building was interrupted. In less than three years he sold 18 players and bought 15.

In 1992, Liverpool would win the FA Cup against Second Division Sunderland, but Souness was forced to step out at Wembley flanked by doctors.

After the semi-final against Portsmouth, a sensational announcement revealed that the >

'He had transformed Glasgow **Rangers** and arrived full of confidence. Many believe Souness went **too far, too quickly,** in trying to re-shape Liverpool in his **own image'**

Hall of Fame

1990s

SCROLL OF FAME

1990-1999: Men who made a first team appearance, players in bold shortlisted for Hall of Fame

ABLETT Gary
BABB Phil
BARNES John
BEARDSLEY Peter
BERGER Patrik
BJORNEBYE Stig Inge
BURROWS David
CAMARA Titi
CARRAGHER Jamie
CARTER Jimmy
CHARNOCK Phil
CLOUGH Nigel
COLLYMORE Stan
DALGLISH Kenny
DICKS Julian
DUNDEE Sean
FERRI Jean-Michel
FOWLER Robbie
FRIEDEL Brad
GERRARD Steven
GILLESPIE Gary
GROBBELAAR Bruce
HAMANN Dietmar
HANSEN Alan
HARKNESS Steve
HEGGEM Vegard
HENCHOZ Stephane
HOOPER Mike
HOUGHTON Ray
HUTCHISON Don
HYSEN Glenn
HYYPIA Sami
INCE Paul
JAMES David
JONES Barry
JONES Lee
JONES Rob
KENNEDY Mark
KIPPE Frode
KOZMA Istvan
KVARME Bjorn Tore
LEONHARDSEN Oyvind
MARSH Mike
MATTEO Dominic
MAXWELL Leyton
McATEER Jason
McMAHON Steve
McMANAMAN Steve
MEIJER Erik
MOLBY Jan
MURPHY Danny
NEWBY Jon
NICOL Steve
OWEN Michael
PIECHNIK Torben
REDKNAPP Jamie
RIEDLE Karlheinz
ROSENTHAL Ronnie
RUDDOCK Neil
RUSH Ian
SAUNDERS Dean
SCALES John
SMICER Vladimir
SONG Rigobert
SPEEDIE David
STAUNTON Steve
STEWART Paul
TANNER Nick
THOMAS Michael
THOMPSON David
TRAORE Djimi
VENISON Barry
WALTERS Mark
WESTERVELD Sander
WHELAN Ronnie
WRIGHT Mark

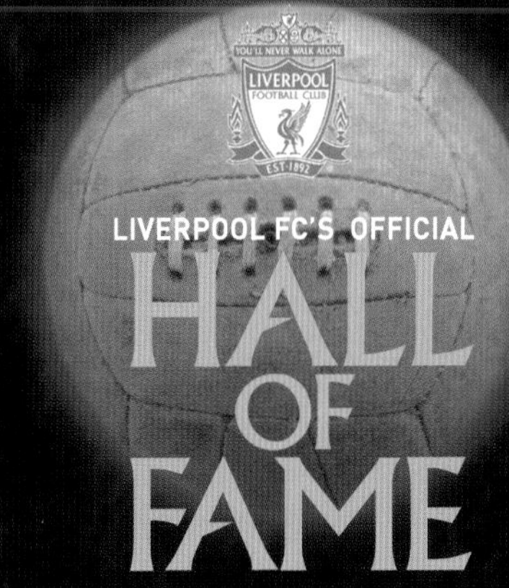

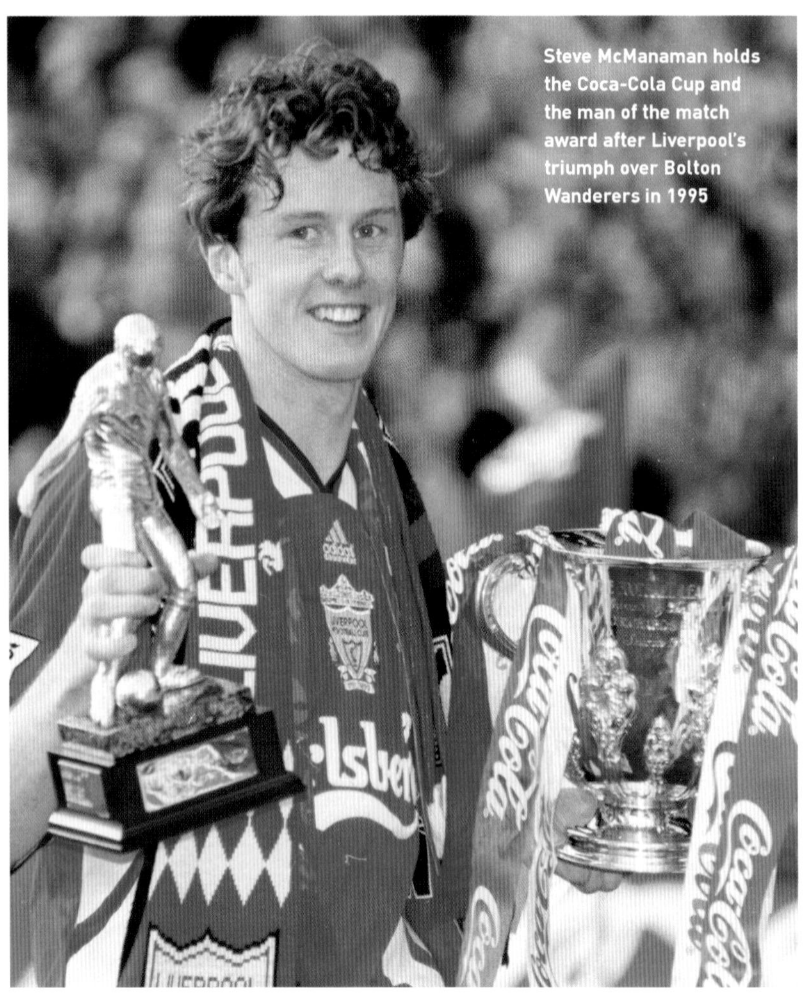

Steve McManaman holds the Coca-Cola Cup and the man of the match award after Liverpool's triumph over Bolton Wanderers in 1995

manager would need heart surgery. It was remarkable and courageous that less than a month after that procedure, Souness was able to walk out under the Twin Towers. But he made an error by selling an exclusive about his recovery to *The Sun* newspaper, still reviled on Merseyside after their reporting of the Hillsborough Disaster.

Souness would later apologise and donate his fee to Alder Hey Hospital. For now the FA Cup win, inspired by the brilliant McManaman, suggested a spell of reasonable calm would follow. However, defender **Glenn Hysen** returned to Sweden, **Houghton** was sold to Aston Villa, **Barry Venison** went to Newcastle United and signings were made like **David James** and **Paul Stewart.**

The manager continued to court controversy by dismissing reserve-team coach Phil Thompson, who had massive support among the fans. The 1992 centenary year was not significant for further Liverpool progress, but for the emergence of rivals Manchester United as a force.

The Reds would finish sixth in the league (the first year of the FA Premier League), go out of the European Cup Winners' Cup to Spartak Moscow and crash out of the FA Cup at home to Second Division Bolton Wanderers. The players felt Souness' anger, the board urged calm and asked fans to support the under-fire manager and one positive step was taken to try and improve matters.

Roy Evans, one of the Shankly boys, was appointed assistant manager. The hope was that things would stabilise, but transfer dealings continued to cause controversy, not least when youngsters **David Burrows** and **Mike Marsh** were exchanged for West Ham hard man **Julian Dicks.**

With injuries adding to his problems, the 1993-94 season was soon testing Souness' resolve, not least as the Reds trailed Manchester United by 20 points. The final straw was a 1-0 FA Cup third-round defeat at Anfield to Bristol City. Three days later, chairman David Moores announced the club was parting company with the manager.

It marked the beginning of the Evans era. Roy was the last of the famous 'Boot Room Boys', a local lad whose pride in his promotion to the hot seat was all too clear. This was an emotional time, not least because at the end of the 1993-94 campaign the Kop stood for the last time. It was April 30, 1994, and although Norwich City spoiled the party on the field with a shock 1-0 victory, over 16,000 Kopites in a full house sung their hearts out to recall greater days.

Before the game, Joe Fagan had led Jessie Paisley and Nessie Shankly onto the field to meet a host of Anfield legends. The Kop roof nearly shattered with the roar that followed. Fittingly, the man now in charge had stood on the Kop as a boy and was red through and through. Evans took some tough, but necessary decisions. Dicks and **Torben Piechnik** were sold and first team changes made.

The 1994-95 season held much more promise, not least when **Robbie Fowler** scored a hat-trick in four minutes, 33 seconds against Arsenal - the fastest on record. Ironically, when the championship was won that season, it was Kenny Dalglish who was celebrating, now rejuvenated and leading Jack Walker's Blackburn Rovers. Remarkably, Kenny's moment of triumph happened at Anfield!

However, Liverpool could look back on a 1995 Coca-Cola Cup win over Bolton Wanderers. Again, McManaman was a key figure and his opening goal was one of the best ever seen at Wembley. Steve would add a second in a 2-1 win.

Looking to build on this success, Evans added the likes of Bolton's **Jason McAteer** and **Stan Collymore** to his squad, smashing the English transfer record to secure the Nottingham Forest striker by paying £8.5m.

In May 1996, the chance to secure more silverware beckoned with an FA Cup final against Double-chasing Manchester United. Unhappily, it would end in defeat and the white suits and sunglasses controversially worn by the players beforehand, inspiring some to call them the 'Spice Boys', would become the abiding memory of a disappointing day. It was just not Liverpool's style. The game was also significant as Ian Rush's last for the Reds.

Liverpool finished fourth in 1996-97 and Evans spent more money on **Oyvind Leonhardsen** and **Karlheinz Riedle.** Collymore was sold and **John Barnes** allowed to leave on a free.

> 'The **1994-95** season held more promise, not least when **Robbie Fowler** scored a hat-trick inside **four minutes,** 33 seconds against Arsenal'

Paul Ince also became an influential figure within the club, but another year ran by without any silverware. One major bonus in 1997 was the emergence of a young man called **Michael Owen,** but Evans was still searching for the wider winning formula and in 1998 he had to accept a joint managerial role as the thoughtful and highly respected French coach Gerard Houllier arrived at the club.

It was hoped the partnership would work, but only one man can have the final say and the experiment ended in November 1998 with Houllier put in sole control. Roy Evans, without a doubt, had been a wonderful Liverpool servant. He stepped aside with honour and good grace. Now it would be time for a new era.

The 1990s would be consigned to the history books, but for Hall of Fame purposes still have some outstanding candidates.

How the panel called it:

There was a consensus amongst the Hall of Fame panel that John Barnes and Ian Rush would fit the bill in this decade.

Robbie Fower and Steve McManaman came into the debate as part of the new order and both had very strong claims for the decade.

However, Barnes was the only one to be named Footballer of the Year in this decade.

Of course, John also had three great years at the end of the 1980s.

The claims for Rush, another whose career bridged the 1980s and 1990s, needed no further justification.

This was highlighted by the panel's 100 per cent support for an individual who was, without a doubt, one of the club's all-time greats.

Below: Michael Owen broke into the Reds team towards the end of the decade

Wing wizard better than the **Brazilians**

No. 22: **JOHN BARNES**

John Barnes brought something very special to Liverpool Football Club. He was one of the most skilful players ever to grace the English game, good enough to win both the Footballer of the Year award in 1988, voted for by the media, and the PFA Player of the Year award, nominated by his peers. John would claim the Footballer of the Year trophy for a second time in 1990, highlighting the fact that he could bring a crowd to its feet with one moment of magic while also contributing efficiently to the team play that was crucial to the Liverpool Football Club success story.

Kenny Dalglish had width and star quality on his mind early in 1987 when news broke that Liverpool were tracking Watford's highly-rated young star Barnes, already an established England player at that time with some 30 caps to his name. The fact that the winger appeared to be reticent about making a quick decision to come to Anfield sparked scepticism on Merseyside that he might have another agenda.

Some newspapers suggested that he was holding out for a better offer from a top Continental club. The 'will he or won't he sign' headlines continued for some time, but the truth of the matter was that the intelligent winger had made a common sense decision to join the Reds in the summer when he would have time to adjust his highly individual game to the more focused team ethic of a club like Liverpool, without dulling his natural skills of course.

Dalglish's patience in waiting for the player and Barnes' logic relating to the timing of his move paid off handsomely. It was once written that the Jamaican-born star stood for everything that was special about the game played at its most attractive. In the same way that George Best's name had become a symbol for sheer football brilliance, John Barnes also generated intense excitement on a football pitch, summed up at its most majestic by that now legendary episode in the world famous Maracana Stadium when he scored a goal for England that even many Brazilians believe was the greatest ever scored, on a stage that had witnessed some truly remarkable moments in football history.

That says everything about the brilliance of John Barnes, whose elevation into the official Liverpool Hall of Fame for the 1990s, alongside the unstoppable Ian Rush, was richly deserved.

John said: "I had won 30 England caps by the time I came to Anfield, but my career really took off from that point. It did not just elevate me nationally and globally, but was crucial in my development as a player.

"The way I played changed completely when I joined Liverpool who had a very different style to Watford. That was the question mark that was posed by many. Could I make a success of the switch? That was where Kenny Dalglish was the best in the business, not just for spotting talent but understanding how a player would fit into the team.

"Terry Venables might have had more in a coaching sense, but Kenny really understood what was needed to bring the very best out of a team. That is why the likes of Peter Beardsley and Ray Houghton just fitted in nicely. >

'First he was a **brilliantly skilful** winger, and then he **adapted** to become a **playmaker**'

– Brian Hall, Panel member

"The question was still asked about how I would adapt to the Liverpool way of doing things.

"I was a ball player. Liverpool's strength was keeping possession. Technically, they were the best.

"For me, Alan Hansen summed up the way Liverpool approached the game at that time in terms of starting attacks and getting the fluidity going. Liverpool defenders had to be confident on the ball which players like Alan, Gary Gillespie, Mark Lawrenson and Steve Nicol all were.

"They had quality in midfield with the likes of Ronnie Whelan and Steve McMahon. Rushie was the best striker around and then John Aldridge arrived, who was also a fantastic goalscorer.

"When you talk about quality strikers and look at great players like Gary Lineker and Michael Owen, what makes them stand out is their understanding of the game.

"As I said, Liverpool were the best footballing side in the country because of their team play. The fact that individual players like Peter Beardsley and myself came to the club and fitted so well into that style of play is a tribute to people like Kenny Dalglish.

'Liverpool were **the best** footballing side in the country because of their **team play.** The fact that individual players like Peter Beardsley and myself **fitted so well** into that style of play is a tribute to people **like Kenny'**

"For four years I expected us to do the Double every season. People will remember that we lost out to Wimbledon at Wembley and Arsenal at Anfield when we stood on the brink of that level of domestic success, but we were a great team."

John reflected on the delay in initially signing for Liverpool. He said: "I believe it was correct to come to the club during the pre-season, rather than in the January or February. People suggested that I did not want to come at all, but this was not the case. I wanted to see the season out with Watford and then get to know my new team-mates in the summer.

"The pre-season gave me a better opportunity to adapt my game to Liverpool's style of play instead of trying to go straight in and do that in league action. Of course, there was a lot of adverse publicity at that time over the transfer delay and so a good start was important because there was a chance people might not have taken to me.

"My first three games were all away at Arsenal, Coventry and West Ham. We won the first two and drew at Upton Park. I played well and it meant I could really look forward to my home debut against Oxford. I scored in that game along with John Aldridge in a 2-0 win.

"I was playing in that left-sided role that Ronnie Whelan had played in. Of course, I was a very different player. Fans were wondering how I would perform. The other big question was whether Peter Beardsley could replace Kenny.

"These were two big issues and very difficult challenges. Peter was the club's most expensive player at that time, having been signed for £1.8m. Kenny paid £900,000 to get me. It was a big double >

JOHN CHARLES BRYAN BARNES MBE

Born 7.11.1963, at Up Park, Kingston, Jamaica.

Career: Sudbury Court as an amateur, Watford (295 appearances, 85 goals) FA Youth Cup winner 1982, Football League Trophy winner in 1982-83. Under 21 caps (3) v Denmark, Greece, Hungary. 31 caps for England; 3 goals

Signed for Liverpool on 19.06.1987.
Fee £900,000. Position: midfield/striker.
Liverpool captain November 1995 to April 1997
League championship winner (2) 1987-88; 1989-90.
FA Cup winner 1988-89.
League Cup/ Coca Cola Cup winner 1994-95.
Charity Shield winner (3) 1988; 1989; 1990 (jointly).
Football Writers Player of the Year, (2) 1988; 1990.
PFA Player of the Year, 1988.
48 caps for England with Liverpool, scoring 8 goals
England total: 79 caps, 11 goals.
Representative game: Football League v Italian League, Naples 16.01.1991.
Awarded M.B.E.

Signed for Newcastle on 13.08.1997; free transfer. 40 appearances, 7 goals.
Signed for Charlton Athletic from January 1999 to May 1999. 12 appearances.
Glasgow Celtic head coach from 10.06.1999 to February 2000.

Liverpool appearances and goals.

	League		**FAC**		**Lge C**		**ECWC**		**UEFA**		**Ch Sh**	
	App	Gls	App	Gls	App	Gls	App	Gls	App	Gls	App	Gls
1987-88	38	15	7	2	3	0	0	0	0	0	0	0
1988-89	33	8	6	3	3	2	0	0	0	0	1	0
1989-90	34	22	8	5	2	1	0	0	0	0	1	0
1990-91	35	16	7	1	2	0	0	0	0	0	1	1
1991-92	12	1	4	3	0	0	0	0	1	0	0	0
1992-93	27	5	2	0	2	0	0	0	0	0	0	0
1993-94	26	3	2	0	2	0	0	0	0	0	0	0
1994-95	38	7	6	2	6	0	0	0	0	0	0	0
1995-96	36	3	7	0	3	0	0	0	4	0	0	0
1996-97	35	4	2	0	3	0	7	3	0	0	0	0
Total	**314**	**84**	**51**	**16**	**26**	**3**	**7**	**3**	**5**	**0**	**3**	**1**

Also Mercantile Credit Centenary Trophy, 1 app, 1 goal. 69 testimonial and friendly games, 15 goals.

Overall: 407 appearances, 108 goals.

Additional notes:
First appearance as captain on 10.04.1995 v Arsenal (a) won 1-0.
Regular captain from 22.11.95 v West Ham U (a), drew 0-0.
Last appearance as captain on 19.04.1997 v Manchester U, lost 1-3.
Last appearance for Liverpool on 11.05.1997 (as sub) v Sheffield Wednesday (a), drew 1-1.

investment and we had that tag to live up to.

"When I reflect on my success, I think immediately about the other players. We were a real passing team. Maybe I would get the ball, go on a dribble and get a bit of glory, but no individual could perform if the other players were not there.

"I believe the late 1970s side and the mid-1980s team were more efficient as a unit. Players like McDermott, Kennedy, Case and Souness were fantastic in the midfield area and probably more consistent, but we had that little bit of individuality. Our team possibly had a bit more flair."

John does not under-estimate how he had to adapt his own game. He said: "At Watford, Graham Taylor always encouraged me to take on defenders. The same emphasis was not on keeping the ball. At Liverpool, if there was any doubt, we would pass the ball. Steve Nicol would go on the overlap and I would do the simple thing.

"My style had to change. We played a high-tempo game. If we gave the ball away, which was not very often, we quickly won it back."

Barnes was still showing the individual brilliance for which he was famous, but the Liverpool way and the down-to-earth nature of everyone at the club made an immediate impression on him. He said: "When we won the league in 1987-88, the thing I remember was not so much the action along the way as the reaction after we had won it. Ronnie Moran came in and simply said: 'Pre-season training starts in July.' There was no big deal about our success and it was not arrogance.

"If you think everything comes as a matter of right, you will not be focused on the next season."

Liverpool went an astonishing 29 games unbeaten in the league at the start of the 1987-88 season before they were finally defeated and by the end of the campaign, Barnes had been voted Footballer of the Year and PFA Player of the Year. He said: "Winning the historic sports writers' award was fantastic, but to be voted as PFA Player of the Year by my peers was very special. Equally, there

were six or seven in the Liverpool team who might have won it, which says a lot about our all-round strength.

"It might seem a cliché, but football is a team sport. You cannot achieve anything without your colleagues. Okay, maybe Diego Maradona might have been an exception, but even he understood the importance of the people around him."

Of course, Barnes was a member of the Liverpool team that came through the Hillsborough experience. He put in a tremendous amount of work with the families at that time to earn the respect of the entire city.

He recalls the FA Cup final that followed and believes it was very fitting that the opposition was Everton. He said: "They went through the loss with us. We wanted to come out on top, not because we wanted to beat Everton, but because of our fans."

Of course, John had a clear understanding of the pain of losing a cup final and so that 1989 triumph was special in many ways.

Likewise, he will never forget the legend of Brazil. He said: "For me, to play in the Maracana where Pele and the rest had performed so magnificently was a great experience in itself."

Fans remember Barnes' long, mazy run in which he ghosted effortlessly past Brazilian players before finishing with tremendous skill inside the area. He smiles at the memory, saying: "It was a wonderful experience."

As for his Hall of Fame accolade, he is extremely proud to be in there amongst 22 Anfield giants. He said: "It's special because Liverpool have had so many great players down the years. The only pity is that so many fantastic players have had to be left out. We could have had 100 'Hall of Famers', which says everything about the history of the club."

'It's special because Liverpool have had **so many** great players down the years. The **only pity** is that so many fantastic players have had to be left out. We could have had **100 'Hall of Famers"**

John certainly contributed to the legend that is Anfield, captaining the side and developing his game to become a key playmaker rather than the electrifying winger of his earlier days.

The stamp on his game was that he was always pure class and while he went on to play for Newcastle, where he joined up again with Kenny Dalglish, he will be remembered as a Red of true star quality and intelligence by all of his Anfield admirers.

All smiles: Celebrating another goal with Ian Rush in April, 1992 and (opposite page) giving Aston Villa defenders a hard time in a 2-1 win from September 1990

All you need is **Rush, Rush . . .**

No. 21: IAN RUSH

Who has been the greatest marksman in the history of Liverpool Football Club? It's not so much a question as an invitation to revel in some of the most inspirational moments ever witnessed at Anfield.

Pose this teaser to modern fans and the debate will be interesting with the likes of Robbie Fowler and Michael Owen having made a major impact in recent years. Roger Hunt will earn powerful support from the revivalist years of the 1960s.

However, the verdict on the greatest will be unanimous - IAN RUSH.

In naming the first of Liverpool's two Hall of Fame heroes for the 1990s, we salute the remarkable qualities of Rushie, who stands out as one of British football's true superstars.

Many of his finest years, of course, were in the 1980s - the era in which Messrs Dalglish and Hansen secured entry in Liverpool's official Hall of Fame. The panel had the chance to consider Rushie for both decades and had no hesitation in finding a place for Ian in the 1990s.

Between 1981-82 and 1993-94, the Welsh predator appeared top of the Anfield goalscoring charts on no fewer than eight occasions, even taking into account his short spell in Italy with Juventus.

His first league goal for Liverpool came on October 10, 1981, when he bagged a double against Leeds United. Fittingly, he scored his 200th league goal against Leeds, on August 28, 1993.

One remarkable statistic stands out in Rushie's famous career. Until Arsenal broke the sequence in the 1987 League Cup final, Liverpool had never lost a match in which Ian had scored. The run reached 144 games with the Reds winning 122 and drawing 22.

When he scored at Old Trafford in October 1992, it was his 287th in all competitions, breaking the club record previously held by Roger Hunt. To complete the stats, Ian's 346th and final goal for Liverpool came on the final day of the 1995-96 season at Manchester City. After the 2-2 draw, City were relegated.

To confirm Rushie's standing in the world of Anfield strikers, he tops a league scoring chart ahead of Roger Hunt, Gordon Hodgson, Billy Liddell, Robbie Fowler, Kenny Dalglish, Michael Owen, Harry Chambers, Jack Parkinson, Sam Raybould, Dick Forshaw, Ian St John, Jack Balmer, John Barnes and Kevin Keegan. That's quite a list.

Of course, Ian is one of just four players who have scored five in one game, his feat coming against Luton in 1983. We could go on and on.

It's enough to say that Ian Rush was a master of his craft, yet he remains one of the most modest individuals in the world of football.

He said: "Liverpool FC is such a great club that it was just a privilege to be part of the success story. If a club is going to be successful at the highest levels of the game, a lot depends on its ability to score goals. I was fortunate enough to be in a great team and the man up front who was regularly putting the ball in the back of the net. The fans never forget that.

"Supporters always have a special affinity with goalscorers and Liverpool FC has had its fair share >

‘Ian Rush was a **master** goal poacher, but remains very **modest’**

– Brian Hall, Panel member

Goal Rush: Celebrating a vintage strike in the 1984 European Cup semi-final against Dynamo Tbilisi

'It was a really **exciting time.** We'd be **4-0 up** and Graeme Souness would still be urging us to get **five** and then **six.** The players around me were **brilliant.** They would help make things **happen** for me'

of greats, men like Liddell, Hunt and Keegan, to name just three. I was lucky enough to play alongside another, who just happened to be a great provider as well - Kenny Dalglish.

"In the first year that I joined the club, I actually struggled in the reserves. Obviously, I could not even begin to dream at that time that one day I would become the club's top goalscorer. Sometimes the penny suddenly drops and things change dramatically for you.

"It happened to me. As I said, I was not doing particularly well. In fact, I was at the point at which I was playing for a move because I felt I was never going to make the breakthrough. I suppose that made me a little more selfish in front of goal.

"At that time, I really grasped the magic of Bob Paisley. I had it in my mind that football at Liverpool was a team game and that I had possibly done enough because I had finally secured a run in the side and played in seven games during which the team had done reasonably well.

"Because of this, I told Bob that I felt I had played well. His response stunned me in a way. He said I'd not achieved anything if I was not scoring goals. He added that if I wanted to leave the club then it was up to me.

"I didn't realise at the time that Bob was really throwing down a challenge to me. As a young player, I was very shy. Bob managed to make me very angry and I left his office determined to show him that I could score goals. He got to me with his directness and actually told me that I was on the transfer list, even though he never formalised it.

"There was interest from Crystal Palace, who were going to be the so-called team of the 1980s.

"Then I suddenly got a chance because David Johnson was injured. I had been scoring goals for fun in the reserves and it all started from there."

Rushie admits that he was in awe of all the other stars around him when he first arrived at the club and this affected his self-belief at that time. He said: "When I first found myself in the first team dressing room, I questioned whether I was good enough to be in there amongst such great players. I would be getting changed next to Hansen and Souness and thinking that I was not worthy to be in such prestigious football company.

"Then, as the games went on, I began to realise that I was in there on merit and good enough to compete with the best. If I hadn't been good enough, Bob would not have selected me."

Ian looks back with great pride at his glory days in a red shirt. He says: "It was a really exciting time. We'd be 4-0 up and Graeme Souness would still be urging us to get five and then six. The players around me were brilliant. They would help to make things happen for me. With my pace and the skill of Kenny Dalglish, all the lads knew we could turn opponents and win games.

"They would play to those strengths and it all started to take off for me. Kenny just said to me: 'You get into that space and I will put the ball in there for you.'

"Nine times out of 10 he would thread balls through from what appeared to be impossible situations. He would be surrounded by three players, but still get the pass into space for me to run onto. I started to do really well.

"It reached the point at which our reputation sometimes went before us. Teams were worried about how to handle us, even before a ball was kicked. Sometimes Joe Fagan would ask me to play when I was not 100 per cent fit. He would say: 'Just having you out there gives us a psychological advantage over the opposition.'

"It filled me with confidence that he could think so highly of me. By 1984 the goals were really flowing and I won an award that still fills me with pride - the European Golden Boot. It went to the player who scored the most league goals in Europe. More often than not the recipient was someone from a tiny nation like Malta where a leading club would be totally dominant.

"I remember Franz Beckenbauer saying that the Golden Boot would never go to one of the leading strikers in Germany, England, Spain and Italy where goals were much harder to come by. I recall that Marco van Basten, at Ajax at the time, was two or three goals behind me that season. I finished with 32 league goals and as well as winning the Golden Boot, I was joint runner-up in the search to find Europe's Player of the Year. The great Michel Platini was number one.

"It was all pointing to the fact that I was up there amongst the best and that is when clubs in Italy and Germany started to take an interest in me."

As far as Liverpool fans were concerned, it was unthinkable that British football's finest striker might be transferred abroad, but in June 1987, Rush >

Wembley wonder: Rushie nets in the 1992 FA Cup final against Sunderland. It was the third consecutive FA Cup final in which he found the net

> signed for Turin giants Juventus in a record-breaking £3m deal.

Ian is extremely honest about his decision to go. He reveals: "Obviously, with Wales not qualifying for the major tournaments, I wanted the chance to play against the best in the world. I was not getting that chance on an international stage and Liverpool were out of Europe after Heysel. I don't deny that the financial opportunity, which was considerable, also encouraged me."

The irony, of course, was that the Reds were willing to sell their prized asset to Juventus, their opponents two years earlier in Brussels where 39 mainly Italian supporters died in what remains one of the blackest episodes in the history of Liverpool Football Club.

Liverpool had worked tirelessly between 1985 and 1987 to do everything they possibly could to rebuild relations with the Italians and, indeed, the links between the clubs at the highest levels had become intimate because of the diplomacy and work that had gone on. Whether this encouraged Liverpool to sanction this deal of deals is an interesting thought.

The reality is that Rush was one of the hottest properties in the world of football at that time. Juventus stood out as one of the game's true giants, inspired by talents like Platini and Zbigniew Boniek.

The unfortunate thing from Rushie's perspective was that these outstanding playmakers would depart the Turin scene and Ian never really exploited his ability in the Italian game.

However, he says he has no regrets about the move. He said: "In some respects, it was the best thing that ever happened to me. I learned a lot about European football. I felt that I grew as a person in the 16 months I was there. I was spoiled at Liverpool because of the success we enjoyed. I found out a lot about myself at Juventus, where things were personally tougher.

"The loss of key players clearly didn't help that first year. Platini told me that I had joined Juventus at the wrong time. They tried to get him to stay, but he had decided to retire. It was always going to be difficult for me, but I have no regrets.

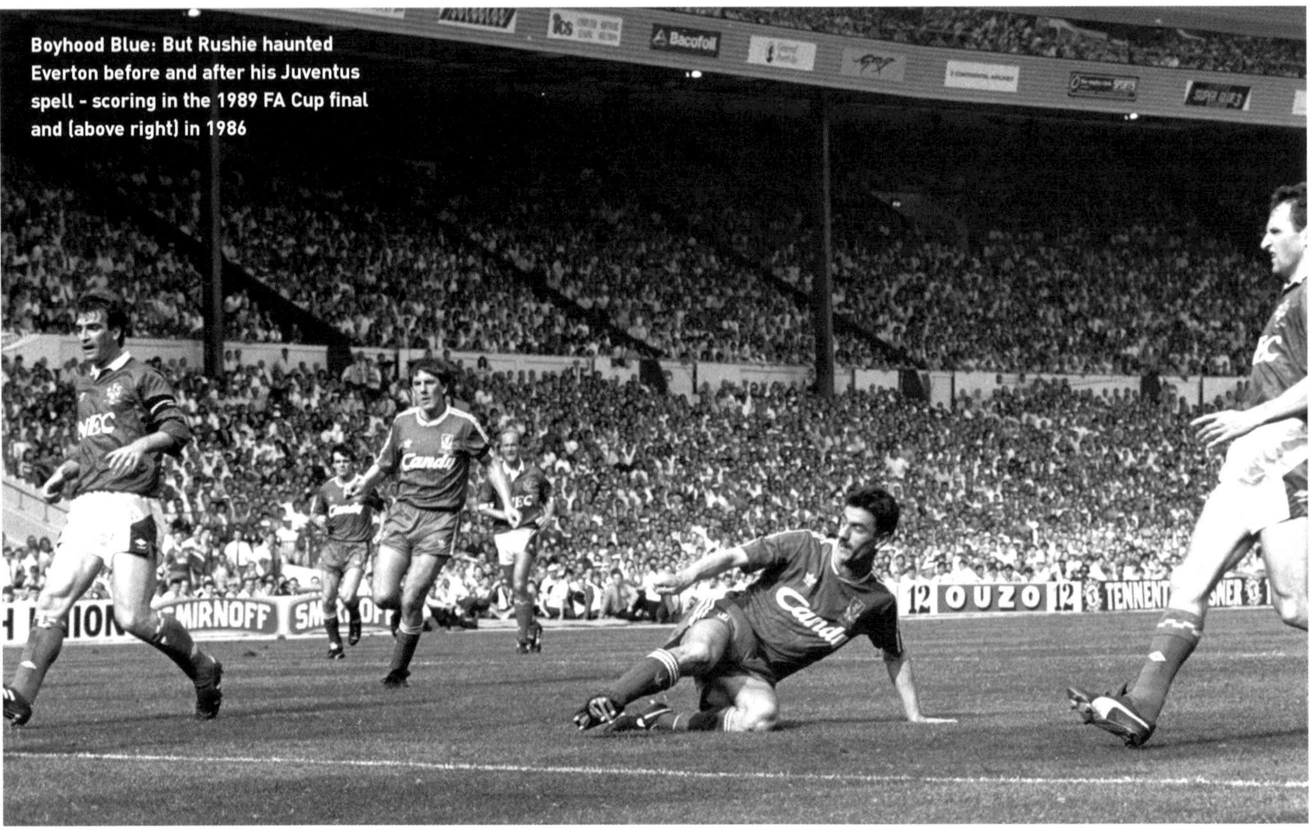

Boyhood Blue: But Rushie haunted Everton before and after his Juventus spell - scoring in the 1989 FA Cup final and (above right) in 1986

"In a way, it also helped me to appreciate Liverpool and everything about the club. When I returned, I got an unbelievable welcome back. I remember playing in Alan Hansen's testimonial game at Anfield and scoring three goals against an England XI.

"It was great for me to be back out on the pitch and to hear the fans chanting my name. I never thought twice when the chance came for me to return to Liverpool. Again, the closeness between Liverpool and Juventus was emphasised by the fact that the deal was done over the phone."

So what are the truly great memories Rushie carries around with him about those wonderful days when he was king of the Liverpool goalscorers? He says: "My last game at Anfield before moving to Juventus sticks out. We played against Watford and I scored the winner from a Kenny Dalglish pass. I remember that because at the time I thought that I would never be coming back.

"Of course, goals in FA Cup finals are always special and I scored two against Everton in 1986 as we won the Double.

"I have so many memories. I remember my final game at Anfield second time round in April 1996 against Boro. I was sub, but both teams formed a tunnel and I was tremendously proud to walk out with my son alongside me. I will never forget that. You simply can't buy such memories."

Of course, Ian didn't need much reminding about famous moments against arch-rivals Everton. He said: "Yes, there were a few of those down the years. Everyone knows that I supported Everton as a lad. Equally, two of my best mates when I was at Liverpool were Blues skipper Kevin Ratcliffe and goalkeeper Neville Southall, who were international >

IAN JAMES RUSH MBE

Born 20.10.1961, St Asaph, Flintshire, Wales. (Family home - Flint.)

Career: Chester City. Apprentice August 1978; professional 25.12.1979.
Appearances 40/1; 19 goals.
Signed for Liverpool on 1.05.1980. Fee £300,000. Position - striker
Juventus, Italy 6.06.1986. Fee £3,200.000.
Loan to LFC 1.07.1986 to May 1987.
Juventus appearances 29; 7 goals.
Transferred back to Liverpool on August 1988 £2,800,000.
Club captain: 1993-94; 1994-95; 1995-96 (part).
First Division championship winner (5): 1981-82; 1982-83; 1983-84*; 1985-86; 1989-90.
FA Cup winner (3): 1985-86; 1988-89; 1991-92. Finalist 1995-96.
League/Milk Cup winner (5): 1980-81; 1981-82; 1982-83; 1983-84*; Coca-Cola 1994-95*
(*only LFC player with these 5 medals).
European Cup winner: 1983-84*.
Charity Shield winner (4): 1982; 1989; jointly 1986; 1990.
Screen Sport Super Cup winner: 1986-87.
*Treble winner in 1983-84.
73 caps for Wales: 28 goals.
Golden Boot Award for Europe's top scorer 1984.
Awarded MBE.
Testimonial game 6.12.1994 v Glasgow Celtic; won 6-0.
Leeds United May 1996 - free transfer. 38/4 appearances, 3 goals.
Newcastle United 15.08.1997. 9/5 appearances, 2 goals.
Sheffield United - loan 23.02.1998 to March 1998. 4 appearances.
Wrexham loan - July 1998 18/5 appearances.
Player/trainer August 1998 to May 1999.
Sydney Olympic – November 1999.
Barnsley part time trainer February 2001
LFC part-time attacker coach 2002

Liverpool appearances and goals:

	League		FAC		Lge C		EC		ECWC		UEFA	
	App	Gls	App	Gls	App	Gls	App	Gls	App	Gls	App	Gls
1980-81	7	0	0	0	1	0	1	0	0	0	0	0
1981-82	32	17	3	3	10	8	4	2	0	0	0	0
1982-83	34	24	3	2	8	2	5	2	0	0	0	0
1983-84	41	32	2	2	12	8	9	5	0	0	0	0
1984-85	28	14	6	7	1	0	6	5	0	0	0	0
1985-86	40	22	8	6	6	3	0	0	0	0	0	0
1986-87*	42	30	3	0	9	4	0	0	0	0	0	0
1988-89	24	7	2	3	4	1	0	0	0	0	0	0
1989-90	36	18	8	6	3	2	0	0	0	0	0	0
1990-91	37	16	7	5	3	5	0	0	0	0	0	0
1991-92	18	4	5	1	3	3	0	0	0	0	5	1
1992-93	32	14	1	1	4	1	0	0	4	5	0	0
1993-94*	42	14	2	1	5	4	0	0	0	0	0	0
1994-95	36	12	7	1	7	6	0	0	0	0	0	0
1995-96	20	5	4	1	2	1	0	0	0	0	3	0
Total	**469**	**229**	**61**	**39**	**78**	**48**	**25**	**14**	**4**	**5**	**8**	**1**

Also: 7 Charity Shield appearances with 3 goals. 1 World Club Championship game, 1 European Super Cup game, 4 Screen Sports Super Cup games and 7 goals. 2 Mercantile Credit Centenary Trophy games.
Overall: 660 appearances; 346 goals.
* denotes ever-present in all competitions.

'It's ironic that I scored so many goals **against Everton,** not least because Kevin was acknowledged as one of the **quickest** defenders in the game and Nev was possibly the best goalkeeper **in the world'**

> team-mates.

"It's ironic that I scored so many goals against Everton, not least because Kevin was acknowledged as one of the quickest defenders in the game and Nev was possibly the best goalkeeper in the world at his peak. But I kept scoring against them.

"People remember the four goals I scored at Goodison in November, 1982, in a 5-0 win. The 'Rush scored one, Rush scored two…' chant evolved from that.

"I'm thankful for that. Liverpool will always be close to me. I enjoyed having an input in my role as part-time coach to the strikers and I've done all my coaching badges. I enjoyed working with the likes of Michael Owen and Milan Baros, passing on little things and improving them. I had the support of the likes of Gerard Houllier, Phil Thompson and Sammy Lee. I've never known anyone with the same knowledge of football as Gerard."

The efforts of Rush as a coach were very much appreciated, but the achievements of Rush the player will live forever in the minds of every Liverpudlian.

He said: "I remember someone telling me to play as long as possible because there is nothing better than scoring goals at the Kop end. When you find the net and hear that roar, the adrenalin pumps through your body. It's something that I will never forget."

'Goal after goal showed what everyone knew - that Fowler was a special talent'

Having the task of picking out just two players from some outstanding decades of football for Liverpool was incredibly difficult.

If I were choosing two from the 1990s, however, I'd go for Robbie Fowler and John Barnes.

Fowler was a boy from the poorer part of Liverpool who grew into one of the best players the club has ever produced. Goal after goal proved what everyone who saw him knew. The boy was a special talent.

He carried the hopes of the fans through a difficult spell in the history of the club.

No-one could touch John Barnes in his early days with Liverpool. But injuries took his pace away. In the Nineties he showed, under Roy Evans, what a talented player he was. He controlled the traffic in the middle of the park for a few seasons and guided younger players along. He was a great player in more ways than one.

Mike Galvin, Liverpool.

There are many greats who played for the Reds but one of my top players was Alan Hansen, who was the perfect defender - cool, calm and dominant.

Apart from the greats of Rushie, King Kenny and Souness, another outstanding star was Craig Johnston, who was one of the most dedicated Reds I've ever seen. 'Skippy' never stopped running, gave 110% every game and most importantly scored against the Blues in the cup final!

I would like to salute all of the Anfield Legends.

Graham May, North Wales.

My first pick for the Hall of Fame in the 1900s would be Joe Hewitt for his

Goal after goal: Robbie Fowler carried the hopes of the fans, according to Mike Galvin of Liverpool

many years of loyalty to Liverpool Football Club.

Winger Jack Cox gets my second nomination. For a winger to average one goal in every four-and-a-half matches is incredible. That's not including the ones he set up for other players.

Peter Chambers, Liverpool.

It was almost impossible to pick just two Liverpool greats for the 1980s when the club enjoyed so much success and had so many outstanding players, but my nominations were Ian Rush and Alan Hansen.

Both players were at Anfield throughout the Eighties, apart from Rushie's one season in Italy, and both gave fantastic service.

Rush was undoubtedly the best goalscorer of his generation and his partnership with Kenny Dalglish was possibly the best strikeforce that Liverpool fans have ever seen.

Hansen was a superb defender who read the game well and always made it look simple.

Alan Molyneux, Prescot.

Putting together a Liverpool FC Hall of Fame was an almost impossible task.

But, I wanted Kevin Keegan and Ray Clemence for the Seventies and Kenny Dalglish and Graeme Souness for the Eighties.

Vish Unnithan, New York.

My two choices for the Eighties were Kenny Dalglish (the best player to pull on a red shirt) and Ian Rush because of his goalscoring record for the Reds and his winning goals in the '86 and '89 cup finals.

Chris Harrison, Merseyside.

IT was difficult choosing two players for each decade in the Hall of Fame, but the first names on my teamsheet would be Dalglish for the Eighties, Callaghan for the Sixties or Seventies, Liddell for the Fifties and Scott for the Twenties.

I suppose we should think ourselves lucky that we support a club where there are so many brilliant players and characters to choose from.

Wayne Rayner, Aigburth.

The men behind the winning teams

Liverpool Football Club - in selecting its Hall of Fame - chose not to extend the exercise to formally debate the merits of the 17 managers who have occupied the Anfield hot seat.

However, it's impossible to conduct any analysis of playing heroes without referring to the impact of those leaders of men who have helped to mould the world class status of the club.

When assessing the claims of all of these great club servants, you need to reflect on longevity, inspirational and leadership qualities, and honours won as you consider who would be the top two in any managerial Hall of Fame.

Tom Watson heads the list for longevity. He was in control for an astonishing 19 years during which time the Reds won two league championships. In sharp contrast, Ronnie Moran and Phil Thompson both responded in emergencies to act in a caretaker capacity for a matter of months, although each gave the club marathon service.

Bob Paisley is untouchable when it comes to honours won, with three European Cups, one UEFA Cup, one European Super Cup, six championships, three League Cups and six Charity Shields (one shared).

Bill Shankly is without a shadow of a doubt the father of modern Liverpool, the most inspirational boss of all time and the definitive man of the people. His honours list never included the European Cup, but he won one UEFA Cup, three league championships, two FA Cups and three Charity Shields (two shared).

Other managers who won the league championship include, as we have mentioned, Watson (2), David Ashworth (1), Matt McQueen(1), George Kay (1), Joe Fagan (1) and Kenny Dalglish (3).

Others with a European pedigree are Joe Fagan (1 European Cup), Gerard Houllier (1 UEFA Cup) and, of course, Rafael Benitez (1 European Cup). >

'**Two men** would automatically **rise to the top** of the pack amongst the managers in the shape of the **legendary** Bill Shankly and Bob Paisley'

LFC Hall of Fame

LEGACY

THE HALL OF FAME

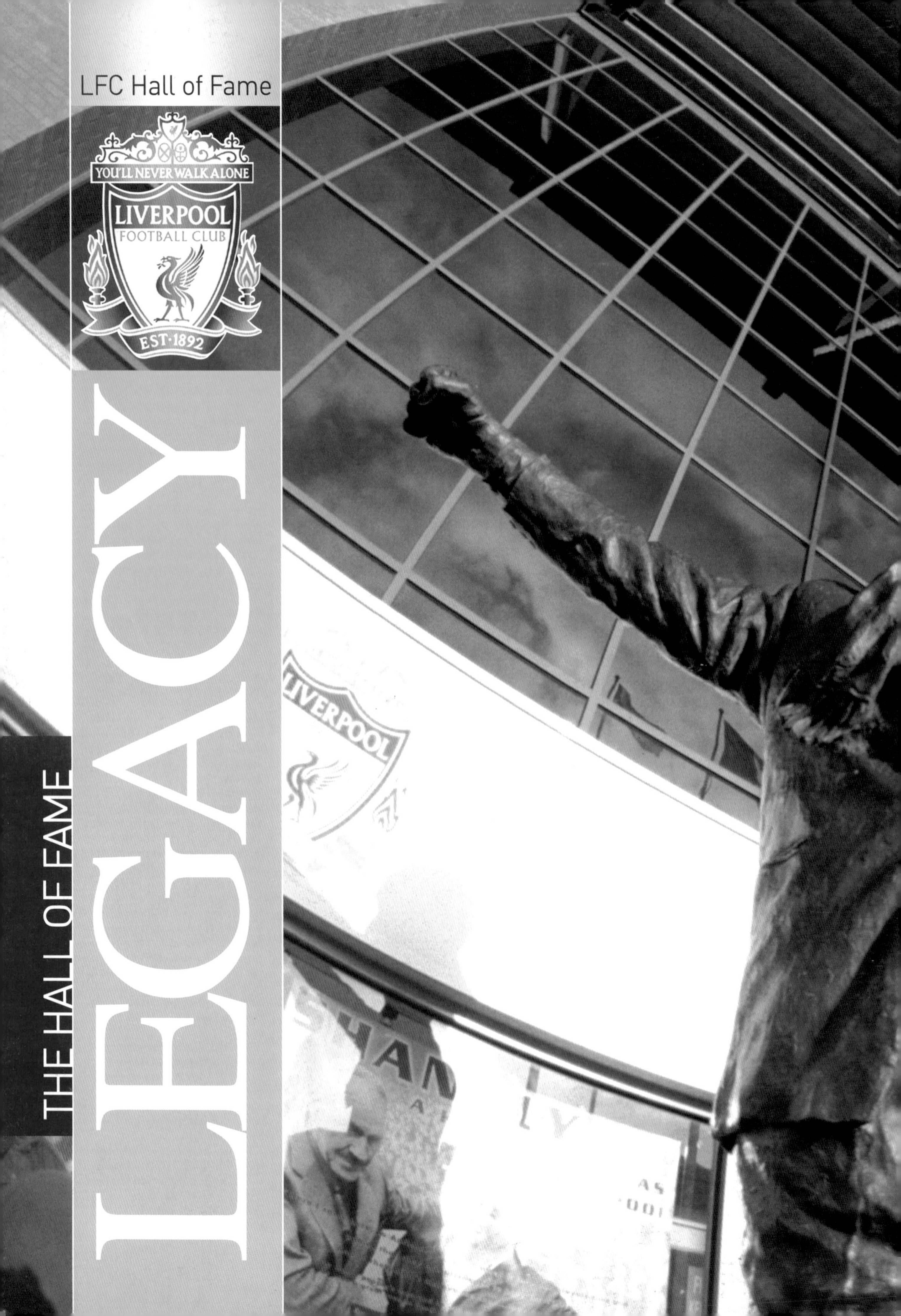

Dalglish

A glorious history . . . a famous future

The 22 legends have been selected for the official Liverpool Football Club Hall of Fame. The debate is over – for now – so what happens next?

The Liverpool Hall of Fame is now in place with 22 absolute legends standing side by side, a tribute to everything that is great about the Reds.

These are contrasting heroes, bridging every decade since 1892.

Some of them played in more successful eras than others, but every single one of them deserves his Hall of Fame accolade, having been nominated at the end of a highly emotive and well-researched project that took an entire season of deliberation to deliver.

The panel - Rick Parry, Phil Thompson, Alan Hansen, Ian Callaghan and Brian Hall - listened to the views of the fans and studied the statistical and emotional claims of a whole host of legends and immortals over a 10-month period.

While the Reds did not need confirmation that Liverpool FC has been represented by an unmatchable array of talent down the years, 'Hall of Fame' helped everyone connected with the club to revel in a famous history (which is always a highly enjoyable experience).

The process brought back into sharp focus the football genius of an army of individuals, not least those pioneers who had a football vision

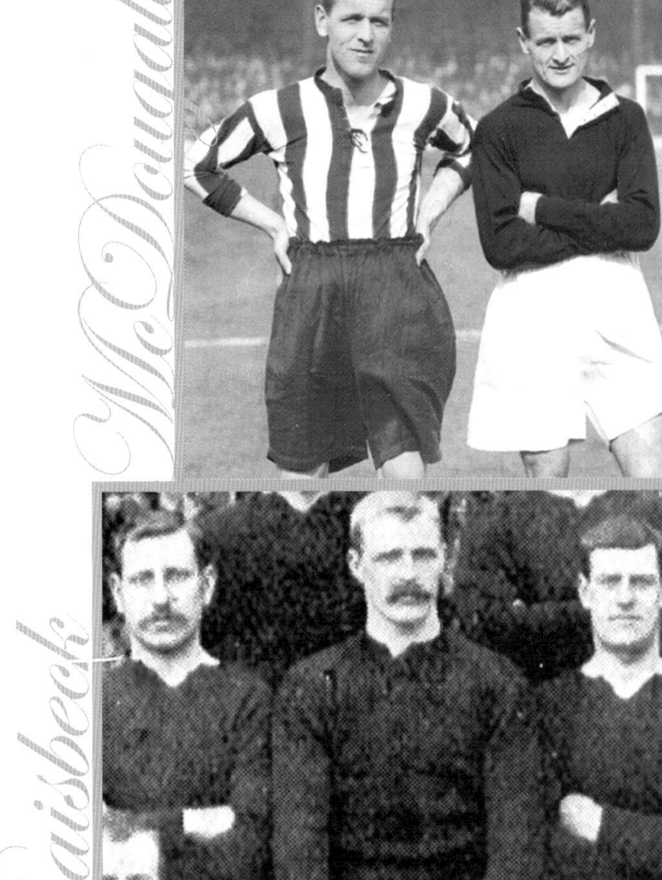

'In some cases, the names of these **early heroes** had not been uttered in the corridors of Anfield for **generations . . .** However, this did not mean their deeds were **forgotten**'

and helped LFC fulfil all of its dreams.

In some cases, the names of these early heroes had not been uttered in the corridors of Anfield for generations as new stars came to the fore to focus the hearts and minds of the fans.

However, this did not mean their deeds were forgotten. Indeed, Hall of Fame has provided the platform to bring their careers back into sharp focus and so Liverpudlians were able to discuss the merits of men like Harry Bradshaw and Matt McQueen,

who were the heroes of Victorian Liverpool in the 1890s.

The club then researched the international quality of early 20th century heroes like Alex Raisbeck, Jack Cox, Eph Longworth and Arthur Goddard and then marvelled at the marathon achievements of the one and only Elisha Scott.

The Liverpool story unfolded either side of two World Wars as this Anfield football 'Time Machine' stopped at intervals to salute the feats of Don Mackinlay, Gordon Hodgson, Jim McDougall, Albert Stubbins and Jack Balmer.

Then it was time to applaud Mr Liverpool himself - Billy Liddell - before completing the first half of an eventful century with a salute to Alan A'Court, a Liverpool and England World Cup star in the challenging Fifties.

The focus then turned to fairly modern times - captivated by the Shankly Revolution and the folklore of his Colossus Ron Yeats and World Cup-winning hero Roger Hunt. Bob Paisley's era was the most glittering in the club's history and no prompting was needed to celebrate the achievements of Ray Clemence, Ian Callaghan, Kenny Dalglish and Alan Hansen.

This remarkable Hall of Fame exercise ended with a double vote for the Nineties, bringing goal machine Ian Rush and double Footballer of the Year John Barnes into the spotlight.

The die is cast on the first phase of the Hall of Fame with 22 giants now in place, but in many ways the process is only just beginning and it will go on with further elections due for the period 2000-2010.

Then there is the legacy to consider. The whole issue of where Liverpool FC's prestigious "Hall of Fame" should be housed and what form it should take is the subject of another major project.

Certainly, Hall of Fame and the giants who now stand within it are helping to focus the club as it begins to consider the reality of moving to a new home in Stanley Park, leaving behind one of the most historic football sites in Britain, indeed in world football.

Can Hall of Fame be used to link the old and the new?

All of this indicates that this project, while completed at the first phase, still provides every fan with real food for thought as the club powers forward.

Should there be a Hall of Fame statue of some sort, around the base of which the names of each legend could be featured?

Should there be a special area in a regenerated Anfield Museum and Visitors' Centre?

'Hall of Fame is helping to **focus the club** as it begins to consider the reality of moving to a **new home** in Stanley Park, leaving behind one of the most historic sites in **world football'**

Balmer

Barnes

Cox

Hansen

Should there be a legends picture gallery within one of the main public walkways within the new stadium? How about the 'Walk Of Fame' proposal, linking the site of the present historic stadium with the proposed arena giant in the Park. This could be a "Hall of Fame Avenue Of The Stars." Special markers could be embedded in the ground at various points, recording the name of each Hall of Fame super hero.

When the club ultimately moves, these points could also mark out the geography of historic Anfield - players' tunnel, centre-circle, Anfield Road end etc.

Those Hall of Fame legends who are still alive could put their famous footprints in the concrete along the "Walk of Fame" - just as the stars of the film world put their handprints down outside the famous Graumanns Chinese Theatre in Hollywood.

Should there be a Hall of Fame window integrated into the fabric of the new stadium, as suggested by one official fan club member?

The ideas are endless and they are very exciting. Certainly, Hall of Fame will provide Liverpool FC with a fitting opportunity to mark the site of the original Kop when the time comes to demolish the legendary old stand as part of the bold new stadium development. All of these ideas are on the table and the club has made it clear that it will welcome any other ideas from the fan base.

For now, it's enough to congratulate every member of the new Hall of Fame and celebrate the memory of every player to have worn Liverpool's famous Red with pride and passion.

LIVERPOOL FC OFFICIAL HALL OF FAME

1890s

HARRY BRADSHAW and MATT McQUEEN

1900s

ALEX RAISBECK and JACK COX

1910s

ARTHUR GODDARD and EPHRAIM LONGWORTH

1920s

ELISHA SCOTT and DON MACKINLAY

1930S

GORDON HODGSON and JIMMY McDOUGALL

1940s

ALBERT STUBBINS and JACK BALMER

1950s

BILLY LIDDELL and ALAN A'COURT

1960s

ROGER HUNT and RON YEATS

1970s

RAY CLEMENCE and IAN CALLAGHAN

1980s

ALAN HANSEN and KENNY DALGLISH

1990s

JOHN BARNES AND IAN RUSH

Who played when -

1892-1899 Scroll of Fame

(Where players appeared for Liverpool over a series of decades, they have been honoured on the scroll for each decade they have represented the club)

Name	First name	Date signed	Seasons
Allan	George	13.06.1895	1895-99
Battles	Ben	4.01.1895	1895-98
Becton	Francis	18.03.1895	1894-98
Bradshaw	Harry	14.10.1893	1893-98
Bull	Ben	15.12.1895	1895-96
Cameron	J (seenotes)	1892	1892/93
Cameron	James	9.05.1894	1894-95
Cleghorn	Thomas	14.03.1896	1895-99
Cleland	James	1.03.1895	1894-95
Colvin	Robert	6.11.1897	1897-98
Cox	Jack	24.02.1898	1897-1909
Cunliffe	Daniel	2.05.1897	1897-98
Curran	John	13.10.1894	1894-96
Dewhurst	Gerald	28.02.1894	1893-94
Dick	Douglas	14.10.1893	1893-94
Donnelly	William	4.01.1895	1895-97
Drummond	John	21.08.1894	1894-95
Dunlop	William	12.10.1894	1894-1909
Finnerhan	Patrick	6.05.1897	1897-98
Foxall	Abraham	27.04.1899	1899-1900
Geary	Frederick	18.05.1895	1895-99
Givens	John	1.03.1894	1893-95
Goldie	Archibald	1895	1895-1900
Goldie	William	26.11.1897	1897-1903
Gordon	Patrick	16.08.1893	1893-95
Hannah	Andrew	1.09.1893	1892-95
Hannah	David	3.11.1894	1894-97
Hartley	Abraham	18.12.1897	1897-98
Henderson	David (see notes)	16.09.1893	1893-94
Henderson	James	23.08.1893	1893-94
Henderson	Hugh	20.10.1894	1894-95.
Holmes	John	June 1895	1895-98
Howell	Raby	7.04.1897	1897-1901
Hughes	William	16.09.1893	1893-95
Hunter	'Sailor'	10.05.1899	1899-1902
Hunter	Thomas	27.09.1899	1899-1902
Jowitt	Charles	14.03.1896	1896-97
Keech	William	11.09.1895	1895-96
Kelly	P	1892	1892/93
Kelso	J	1892	1892/93
Kelvin	Andrew	1892	1892/93
Kerr	Neil	5.06.1894	1894-85
Kyle	Peter	1.05.1899	1899-1900
Lumsden	Joseph	12.06.1897	1897-98
Marshall	Robert	9.01.1897	1897-99
McBride	James (notJohn)	7.08.1893	1892-95
McCann	William	26.05.1894	1894-95
McCartney	John	23.08.1892	1892-98
McCowie	Andrew	27.10.1896	1896-99
McLean	Duncan	16.08.1893	1893-95
McLean	John (see note)	22.05.1894	1894-97
McOwen	William	26.08.1892	1892-94
McQue	Joseph	5.08.1893	1892-98
McQueen	Hugh	8.07.1893	1892-95
McQueen	Matthew	14.08.1893	1892-99
McVean	Malcolm	5.08.1893	1892-97
Michael	William	23.01.1895	1895-97
Miller	John	1892	1892/93
Morgan	Hugh	26.03.1898	1897-1900
Neill	Robert	4.01.1895	1894-97
Parkinson	John	22.05.1899	1899/1900
Pearson	No details	1892	1892/92
Perkins	William	26.03.1898	1898-1903
Richardson	Nodetails	1892	1892/93
Raisbeck	Alexander	6.05.1898	1898-1909
Robertson	Thomas	31.03.1898	1897-1902
Ross	James	20.08.1894	1894-97
Ross	Sydney	1892	1892/93
Satterthwaite	Charles	8.12.1899	1899-1901
Smith	Jock	1892	1892/93
Stevenson	William	May 1896	1896-99
Storer	Harry	25.12.1895	1895-1901
Stott	James	7.08.1893	1893-94
Walker	John (see notes)	31.03.1898	1897-1902
Walker	William	2.05.1897	1897-98
Whitehead	John	29.03.1894	1894-95
Wilkie	Thomas	19.01.1895	1895-98
Wilson	Charles	16.12.1897	1897-1905
Wilson	David	7.05.1899	1899-1900
Worgan	A	17.08.1893	1893-94
Wyllie	Thomas	1892	1892/93

Notes: Lancashire League 1892-93, players not registered with the Football League. In the early seasons, registrations had to be received seven days before becoming eligible. Signings in the summer were deemed eligible for the first game of the new season.
J.Cameron signed 1892 from Aston Villa. Formerly with Renton.
James Cameron signed 8.05.1894 from Glasgow Rangers. Formerly an amateur with Linthouse.
David Henderson from Kings Park, Stirling, signed 15.09.1893, eligible 23.09.1893 (debut). 20 games at centre forward.
James Henderson from Annbank, signed 22.08.1893, eligible 1.09.1893. One appearance on 2.09.1893 as centre forward.
Hugh Henderson from Third Lanark, signed 19.10.1894, eligible 27.10.1894 (debut). Played as centre forward.
William Hughes signed from Bootle summer 1893 as a centre-half and captain of reserve side in 1893/94. 1 appearance 3.02.1894.
John McLean registered in 10.10.1894, eligible 18.10.1894.
John Walker from Hearts. registered in 30.03.1898, eligible on 7.04.1898. 1897/8 to 1901/2. Three appearances at outside-right on April 11,12,&16,1898.
William Walker from Leith registered 2.05.1897, eligible 1.09.1897. 12 appearances in 1897/8 as inside-forward to 1.01.1898.
Sources - Football League registers, Association of Football Statisticians and local papers.

1900s Scroll of Fame

Name	First name	Date signed	Seasons
Allman	Messina	7.07.1908	1908-1909
Beeby	Augustus	15.12.1908	1908-1911
Berry	Arthur	27.03.1908	1907-1908
Blanthorne	Robert	2.11.1905	1905-1907
Bowen	George	3.05.1901	1901-1902
Bowyer	Samuel	5.03.1907	1907-1912
Bradley	James	17.09.1905	1905-1911
Buck	Frederick	May 1903	1903-1904
Carlin	John	5.12.1902	1902-1907
Chadburn	John	11.05.1903	1903-1904
Chadwick	Edgar	May 1902	1902-1904
Chorlton	Thomas	15.05.1904	1904-1912
Cotton	Charles	4.12.1903	1903-1904
Cox	Jack	24.02.1898	1897-1909
Craik	Herbert	15.05.1903	1903-1904
Crawford	Robert	21.01.1909	1909-1915
Davies	John	1.09.1902*	1902-1903
Doig	Teddy	17.08.1904	1904-1908
Dunlop	William	12.10.1894	1894-1909
Fitzpatrick	Harold	3.05.1907	1907-1908
Fleming	George	26.08.1901	1901-1906

a complete record

Garside	James	9.03.1904	1904-1906
Glover	John	14.06.1900	1900-1903
Goddard	Arthur	24.02.1902	1902-1914
Goldie	Archibald	1895	1895-1900
Goldie	William	26.11.1897	1897-1903
Goode	Bertram	7.07.1908	1908-1910
Gorman	James	14.09.1905	1905-1908
Green	Thomas	4.09.1901	1901-1903
Griffin	Michael	20.09.1907	1907-1909
Griffiths	Harold	17.09.1905	1905-1908
Hardy	Samuel	18.05.1905	1905-1912
Harrop	James	16.01.1908	1908-1912
Hewitt	Charles	5.06.1907	1907-1908
Hewitt	Joseph	9.02.1904	1904-1910
Hignett	Samuel	4.10.1907	1907-1910
Hoare	Joseph	25.05.1903	1903-1904
Howell	Raby	7.04.1897	1897-1901
Hughes	James	14.06.1904	1904-1909
Hughes	John	7.05.1903	1903-1906
Hunter	'Sailor'	10.05.1899	1899-1902
Hunter	Thomas	27.09.1899	1899-1902
Hunter	William	22.12.1908	1908-1909
Kyle	Peter	1.05.1899	1899-1900
Lathom/Latham	George	25.10.1902	1902-1909
Lipsham	John	3.01.1907	1906-1907
Livingston(e)	George	28.05.1902	1902-1903
Marshall	William	3.12.1901	1901-1902
McCallum	Donald	31.06.1901	1901-1903
McConnell	John	15.04.1909	1909-1912
McDonald	John	11.05.1909	1909-1912
McGuigan	Andrew	19.05.1900	1900-1902
McKenna	John	9.09.1905	1905-1907
McLean	James	21.05.1903	1903-1904
McPherson	William	31.08.1906	1906-1908
Morgan	Hugh	25.03.1898	1897-1900
Morris	Richard	29.03.1902	1902-1905
Murray	David	29.08.1904	1904-1905
Orr	Ronald	2.04.1908	1908-1912
Parkinson	John	22.05.1899	1899/1900
Parkinson*	John 'Jack'	4.10.1902	1902-1914
Parry	Maurice	13.08.1900	1900-1909
Peake	Ernest	30.05.1908	1908-1914
Perkins	William	26.03.1898	1898-1903
Platt	Peter	May 1902	1902-1904
Raisbeck	Alexander	6.05.1898	1898-1909
Raybould	Samuel	3.01.1900	1900-1907
Robertson	John	24.04.1900	1900-1902
Robertson	Thomas	31.03.1898	1897-1902
Robinson	Robert	11.02.1904	1904-1912
Rogers	Thomas	25.04.1907	1907-1912
Satterthwaite	Charles	8.12.1899	1899-1901
Saul	Percy	16.08.1906	1906-1909
Sloan	Donald	4.05.1908	1908-1909
Smith	Sydney	16.04.1903	1903-1904
Speakman	James	5.02.1909	1909-1912
Stewart	James	17.04.1909	1909-1914
Storer	Harry	25.12.1895	1895-1901
Uren	Harold	4.10.1907	1907-1912
Walker	John	31.03.1898	1897-1902
West	Alfred	4.11.1903	1903-1909
White	William	20.05.1901	1901-1902
Wilson	Charles	16.12.1897	1897-1905

Notes: In the early seasons players had to be registered for 7* days before being eligible. If registered in the summer then the first league game was given as eligible date (Football League).
*This was later reduced to 2 days.
John Davies was said to have made his debut 9.03.1901 (Liverpool Echo) but Football League Register states Morris who Echo shows playing in reserves on this day. James Hughes 15 appearances 1904/05 to 1908/09.
John Hughes 32 appearances 1903/04 (Source FLR).
William Hunter 1 appearance 20.03.1909. (FLR).
T.J. Hunter 5 appearances 1899/90 to 1901/02.
*There are two John Parkinsons in this scroll.

1910s Scroll of Fame

Name	First name	Date signed	Seasons
Bamber	John	4.12.1915	1915-1924
Banks	William	29.09.1913	1913-1919
Bartrop	Wilfred	18.05.1914	1914-1918*
Beeby	Augustus	15.12.1908	1908-1911
Bennett	Thomas	13.11.1919(P)	1916-1920
Bovill	John	20.04.1911	1911-1914
Bowyer	Samuel	5.03.1907	1907-1912
Bradley	James	17.09.1905	1905-1911
Bratley	Philip	14.05.1914	1914-1915
Bromilow	Thomas	May1919	1919-1930
Brough	Joseph	7.08.1910	1910-1912
Campbell	Kenneth	9.05.1911	1911-1920
Chambers	Henry	13.04.1914	1914-1928
Chorlton	Thomas	15.05.1904	1904-1912
Crawford	Robert	21.01.1909	1909-1915
Dawson	James	25.12.1912	1912-1916
Dines	Joseph	28.05.1912	1912-1913
Fairfoul(l)	Thomas	3.05.1913	1913-1915
Ferguson	Robert	15.05.1913	1913-1915
Forshaw	Richard	31.07.1919	1919-1927
Gilligan	Samuel	30.04.1910	1910-1913
Goddard	Arthur	24.02.1902	1902-1914
Gracie	Thomas	23.02.1912	1912-1914
Grayer	Frank	16.07.1912	1912-1915
Hafekost	Charles	7.05.1914	1914-1915
Hardy	Samuel	18.05.1905	1905-1912
Harrop	James	16.01.1908	1908-1912
Hewitt	Joseph	9.02.1904	1904-1910
Hignett	Samuel	4.10.1907	1907-1910
Holden	Ralph (not A.)	24.08.1911	1911-1914
Jenkinson	William	13.05.1919	1919-1921
Lacey	William	28.02.1912	1912-1924
Leavey	Herbert	18.08.1910	1910-1911
Lester	Henry	1.12.1911	1911-1913
Lewis	Henry	Sept 1916	1916-1923
Longworth	Ephraim	9.06.1910	1910-1928
Lowe	Henry	5.05.1911	1911-1920
Lucas	Thomas	May 1916	1916-1933
Mackinlay	Donald	27.01.1910	1910-1929
Matthews	Robert	1918	1918-1922
McConnell	John	15.04.1909	1909-1912
McDonald	John	11.05.1909	1909-1912
McDougall	Robert	15.11.1913	1913-1915
Metcalf	Arthur	25.05.1912	1912-1919
Miller	John	1.07.1918	1918-1921
Miller	Thomas	17.02.1912	1912-1920
Nicholl	James	23.01.1914	1914-1915
Orr	Ronald	2.04.1908	1908-1912
Pagnam	Frederick	21.05.1914	1914-1919
Parkinson	John 'Jack'	4.10.1902	1902-1914
Peake	Ernest	30.05.1908	1908-1914
Pearson	Albert	29.04.1919	1919-1921
Pursell	Robert	29.08.1911	1911-1920
Robinson	Robert	11.02.1904	1904-1912
Rogers	Thomas	25.04.1907	1907-1912
Scott	Elisha	3.09.1912	1912-1934
Scott	James	20.08.1910	1910-1915

Sheldon	Jackie	27.11.1913	1913-1922
Speakman	James	5.02.1909	1909-1912
Speakman	Samuel	24.09.1912	1912-1920
Staniforth	Frederick	11.06.1913	1913-1914
Stewart	James	17.04.1909	1909-1914
Stuart	William	2.09.1910	1910-1912
Tosswill	John	4.06.1912	1912-1913
Uren	Harold	4.10.1907	1907-1912
Wadsworth	Harold	13.051919*	1918-1924
Wadsworth	Walter	23.04.1912(A)	1912-1926
Welfare	J.	17.05.1912	1912-1914
West	Alfred	11.08.1910*	1910-1911

Notes: Seasons 1915/16 to 1918/19 not included.
A=amateur signing; P=professional signing (may have been with club earlier)
Wilfred Bartop killed in action 1918. A West 11.08.1910 second time signed. H Wadsworth played some WWI games 1918.

1920s Scroll Of Fame

Name	First name	Date signed	Seasons
Armstrong	Thomas	12.03.1920	1919-1920
Bamber	John	4.12.1915	1915-1924
Baron	Frederick	10.02.1925	1925-1927
Barton	Harold	24.11.1928	1928-1934
Beadles	George	12.05.1921	1921-1924
Bromilow	Thomas	May 1919	1919-1930
Campbell	Kenneth	9.05.1911	1911-1920
Chalmers	William	9.08.1923	1923-1925
Chambers	Henry	13.04.1914	1914-1928
Checkland	Francis	May1919	1919-1923
Clark	John	28.01.1928	1928-1931
Cockburn	William	28.05.1924	1924-1928
Cunningham	William	4.05.1920	1920-1924
Davidson	David	11.07.1928	1928-1930
Devlin	William	7.05.1927	1927-1928
Done	Robert	13.04.1926	1926-1935
Edmed	Richard	22.01.1926	1926-1932
Forshaw	Richard	31.07.1919	1919-1927
Gardner	Thomas	25.11.1927	1927-1931
Garner	James	24.06.1922	1922-1926
Gilhespy	Cyril	22.08.1921	1921-1925
Gray	William	5.10.1926	1926-1930
Harrington	James	29.12.1920	1920-1921
Hodgson	Gordon	15.12.1925	1925-1936
Hopkin	Frederick	22.05.1921	1921-1931
Jackson	James	23.05.1925	1925-1933
Jenkinson	William	13.05.1919	1919-1921
Johnson	Richard	27.01.1920	1920-1925
Jones	John	28.08.1924	1924-1925
Keetley	Joseph	9.11.1923	1923-1925
Lacey	William	28.02.1912	1912-1924
Lawson	Hector	4.01.1924	1924-1926
Lewis	Henry	Sept 1916	1916-1923
Lindsay	John	9.04.1928Am.	1928-1930
Longworth	Ephraim	9.06.1910	1910-1928
Lucas	Thomas	May 1916	1916-1933
Mackinlay	Donald	27.01.1910	1910-1929
Matthews	Robert	1918	1918-1922
McBain	Neil	9.03.1928	1928-1928
McDevitt	William	16.06.1923	1923-1925
McDougall	James	26.04.1928	1928-1938
McFarlane	John	16.11.1928	1928-1930
McKinney	Peter	29.04.1919	1919-1923
McMullan	David	19.10.1925	1925-1928
McNab(McNabb)	John	6.11.1919	1919-1928
McNaughton	Harold	6.07.1920	1920-1921
McPherson	Archibald	21.11.1929	1929-1934
Millar	William	26.03.1928	1928-1930
Miller	John	1.07.1918	1918-1921
Miller	Thomas	17.02.1912	1912-1920
Mitchell	Frank	5.12.1919Am	1919-1923
Morrison	Thomas	10.02.1928	1928-1935
Murray	William	28.11.1927	1927-1930
Oxley	Cyril	29.10.1925	1925-1928
Parry	Edward	5.02.1921	1921-1926
Pearson	Albert	29.04.1919	1919-1921
Penman	James	7.08.1919	1919-1921
Pither	George	26.11.1926	1926-1928
Pratt	David	1.02.1923	1923-1927
Race	Henry	14.02.1928	1928-1930
Rawlings	Archibald	14.03.1924	1924-1926
Reid	Thomas	13.04.1926	1926-1929
Riley	Arthur	18.08.1925	1925-1940
Salisbury	William	26.10.1928	1928-1929
Sambrook	John	16.08.1922	1922-1923
Scott	Alan	26.02.1929Am	1929-1932
Scott	Elisha	3.09.1912	1912-1934
Scott	Thomas	13.02.1925	1925-1928
Shears	Albert	17.09.1924	1924-1930
Sheldon	Jackie	27.11.1913	1913-1922
Shone	Daniel	19.05.1921	1921-1928
Smith	James	20.09.1929	1929-1932
Wadsworth	Harold	13.051919*	1918-1924
Wadsworth	Walter	23.04.1912(A)	1912-1926
Walsh	James	17.07.1922	1922-1928
Whitehurst	Albert	26.05.1928	1928-1929

Note: Most dates given are professional signings but some players were signed as amateurs earlier.

1930s Scroll of Fame

Name	First name	Date signed	Seasons
Aitken	Andrew	15.03.1930	1930-1931
Balmer	Jack	23.09.1935	1935-1952
Barkas	Henry	31.12.1930	1930-1932
Barton	Harold	24.11.1928	1928-1934
Blenkinsop	Ernest	16.03.1934	1934-1937
Bradshaw	Thomas 'Tiny'	27.01.1930	1930-1938
Bromilow	Thomas	May 1919	1919-1930
Browning	John	21.03.1934	1934-1939
Bruton	Leslie	13.02.1932	1932-1933
Busby	Matthew	11.03.1936	1936-1945
Bush	Tom	21.03.1933	1933-1947
Carr	Leslie	12.09.1933	1933-1936
Charlton	John	18.09.1929	1929-1932
Clark	John	28.01.1928	1928-1931
Collins	James	18.01.1936	1936-1937
Cooper	Thomas	4.12.1934	1934-1940
Crawford	Edmund	27.05.1932	1932-1933
Dabbs	Benjamin	7.06.1932	1932-1938
Davidson	David	11.07.1928	1928-1930
Done	Robert	13.04.1926	1926-1935
Eastham	Harold	27.02.1936	1936-1948
Edmed	Richard	22.01.1926	1926-1932
English	Samuel	27.07.1933	1933-1935
Fagan	William	22.10.1937	1937-1952
Fitzsimmons	Matthew	16.10.1936	1936-1939
Gardner	Thomas	25.11.1927	1927-1931
Glassey	Robert	9.03.1933	1934-1937
Gunson	Joseph	13.03.1930	1930-1934
Hancock	Edmund	5.01.1931	1931-1933
Hanson	Alf	19.11.1931	1931-1938
Harley	James	30.04.1934	1934-1949
Harston	Edwin	22.06.1937	1937-1939
Hartill	William	11.01.1936	1936-1936
Henderson	Alastair	7.07.1931	1931-1933
Hobson	Alfred	27.04.1936*	1936-1938*
Hodgson	Gordon	15.12.1925	1925-1936
Hood	William	9.03.1937	1937-1938
Hopkin	Frederick	22.05.1921	1921-1931
Howe	Frederick	19.03.1935	1935-1938
Ireland	Robert	25.11.1929	1929-1931
Jackson	James	23.05.1925	1925-1933
James	Norman	9.05.1928	1928-1933
Johnson	Thomas	3.03.1934	1934-1936
Jones	Ronald	10.03.1938	1938-1939
Kane	Stanley	2.07.1934	1935-1936
Kemp	Dirk	8.12.1936	1936-1944
Kinghorn	William	19.04.1939	1939-1945
Low	Norman	30.10.1933	1933-1936
Lucas	Thomas	1916	1916-1933
McDougall	James	26.04.1928	1928-1938

McInnes	James	15.03.1938	1938-1946
McPherson	Archibald	21.11.1929	1929-1934
McRorie	Daniel	27.11.1930	1930-1933
Morrison	Thomas	10.02.1928	1928-1935
Nieuwenhuys	Berry	11.09.1933	1933-1947
Paterson	George	20.05.1937	1937-1946
Peters	Keith	4.05.1936	1936-1940
Race	Henry	14.02.1928	1928-1930
Ramsden	Bernard	7.03.1935	1935-1948
Riley	Arthur	18.08.1925	1925-1940
Roberts	John	27.05.1933	1933-1934
Roberts	Sydney	15.12.1931	1931-1937
Rogers	Frederick	17.03.1933	1933-1940
Savage	Robert	7.05.1931	1931-1937
Scott	Alan	26.02.1929Am	1929-1932
Scott	Elisha	3.09.1912	1912-1934
Shafto	John	26.11.1936	1936-1943
Shield	John	12.12.1935	1935-1937
Smith	Alexander	6.03.1937	1937-1939
Smith	James	20.09.1929	1929-1932
Steel	William	25.09.1931	1931-1935
Taylor	Harold	30.07.1932	1932-1936
Taylor	Phil	14.03.1936	1936-1954
Tennant	John	6.05.1933	1933-1936
Thompson	Charles	10.05.1929	1929-1931
Van Den Berg	Harman	18.10.1937	1937-1940
Wright	David	13.03.1930	1930-1934
Wright	Vic	5.03.1934	1934-1937

1940s Scroll Of Fame

Name	First name	Date signed	Seasons
Ashcroft	Charles	24.12.1945	1943-1955
Balmer	Jack	23.09.1935	1935-1952
Baron	Kevin	25.08.1945	1944-1954
Brierley	Kenneth	28.02.1948	1948-1953
Bush	Tom	21.03.1933	1933-1947
Carney	Leonard	2.07.1946 prof	1939-1948
Done	Cyril	11.01.1938	1938-1952
Easdale	John	27.02.1937	1937-1948
Eastham	Harold	27.02.1936	1936-1948
Fagan	William	22.10.1937	1937-1952
Finney*	Frederick	6.10.1945 prof	1941-1946
Harley	James	30.04.1934	1934-1949
Hobson*	Alfred	April 1943	1943-1946
Hughes	Laurie	19.02.1943	1943-1960
Jones	William	24.09.1938	1938-1954
Kaye	George	14.04.1941	1941-1947
Kippax	Peter	1948 amateur	1948-1950
Lambert	Raymond	1939 prof	1936-1957
Liddell	Billy	18.04.1939 prof	1938-1961
McAvoy	Douglas	12.12.1947	1947-1949
McLeod	Thomas	18.10.1945	1945-1951
Minshull	Raymond	25.06.1946	1946-1951
Muir	Alexander	25.07.1947	1947-1949
Nickson*	Harry	15.12.1945	1945-1946
Nieuwenhuys	Berry	11.09.1933	1933-1947
Paisley	Bob	12.05.1939	1939-1954
Palk^	Stanley	23.03.1940	1940-1948
Payne	James	2.11.1944	1942-1956
Priday	Robert	1.12.1945	1945-1949
Ramsden	Bernard	7.03.1935	1935-1948
Shannon	Leslie	7.11.1944	1943-1949
Shepherd	Bill	14.12.1945	1945-1952
Shields	Samuel	2.05.1949	1949-1951
Sidlow	Cyril	21.02.1946	1946-1952
Spicer	Eddie	6.10.1939 prof	1937-1953
Stubbins	Albert	14.09.1946	1946-1953
Taylor	Phil	14.03.1936	1936-1954
Watkinson	Bill	18.02.1946	1946-1951
Williams	Bryan	7.08.1945	1945-1953

*Played in the FA Cup in season 1945/46.

Notes: Although 1945-1946 was called a post-war transitional season, the FA Cup was resumed immediately. There are three more players therefore that must be considered for this period. Fred Finney signed as an amateur in 1941 and turned professional on 6.10.1945. He played at left-half in two of the four FA Cup games. The other two were both goalkeepers.

Alfred Hobson played 25 games in the 1936/37 season but was transferred to Chester in 1938. He 'guested' in goal for Liverpool in the early war years but re-signed for the Reds in 1942/43. He played regularly in the later war years but only appeared 'officially' in one FA Cup game on 26.01.1946.

Harry Nickson signed as a professional on 15.12.1945 and made 3 appearances in the FA Cup.

^Correct name PALK. Personal communication. Originally a mix-up in birth certificate.

1950s Scroll Of Fame

Name	First name	Date signed	Seasons
A'Court	Alan	24.09.1952	1952-1964
Anderson	Eric	11.12.1951	1951-1957
Arnell	Alan	22.03.1954 prof	1953-1961
Ashcroft	Charles	24.12.1945	1943-1955
Balmer	Jack	23.09.1935	1935-1952
Banks	Alan	5.05.1958	1956-1961
Baron	Kevin	25.08.1945	1944-1954
Bimpson	Louis	30.01.1953	1953-1959
Blore	Reginald	13.05.1959	1957-1960
Brierley	Kenneth	28.02.1948	1948-1953
Burkinshaw	Keith	16.11.1953	1953-1957
Byrne	Gerry	30.08.1955	1955-1969
Cadden	Joseph	12.06.1948	1948-1952
Campbell	Bobby	11.05.1954	1954-1961
Campbell	Donald	28.11.1950	1950-1958
Carlin	William	5.05.1958	1958-1962
Childs	Albert	19.09.1953	1953-1954
Christie	Frank	29.03.1949	1949-1950
Crossley	Russell	21.06.1947	1947-1954
Dickson	Joseph	3.06.1952	1952-1958
Done	Cyril	11.01.1938	1938-1952
Evans	John	28.12.1953	1953-1957
Fagan	William	22.10.1937	1937-1952
Gerhardi	Hugh	4.08.1952	1952-1953
Haigh	John	31.10.1949	1949-1952
Harrower	James	3.01.1958	1958-1961
Heydon	John	1.01.1949	1949-1953
Hickson	Dave	6.11.1959	1959-1961
Hughes	Laurie	19.02.1943	1943-1960
Hunt	Roger	29.07.1959	1958-1969
Jackson	Brian	1.11.1951	1951-1958
Jones	Alan	29.04.1957	1957-1963
Jones	Harold	31.01.1952	1952-1954
Jones	Mervyn	1.12.1951	1951-1953
Jones	William	24.09.1938	1938-1954
Lambert	Raymond	1939 prof	1936-1957
Leishman	Thomas	23.11.1959	1959-1963
Liddell	Billy	18.04.1939 prof	1938-1961
Lock	Frank	28.12.1953	1953-1955
Maloney	Joseph	31.01.1951	1951-1954
McNamara	Anthony	14.12.1957	1957-1958
McNulty	Thomas	24.02.1954	1954-1958
Melia	Jimmy	1.11.1954	1953-1964
Minshull	Raymond	25.06.1946	1946-1951
Molyneux	John	23.06.1955	1955-1962
Moran	Ronnie	7.01.1952	1952-1969
Morris	Frederick	5.05.1958	1958-1960
Morrissey	Johnny	29.04.1957	1957-1962
Murdoch	Bobby	14.05.1957	1954-1959
Nicholson	John	8.01.1957	1957-1961
Paisley	Bob	12.05.1939	1939-1954
Parr	Stephen	14.04.1948	1948-1955
Payne	James	2.11.1944	1942-1956
Perry	Frederick	21.07.1954	1954-1957
Price	John	18.10.1954	1954-1957
Rowley	Tony	20.10.1953	1953-1958
Rowley	Arthur	25.05.1951	1951-1954
Rudham	Doug	19.08.1955	1954-1960
Saunders	Roy	20.05.1948	1948-1959
Shepherd	Bill	14.12.1945	1945-1952
Shields	Samuel	2.05.1949	1949-1951
Sidlow	Cyril	21.02.1946	1946-1952
Slater	Bert	12.06.1959	1959-1962
Smith	Jack	4.03.1951	1951-1954
Smyth	Sammy	31.12.1952	1952-1955

South	Alex	20.12.1954	1954-1956
Spicer	Eddie	6.10.1939 prof	1937-1953
Stubbins	Albert	14.09.1946	1946-1953
Taylor	Phil	14.03.1936	1936-1954
Tomley	Fred	25.09.1953	1953-1955
Twentyman	Geoff	19.12.1953	1953-1959
Underwood	Dave	17.12.1953	1953-1956
Watkinson	Bill	18.02.1946	1946-1951
Wheeler	Johnny	8.09.1956	1956-1963
White	Dick	12.11.1955	1955-1962
Whitworth	George	27.02.1950	1950-1953
Wilkinson	Barry	3.09.1953	1953-1960
Williams	Bryan	7.08.1945	1945-1953
Woan	Donald	7.10.1950	1950-1951
Younger	Tommy	7.06.1956	1956-1959

Notes: Most signing dates are professional contract registrations with Football League.
Although he was born in Glasgow, Joseph Cadden was spotted by Liverpool when selected for New York All Stars in their game against the Reds on 16.05.1948 during the American tour of 1948. He was an amateur with Brooklyn Wanderers and signed professionally for Liverpool on 12.06.1948. Although playing regularly at centre-half in the reserves he only managed four league games in 1950-51 and one FA Cup game in 1952. Known as Jersey Joe he went to Grimsby in July 1952 and later to Accrington Stanley. He settled in Liverpool after retiring from the game, taking over a tobacconist/newsagent shop in the Smithdown Road area. Billy Watkinson made the last of his 24 appearances on 22.4.1950 - his only one of the season.
George Whitworth signed on 25.02.1950 and played at right-back for nine games in March/April 1952.
Full-back John Price managed only one game in November 1955 before moving to Aston Villa and Walsall.

1960s Scroll of Fame

Name	First name	Date signed	Seasons
A'Court	Alan	24.09.1952	1952-1964
Arnell	Alan	22.03.1954 prof	1953-1961
Arrowsmith	Alf	30.08.1960	1960-1968
Banks	Alan	5.05.1958	1956-1961
Boersma	Phil	11.09.1968	1965-1975
Byrne	Gerry	30.08.1955	1955-1969
Callaghan	Ian	28.03.1960	1957-1978
Campbell	Bobby	11.05.1954	1954-1961
Chisnall	Phil	16.04.1964	1964-1967
Clemence	Ray	12.06.1967	1967-1981
Evans	Alun	17.09.1968	1968-1972
Ferns	Phil	8.08.1961	1961-1965
Furnell	James	23.02.1962	1962-1963
Graham	Bobby	24.11.1961	1960-1972
Hall	Brian	26.06.1968	1968-1976
Harrower	James	3.01.1958	1958-1961
Hateley	Tony	5.07.1967	1967-1968
Hickson	Dave	6.11.1959	1959-1961
Hignett	Alan	4.11.1963	1962-1966
Hughes	Emlyn	2.03.1967	1967-1979
Hunt	Roger	29.07.1959	1958-1969
Jones	Alan	29.04.1957	1957-1963
Lawler	Chris	20.10.1960	1959-1975
Lawrence	Tommy	30.10.1957	1957-1971
Leishman	Thomas	23.11.1959	1959-1963
Lewis	Kevin	16.06.1960	1960-1963
Liddell	Billy	18.04.1939 prof	1938-1961
Lindsay	Alec	13.03.1969	1969-1977
Livermore	Doug	9.08.1965	1965-1970
Lloyd	Larry	22.04.1969	1969-1974
Lowry	Thomas	20.05.1963	1963-1966
Melia	Jimmy	1.11.1954	1953-1964
Milne	Gordon	30.08.1960	1960-1967
Molyneux	Bill	26.11.1963	1961-1967
Molyneux	John	23.06.1955	1955-1962
Moran	Ronnie	7.01.1952	1952-1969
Morrissey	Johnny	29.04.1957	1957-1962
Ogston	John	21.09.1965	1965-1968
Peplow	Stephen	12.01.1966	1965-1970
Ross	Ian	20.08.1965	1965-1972
Sealey	John	30.12.1963	1963-1966
Slater	Bert	12.06.1959	1959-1962
Smith	Tommy	5.04.1962	1960-1978
Stevenson	Willie	22.10.1962	1962-1967
St John	Ian	2.05.1961	1961-1971
Strong	Geoff	7.11.1964	1964-1970
Thompson	Peter	14.08.1963	1963-1974
Thomson	Bobby	6.12.1962	1962-1965
Wall	Peter	10.10.1966	1966-1970
Wallace	Gordon	21.07.1961	1961-1967
Wheeler	Johnny	8.09.1956	1956-1963
White	Dick	12.11.1955	1955-1962
Wilson	David	20.02.1967	1967-1968
Yeats	Ron	22.07.1961	1961-1971

Note: Most signing dates are professional contract registrations with Football League.

1970s Scroll of Fame

Name	First name	Date signed	Seasons
Arnold	Steve	9.09.1970	1970-1973
Boersma	Phil	11.09.1968	1965-1975
Brownbill	Derek	22.02.1975	1972-1974
Callaghan	Ian	28.03.1960	1957-1978
Case	Jimmy	8.05.1973	1973-1981
Clemence	Ray	12.06.1967	1967-1981
Cohen	Avi	18.07.1979	1979-1981
Cormack	Peter	8.07.1972	1972-1976
Dalglish	Kenny	16.08.1977	1977-1990
Evans	Alun	17.09.1968	1968-1972
Evans	Roy	5.10.1965	1965-1974
Fagan	Kit	8.07.1970	1970-1971
Fairclough	David	14.01.1974	1974-1982
Graham	Bobby	24.11.1961	1960-1972
Hall	Brian	26.06.1968	1968-1976
Hansen	Alan	6.05.1977	1977-1990
Heighway	Steve	26.05.1970	1970-1981
Hughes	Emlyn	2.03.1967	1967-1979
Irwin	Colin	7.12.1974	1974-1981
Johnson	David	13.08.1976	1976-1982
Jones	Joey	15.07.1975	1975-1978
Keegan	Kevin	10.05.1971	1971-1977
Kennedy	Alan	14.08.1978	1978-1985
Kennedy	Ray	20.07.1974	1974-1982
Kettle	Brian	14.05.1973	1973-1980
Kewley	Kevin	8.03.1972	1972-1978
Lane	Frank	30.09.1971	1971-1975
Lawler	Chris	20.10.1960	1959-1975
Lawrence	Tommy	30.10.1957	1957-1971
Lee	Sammy	16.04.1976	1975-1986
Lindsay	Alec	13.03.1969	1969-1977
Livermore	Doug	9.08.1965	1965-1970
Lloyd	Larry	22.04.1969	1969-1974
McDermott	Terry	14.11.1974	1974-1982
McLaughlin	John	25.02.1969	1967-1976
Neal	Phil	11.10.1974	1974-1985
Ogrizovic	Steve	7.11.1977	1977-1982
Ross	Ian	20.08.1965	1965-1972
Rylands	David	11.03.1970	1967-1974
Smith	Tommy	5.04.1962	1960-1978
Souness	Graeme	11.01.1978	1978-1984
St John	Ian	2.05.1961	1961-1971
Storton	Trevor	2.08.1972	1972-1974
Strong	Geoff	7.11.1964	1964-1970
Thompson	Max	14.01.1974	1974-1978
Thompson	Peter	14.08.1963	1963-1974
Thompson	Phil	8.02.1971	1971-1985
Toshack	John	12.11.1970	1970-1978
Waddle	Alan	26.06.1973	1973-1977
Wall	Peter	10.10.1966	1966-1970
Whitham	Jack	1.05.1970	1970-1974
Yeats	Ron	22.07.1961	1961-1971

Note: Signing dates are professional contract registrations with Football League.

1980s Scroll of Fame

Name	First name	Date signed	Seasons
Ablett	Gary	19.11.1983	1983-1992
Aldridge	John	27.01.1987	1987-1989
Barnes	John	19.06.1987	1987-1997
Beardsley	Peter	24.07.1987	1987-1991
Beglin	Jim	18.05.1983	1983-1989
Burrows	David	20.10.1988	1988-1993
Case	Jimmy	8.05.1973	1973-1981
Clemence	Ray	12.06.1967	1967-1981
Cohen	Avi	18.07.1979	1979-1981
Dalglish	Kenny	16.08.1977	1977-1990
Durnin	John	29.03.1986	1986-1989
Fairclough	David	14.01.1974	1974-1982
Gayle	Howard	28.11.1977	1977-1983
Gillespie	Gary	July 1983	1983-1991
Grobbelaar	Bruce	12.03.1981	1981-1994
Hansen	Alan	6.05.1977	1977-1990
Heighway	Steve	26.05.1970	1970-1981
Hodgson	David	11.08.1982	1982-1984
Hooper	Mike	25.10.1985	1985-1993
Houghton	Ray	19.10.1987	1987-1992
Hysen	Glenn	14.08.1989	1989-1992
Irvine	Alan	1.12.1986	1986-1987
Irwin	Colin	7.12.1974	1974-1981
Johnson	David	13.08.1976	1976-1982
Johnston	Craig	3.04.1981	1981-1988
Kennedy	Alan	14.08.1978	1978-1985
Kennedy	Ray	20.07.1974	1974-1982
Lawrenson	Mark	15.08.1981	1981-1988
Lee	Sammy	16.04.1976	1975-1986
MacDonald	Kevin	24.11.1984	1984-1989
Marsh	Mike	21.08.1987	1987-1993
McDermott	Terry	14.11.1974	1974-1982
McMahon	Steve	6.09.1985	1985-1991
Molby	Jan	24.08.1984	1984-1996
Money	Richard	2.05.1980	1980-1982
Mooney	Brian	August 1983	1983-1987
Neal	Phil	11.10.1974	1974-1985
Nicol	Steve	26.10.1981	1981-1995
Ogrizovic	Steve	7.11.1977	1977-1982
Robinson	Michael	15.08.1983	1983-1984
Rush	Ian	1.05.1980	1980-1996
Russell	Colin	22.04.1978	1977-1982
Seagraves	Mark	4.11.1983	1981-1987
Sheedy	Kevin	1.07.1978	1978-1982
Souness	Graeme	11.01.1978	1978-1984
Spackman	Nigel	24.02.1987	1987-1989
Staunton	Steve	2.09.1986	1986-2000
Tanner	Nick	8.07.1988	1988-1990
Thompson	Phil	8.02.1971	1971-1985
Venison	Barry	31.07.1986	1986-1992
Walsh	Paul	17.05.1984	1984-1988
Wark	John	19.03.1984	1984-1988
Watson	Alec	18.05.1985	1984-1991
Whelan	Ronnie	1.10.1979	1979-1994

Notes: Ian Rush left Liverpool for Juventus at the end of the 1986/87 season, re-signing for the Reds on 23.08.1988.
Steve Staunton left the Reds in 1991, but re-signed for the club on 3.07.98.

1990s Scroll of Fame

Name	First name	Date signed	Seasons
Ablett	Gary	19.11.1983	1983-1992
Babb	Phil	1.09.1994	1994-2000
Barnes	John	19.06.1987	1987-1997
Beardsley	Peter	24.07.1987	1987-1991
Berger	Patrik	15.08.1996	1996-2003
Bjornebye	Stig Inge	18.12.1992	1992-2000
Burrows	David	20.10.1988	1988-1993
Camara	Titi	14.06.1999	1999-2000
Carragher	Jamie	9.10.1996	1994-
Carter	Jimmy	10.01.1991	1990-1992
Charnock	Phil	16.03.1993	1991-1996
Clough	Nigel	June 1993	1993-1996
Collymore	Stanley	4.07.1995	1995-1997
Dalglish	Kenny	16.08.1977	1977-1990
Dicks	Julian	17.09.1993	1993-1994
Dundee	Sean	June 1998	1998-1999
Ferri	Jean-Michel	Dec 1998	1998-1999
Fowler	Robbie	23.04.1992	1991-2001
Friedel	Brad	23.12.1997	1997-2000
Gerrard	Steven	26.02.1998	1996-
Gillespie	Gary	July 1983	1983-1991
Grobbelaar	Bruce	12.03.1981	1981-1994
Hamann	Dietmar	23.07.1999	1999-2006
Hansen	Alan	6.05.1977	1977-1990
Harkness	Steve	17.07.1989	1989-1999
Heggem	Vegard	27.07.1998	1998-2002
Henchoz	Stephane	20.07.1999	1999-2005
Hooper	Mike	25.10.1985	1985-1993
Houghton	Ray	19.10.1987	1987-1992
Hutchison	Don	27.11.1990	1990-1994
Hysen	Glenn	14.08.1989	1989-1992
Hyypia	Sami	7.07.1999	1999-
Ince	Paul	22.07.1997	1997-1999
James	David	6.07.1992	1992-1999
Jones	Barry	19.01.1989	1989-1992
Jones	Lee	12.03.1992	1992-1997
Jones	Rob	4.10.1991	1991-1999
Kennedy	Mark	21.03.1995	1995-1998
Kippe	Frode	7.01.1999	1999-2002
Kozma	Istvan	8.02.1992	1992-1993
Kvarme	Bjorn Tore	Jan 1997	1997-1999
Leonhardsen	Oyvind	3.06.1997	1997-1999
Marsh	Mike	21.08.1987	1987-1993
Matteo	Dominic	27.05.1992	1990-2000
Maxwell	Leyton	17.07.1997	1996-2004
McAteer	Jason	6.09.1995	1995-1999
McMahon	Steve	6.09.1985	1985-1991
McManaman	Steve	19.02.1990	1988-1999
Meijer	Erik	13.07.1999	1999-2000
Molby	Jan	24.08.1984	1984-1996
Murphy	Danny	17.07.1997	1997-2004
Newby	Jon	23.05.1997	1995-2001
Nicol	Steve	26.10.1981	1981-1995
Owen	Michael	14.12.1996	1996-2004
Piechnik	Torben	17.09.1992	1992-1994
Redknapp	Jamie	15.01.1991	1991-2002
Riedle	Karlheinz	4.08.1997	1997-1999
Rosenthal	Ronny	11.05.1990	1990-1994
Ruddock	Neil	22.07.1993	1993-1998
Rush	Ian	1.05.1980	1980-1996
Saunders	Dean	19.07.1991	1991-1992
Scales	John	2.09.1994	1994-1996
Smicer	Vladimir	14.07.1999	1999-2006
Song	Rigobert	29.01.1999	1999-2000
Speedie	David	1.02.1991	1990-1991
Staunton	Steve	2.09.1986	1986-2000
Stewart	Paul	29.07.1992	1992-1996
Tanner	Nick	8.07.1988	1988-1990
Thomas	Michael	16.12.1991	1991-1998
Thompson	David	8.11.1994	1994-2000
Traore	Djimi	18.02.1999	1999-2006
Venison	Barry	31.07.1986	1986-1992
Walters	Mark	13.08.1991	1991-1996
Watson	Alec	18.05.1985	1984-1991
Westerveld	Sander	18.06.1999	1999-2001
Whelan	Ronnie	1.10.1979	1979-1994
Wright	Mark	15.07.1991	1991-1998

Notes: Signing dates prior to 1992 are based on Football League Registers.
Years of service start from date of professional contract.
Loan periods are excluded. Final date is based on officially leaving club, in some cases a year or more after last appearance.

Statistics compiled by JE Doig